GREEN SUPPLY CHAIN MANAGEMENT

GREEN SUPPLY CHAIN MANAGEMENT

Mohammed Majeed, PhD
Kirti Agarwal, PhD
Ahmed Tijani, PhD
Editors

First edition published 2025

Apple Academic Press Inc.
1265 Goldenrod Circle, NE,
Palm Bay, FL 32905 USA

760 Laurentian Drive, Unit 19,
Burlington, ON L7N 0A4, CANADA

CRC Press
2385 NW Executive Center Drive,
Suite 320, Boca Raton FL 33431

4 Park Square, Milton Park,
Abingdon, Oxon, OX14 4RN UK

© 2025 by Apple Academic Press, Inc.

Apple Academic Press exclusively co-publishes with CRC Press, an imprint of Taylor & Francis Group, LLC

Reasonable efforts have been made to publish reliable data and information, but the authors, editors, and publisher cannot assume responsibility for the validity of all materials or the consequences of their use. The authors, editors, and publishers have attempted to trace the copyright holders of all material reproduced in this publication and apologize to copyright holders if permission to publish in this form has not been obtained. If any copyright material has not been acknowledged, please write and let us know so we may rectify in any future reprint.

Except as permitted under U.S. Copyright Law, no part of this book may be reprinted, reproduced, transmitted, or utilized in any form by any electronic, mechanical, or other means, now known or hereafter invented, including photocopying, microfilming, and recording, or in any information storage or retrieval system, without written permission from the publishers.

For permission to photocopy or use material electronically from this work, access www.copyright.com or contact the Copyright Clearance Center, Inc. (CCC), 222 Rosewood Drive, Danvers, MA 01923, 978-750-8400. For works that are not available on CCC please contact mpkbookspermissions@tandf.co.uk

Trademark notice: Product or corporate names may be trademarks or registered trademarks and are used only for identification and explanation without intent to infringe.

Library and Archives Canada Cataloguing in Publication

....

CIP data on file with Canada Library and Archives

....

Library of Congress Cataloging-in-Publication Data

....

CIP data on file with US Library of Congress

....

ISBN: 978-1-77491-808-1 (hbk)
ISBN: 978-1-77491-809-8 (pbk)
ISBN: 978-1-00356-084-5 (ebk)

About the Editors

Mohammed Majeed, PhD

Mohammed Majeed (PhD, DBA, CBC) is a Senior Lecturer (PhD) at Tamale Technical University, Tamale, Ghana, where he is the current Head of the Department (HoD) of Marketing. His current research interest includes branding, social media in service organizations. He holds degrees that include Doctor of Business Administration (DBA), Certified Business Analyst and Consultant (ICBAC), and MPhil and MBA in Marketing. Dr. Majeed has published with reputable publishers such as Emerald, Taylor & Francis, Apply Academic Press, Asia-Pacific Management Accounting Association, Springer and Palgrave McMillan.

Kirti Agarwal, PhD

Kirti Agarwal, PhD, is currently Professor and Director at ITERC College of Management, Delhi NCR, India, since 2013. She served as a Lecturer at Jain College, Gwalior; rendered her services at BLS Institute of Management, Ghaziabad, ICFAI National Institute, Noida; served as a Department Head at the Institute of Advance Management & Research (IAMR), Ghaziabad; and served as Director at the Greater Noida Institute of Management (GNIT Group), Greater Noida, India. An excellent academician with an overall experience of more than 21 years. Dr. Agarwal has published more than 50 research papers in journals of national and international repute. She has chaired technical sessions at international conferences in Bangkok and Kathmandu. She visited Michigan University, USA, to represent her college and presented a paper. She has also been a guide and supervisor of more than 22 research scholars across the national boundaries. She is also a reviewer for journals published by Inderscience Publishers. Dr. Agarwal received a young entrepreneur research award in 2018 and an award for social work in education in 2019. She is also the recipient of a Vishisht Siksha Samman Award (2019) for her outstanding contribution in the education sector. She has also penned 13 books on different commerce and management subjects for distance learning programs of Nalanda University, Dr. Bhim Rao Ambedkar University, and MD University Rohtak, India. In addition, she is running the Smt. Vimla Devi Education Society (SVDES- National Education Society) and KAAV Media Private Limited. She is associated with many public and private educational institutes and corporate houses in New Delhi. Dr. Agarwal is an editorial board member for 12 national and international journals and Editor-in-Chief of Kaav Publications. She has a postgraduate degree and PhD in Commerce from Jiwaji University, Gwalior, India. She also pursued a Post Graduate Diploma in Financial Management (PGDFM), Executive MBA, and LLB (Bachelor of Laws).

Ahmed Tijani, PhD

Ahmed Tijani, MBA, PhD, is the Manager of Corporate Affairs and Information Technology Department of Minerals Commission, Ghana. His research interests are corporate governance, stakeholder relations, circular economy, local content policies, marketing, development communication, ande xtractive industry policy, regulation, and management. He currently holds a PhD in Marketing from the University of Professional Studies, Accra-Ghana, and an LLM in Extractive Industry Policy, Management and Regulation from the University of Pretoria-South Africa, MA in Development Communication from the University of Media Arts and Communication (UniMAC)-GIJ Campus, Ghana, MBA in Corporate Governance from the University of Professional Studies, Accra-Ghana, a BSc in Business Administration (Banking and Finance) from Data Link University College (KNUST Affiliate)-Ghana, and a Higher National Diploma (HND) in Marketing from the Tamale Technical University-Ghana.

Contents

Contributors .... *ix*
Abbreviations .... *xi*
Preface .... *xiii*

1. **Green Supply Chain Management: Benefits and Challenges** 1
   Abdul Ganiw Hussein, Alhassan Seidu, and Shani Salifu

2. **Factors/Determinants of Green Supply Chain Management (GSCM) Practices** 19
   Mohammed Abdul-Basit Fuseini, Alhassan Seidu, Shani Salifu, and Mohammed Majeed

3. **Key Green Supply Chain Management Practices Today** 35
   Shani Salifu, Alhassan Seidu, and Mohammed Abdul-Basit Fuseini

4. **Key Drivers of Green Supply Chain Management** 57
   Shani Salifu, Alhassan Seidu, and Ibrahim Sulemana

5. **Green Distribution for Green Supply Chain Management** 77
   Alhassan Seidu, Shani Salifu, and Mohammed Abdul-Basit Fuseini

6. **Benefits of Green Transportation** 89
   Ibrahim Sulemana, Shani Salifu, and Alhassan Seidu

7. **Green Marketing Aspect of Green Supply Chain Management** 103
   Alhassan Seidu, Shani Salifu, and Ibrahim Sulemana

8. **Green Warehousing Practices for Firms** 133
   Mohammed Majeed, Awini Gideon, and Ahmed Tijani

9. **Green Manufacturing** 153
   Ahmed Tijani

10. **Green SCM in the Fashion Sector** 169
    Joana Akweley Zanu, Sherifatu Abas, and Rebecca Lartekai Lartey

11. **Impact of Green Structural Capital on Green Supply Chain Agility** 187
    Raseem Abdul Khader and P. Nissar

12. **The Role of Industry 4.0 Software Tools in Creating Sustainable Supply Chain Management in Emerging Markets** 197
    Ketan Rathor

13. **Green Supply Chain Management in the Hospitality Industry** 217
    Fatawu Alhassan, Sherifatu Abas, Stanley Cowther, and Sussana Antwi-Boasiako

14. **Green Procurement** 237
    Fatawu Alhassan, Sherifatu Abas, Stanley Cowther, and Sussana Antwi-Boasiako

15. **Green Logistics** 259
    Mohammed Majeed

16. **A Study on Green Practices and Strategies in Supply Chain Management** 283
    Suja Sundram, Chetan V Hiremath, Madhu Arora, Varsha Agarwal, S. Sekar, and Suja Sundram

Index *305*

Contributors

Sherifatu Abas
Department of Textiles Technology, Tamale Technical University, Northern Region, Ghana
Accra Technical University, Accra, Ghana

Varsha Agarwal
ISME, ATLAS SkillTech University, Mumbai, Maharashtra, India

Fatawu Alhassan
Tamale Technical University, Tamale, Ghana

Sussana Antwi-Boasiako
Accra Technical University, Accra, Ghana

Madhu Arora
Uttaranchal Institute of Management, Uttaranchal University, Dehradun, Uttarakhand, India

Mohammed Abdul-Basit Fuseini
Department of Marketing, Tamale Technical University, Tamale, Ghana

Stanley Cowther
Tamale Technical University, Tamale, Ghana

Awini Gideon
Marketing Department, Tamale Technical University, Tamale, Ghana

Chetan V Hiremath
Department of Operations and Analytics, Kirloskar Institute of Management, Yantrapur, Harihar, Karnataka, India

Abdul Ganiw Hussein
Department of Logistics and Procurement Management, Tamale Technical University, Tamale, Ghana

P. Raseem Abdul Khader
Department of Commerce, Ansar Arabic College Valavannur, Kerala, India

Rebecca Lartekai Lartey
Department of Textiles Technology, Tamale Technical University Northern Region, Ghana

Mohammed Majeed
Marketing Department, Tamale Technical University, Tamale, Ghana
Chicago School of Professional Psychology, Chicago, USA

P. Nissar
Department of Commerce and Management Studies, PSMO College Tirurangadi, Kerala, India

Ketan Rathor
GyanSys Inc.

Shani Salifu
Chicago School of Professional Psychology, Chicago, USA

Alhassan Seidu
Department of Secretaryship and Management, Tamale Technical University, Tamale, Ghana
Department of Marketing, Tamale Technical University, Tamale, Ghana

S. Sekar
Department of Commerce (CA), Govermnent Arts College (Autonomous), Salem, Tamil Nadu, India

Ibrahim Sulemana
Department of Marketing, Tamale Technical University, Tamale, Ghana

Suja Sundram
Department of Business Administration, Jubail Industrial College, Kingdom of Saudi Arabia

Ahmed Tijani
Minerals Commission, Accra, Ghana

Joana Akweley Zanu
Department of Fashion and Design, Tamale Technical University, Northern Region, Ghana

Abbreviations

AI	artificial intelligence
CE	chief executive officer
CO_2	carbon dioxide
CSR	corporate social responsibility
EPA	Environmental Protection Agency
GI	green innovation
GM	green marketing
GSC	green supply chain
GSCM	green supply chain management
ISO	international standard organization
KPIs	key performance indicators
LCA	life cycle assessment
LOHAS	lifestyles of health and sustainability
NGOs	nongovernmental organizations
R&D	research and development
RL	reverse logistics
SC	supply chain
SCM	supply chain management
SMEs	small and medium-sized businesses
SSCM	sustainable supply chain management
UN	United Nations
US	United States

Preface

Green supply chain management (GSCM) is the practice of integrating ecological sustainability processes that integrates the 4Rs concept (reduce, reuse, recycle, reclaim, and degradable) into the production, logistics, and end-of-life management of conventional supply networks. This book is revolutionary because it integrates environmentally friendly aspects of technology, transportation, purchasing/procurement, manufacturing, logistics, and the supply chain. These key issues have only lately been studied by academics. Focusing on how green approaches improve operations in an ecological manner, the field of GSCM focuses the difficulties and rewards of integrating "green" into the fundamental processes of modern businesses.

This book is essential for workers, managers, academics, and advanced students as it summarizes the most important ideas, current developments, and potential futures in the field of GSCM. The book teaches readers how to build a GSC by combining the efforts of operations management, purchasing, logistics, and marketing, and by looking outside the business to create long-term partnerships. The topics covered and linked to green SCM consist of the following: benefits of green SCM, factors/determinants of green SCM, green SCM practices, green distribution, green procurement/purchasing, green logistics, green marketing, green warehousing, green transportation, and green SCM drivers.

CHAPTER 1

Green Supply Chain Management: Benefits and Challenges

ABDUL GANIW HUSSEIN[1], ALHASSAN SEIDU[2], and SHANI SALIFU[3]

[1]Department of Logistics and Procurement Management, Tamale Technical University, Tamale, Ghana

[2]Department of Secretaryship and Management, Tamale Technical University, Tamale, Ghana

[3]Chicago School of Professional Psychology, Chicago, USA

ABSTRACT

Greening is the order of the day. Therefore, the purpose of this study is to look at the benefits and challenges of green supply chain management. This article is treasured since it sheds new light on the topic of GSCM and adds to the existing body of knowledge in the area. Factors affecting GSCM in major pharmaceutical companies have been the subject of very little prior research. When goods in a variety of categories are readily available and delivered to individual homes and businesses, it raises everyone's standard of living. GSCM poses a lot of benefits such as environmental and financial benefits, reduces pollution, precision manufacturing, innovation in technology, monetary gains, transportation, computer technology, reduces waste, heightens consumer awareness, builds brand reputation, lowers gas emissions, and cost cutting/reduction. Challenges of creating a green supply chain include, but are not limited to, lack of financial support, lack of green industry professionals, inadequate backing from the senior executives, expensive implementation, supplier adherence, ignorance/lack of knowledge, a lack of awareness and knowledge, transport optimization, a dearth of green vendors, and arbitrary and rigid stakeholder deadlines. Efficient and effective logistics connects organizations to the domestic and international markets through supply chain networks. Organizations identified as low logistics performance companies incur a higher cost because of transportation costs and unreliable supply chain networks; however, organizations with high logistics performance rankings enjoy low costs and a competitive advantage.

1.1 INTRODUCTION

Corporations' shareholders are paying more attention to environmental issues as a result of expanding competition. Corporations' ability to execute in a sustainable manner is a measure of both their financial success and their contribution to a better world. Manufacturing, transport, logistics, marketing, and sales all contribute to the conventional supply chain management by sharing the same aims of maximizing efficiency and profit for customers. The production cycle can be sped up and expenses are reduced by employing efficient supply chain management. A just-in-time supply chain, in which rising demand at stores triggers the production of more of the product, has become the norm. However, many people still do not realize that being green with their supply chain is good for business and the environment. However, in order to put this into action, you should reevaluate the entire process, from purchasing to the use of materials during shipping, warehousing, picking and packing goods, and many more that can further decrease a firm's carbon footprint (i.e., the total carbon dioxide emission into the atmosphere due to the activities of an individual, community, event, or organization) (20cube, 2018). Success in supply chain management has strong ties to happy clients. Toward that end, the business framework must be coordinated and integrated. The production, purchasing, marketing, logistics, and information system components of the business process need to work together seamlessly. Therefore, customer satisfaction, quality, and environmental sustainability are prioritized in supply chain management methods (De et al., 2020). Having a competitive edge at the conclusion of supply chain management requires the identification and selection of practices (Ikram et al., 2018).

This article aims to evaluate the effect of green supply chain management methods on performance as this aspect of environmental supply chain management plays a significant role in helping businesses achieve sustainable results.

As a result, this article offers a paradigm for practitioners to use in evaluating the symbiotic effects of GSCM activities in their own organizations. Green purchasing, customer collaboration, ecodesign, and investment recovery are all deemed essential steps that must precede the introduction of internal environmental management and green information systems. This chapter corroborates the view that GSCM strategies are beneficial for the environment and profitable for businesses. The findings of the study add to our knowledge of the favorable benefits of GSCM practices on both a company's bottom line and the natural world. The review will aid in the decrease of carbon dioxide and other greenhouse gas emissions, which will have an effect on global warming. Lack of government initiatives and the commitment of enterprises participating in the supply chain continue to discourage the application of GSCM practices, despite rising awareness. The advantages of GSCM will remain elusive unless it is prioritized.

1.2 CONTRIBUTION

This research is valuable because it will likely shed new light on the topic of GSCM and add to the existing body of knowledge in the area. Factors affecting GSCM in major pharmaceutical companies have been the subject of very little prior research. When goods in a variety of categories are readily available and delivered to individual homes and businesses, it raises everyone's standard of living (Catherine, 2015). Socially significant ramifications include the possibility to regulate and eliminate environmental resource wastage, waste of materials, and groundwater pollution due to the destruction of materials from damaged products. The delivery of goods to the public without interruption or harm is another potential social advantage. A community's health, safety, and nutrition can all benefit from the timely, undamaged delivery of essential items that are not prone to spoilage. This can also help the environment. The elements affecting GSCM in the procurement, logistics, and strategic planning divisions are identified. Moreover, this research adds to the existing body of knowledge by proposing solutions to the identified elements that have a detrimental effect on GSCM activities. Other pharmaceutical firms may benefit from implementing the suggested changes to their GSCM processes. This would allow them to keep making useful contributions to the preservation of the natural world. This research lays the groundwork for subsequent studies into the elements that influence GSCM in different businesses and industries. The advantages and disadvantages of this endeavor in practice are demonstrated. This chapter's goal is to help international businesses better grasp the potential of new GSCM processes to boost their bottom lines. The research has provided a solid basis for advancing these practices, removing impediments, and learning more about GSCM efforts.

1.3 LITERATURE

1.3.1 SCM

The handling of a complicated system of processes involved in getting a finished product to the customer or end user is known as supply chain coordination. Supply chain management (SCM) calls for the synchronization of business operations and the alignment of strategies throughout the whole supply chain as a means to an end—the fulfillment of the supply chain's final consumers. It is a crucial economic activity, and the procedure entails obtaining raw materials and components, producing and putting together goods, storing them, entering and tracking orders, distributing them through various channels, and eventually delivering them to the consumer. The components of a corporation's supply chain include external suppliers, internal operations, external distributors, and customers (whether end users or commercial customers) (commercial or end user). Businesses may simultaneously participate in multiple different supply networks. Management and collaboration are made more challenging by the presence of international actors who are dispersed across borders and time zones. Customer expectations, globalization, information technology, governmental regulations, competitiveness, and the environment all have an impact on how successfully a supply chain is managed.

1.3.2 GREEN SUPPLY

When discussing supply chain management and corporate buying advances, the term "green supply" refers to how the environment may be taken into account. The purchasing function participates in operations including material substitution, reduction, recycling, and reuse as part of environmental supply chain control. The process of monitoring and improving the environmental performance of the supply chain involves integrating environmental considerations into all aspects of supply chain management, including product design, material sourcing and selection, manufacturing procedures, final product delivery to the consumer, and the management of a product's end-of-life after it has fulfilled its purpose. We can see from these four definitions that different authors have different goals and points of focus when it comes to managing green supply chains. Given that corporate environmental management and supply chain management, the basic components of the green supply chain, are both relatively new fields of study and practice, the lack of agreement on their definition and application is not surprising.

1.3.3 DEFINITION AND CONCEPT OF GREEN SUPPLY CHAIN MANAGEMENT

Businesses utilize green supply chain management in their everyday operations to protect the environment (Laari et al., 2016). Green supply chain management is the practice of overseeing all business operations while taking the environment into account in order to ensure environmentally friendly manufacturing and delivery procedures. Numerous research studies in the literature back up the beneficial impact of GSCM on the industry's sustainability performance (Khan et al., 2019). Businesses are more likely to adopt the GSCM to improve their performance in terms of sustainability and competitiveness. Delivering goods and services from suppliers, manufacturers, and end customers through material flow, information flow, and payment flow while considering the environment is the focus of green supply chain management.

The rise in awareness and concern about pollution, carbon emissions, and deteriorating environmental circumstances among individuals, governments, and companies is largely responsible for the development of green supply chain management as a technique. Green supply chain management includes not only the production of goods and their distribution to consumers but also the stages of product development before the goods are used (Chiu and Hsieh, 2016). Businesses utilize a variety of strategies to adopt green supply chain management, including internal environmental management, ecodesign, green purchasing, and customer collaboration (Ahmed et al., 2019). The scope of GSCM comprises both proactive procedures done through multiple "R's" and reactive actions taken in accordance with general environment management programs (Reduce, Reuse, Rework, Refurbish, Reclaim, Recycle, Remanufacture, and Reverse logistics). Three crucial elements can be combined to form the green supply: (i) increased understanding of the strategic value of buying; (ii) emphasis on cooperative connections between buyers and sellers; and (iii) knowledge of the link between consumer choices and environmental performance. The implementation of GSCM methods, according to the research of Saade et al. (2019), aids firms in seizing new market opportunities on a national and international scale, which inspires the market to go green and attracts workers. In addition, pressure from outside stakeholders and a lack of government support hindered the introduction of GSCM. Technology innovation, organizational factors, and environmental factors were evaluated by Lin et al. (2020) to determine their effects on the adoption of GSCM. The findings revealed that perceived relative advantage, perceived cost, top management support, complexity, compatibility, firm size, customer pressure, regulatory pressure, and human resources were significantly related to GSCM adoption. The authors, Mathiyazhagan et al. (2018), discovered and ranked a number of parameters that influence the adoption of GSCM. Government was the most important category, followed by market, supplier, customer, internal drivers, and finally the environment. Government laws, customer needs, and supplier performance were identified by Asif et al. (2020) as three high-priority drivers of GSCM adoption.

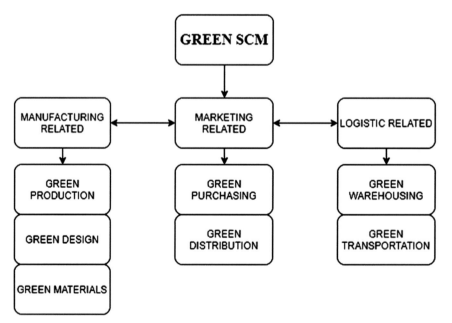

FIGURE 1.1 Scheme of GSCM.

Source: Adapted from Saada, R. (2021). Green Transportation in Green Supply Chain Management. IntechOpen, p. 6. doi: 10.5772/intechopen.93113.

1.3.4 BENEFITS OF GSCM

1. **Environmental and financial benefits**

   Zhu and Sarkis (2004) investigated how GSCM methods in Chinese manufacturing businesses affected their bottom line and the environment. The study discovered a high and favorable correlation between GSCM methods and successful economic and environmental outcomes. It came to the conclusion that adopting GSCM principles would present a major "win-win" potential for Chinese manufacturing businesses. The first empirical study to examine the relationship between GSCM practices and improved economic performance and competitiveness across a sample of Southeast Asian organizations was carried out by Rao and Holt in 2005. According to the study, integrating the supply chain's various phases with environmental considerations results in a chain that is more competitive and performs better economically.

2. **Reduces pollution**

   The first and most important step in putting in place a green supply chain is to choose a manufacturer who can make the product with the least amount of pollution and energy use possible (Champion, 2022). Since they should not be dangerous when dumped outside, they should be made with the environment in mind.

3. **Precision manufacturing**

   Most of the time, buyers choose vendors who use lean manufacturing because it reduces waste without interfering with output. For those who prefer it, this presents an excellent chance because they may obtain high-quality things for a very small price (20cube, 2018). For instance, Toyota created a sociointegrated system that, by removing waste, allowed it to deliver things of higher quality at lower costs and with shorter lead times.

4. **Innovation in technology**

   Geffen and Rothenberg (2000) investigated the contribution of partnerships between original equipment manufacturers (OEMs) and their suppliers in reducing the environmental impact of manufacturing operations, making a compelling case for developing strategic collaborations with suppliers in order to leverage the supply chain and incorporate GSCM practices. The study, which focused on US auto assembly plants, discovered that strong supplier relationships, supported by effective incentive programs, led to the successful implementation of cutting-edge environmental solutions.

5. **Monetary gains**

   Reverse logistics and government regulation and legislation are important drivers that promote cooperation between product designers and suppliers in order to lessen or completely eliminate negative environmental impacts according to Diabat and Govindan (2011) who studied a variety of factors that influence the implementation of green supply chains. According to the study, green design, which has a good impact on the environment without sacrificing costs, profitability, or other features, enhances the efficiency of green supply chains.

6. **Transportation**

   The process that follows production is the transportation of the commodities. Therefore, businesses need to make sure that fuel usage is decreased through better planning and execution. If a company uses the services of a digital freight agency, it will guarantee that you receive the requested items through sea or road in the specified amount of time, and it will be more transparent and cost-effective (20cube, 2018). A digital freight forwarder is preferred because it can offer end-to-end transportation visibility and, with its use of green supply chain techniques, can also recommend the least expensive and most effective method of shipping a firm's goods.

7. **Computer technology**

   The primary benefit of choosing an environmentally friendly digital freight forwarder is that it can make the firm's transactions paperless, thereby lowering the firm's transactions' carbon impact. Additionally, it offers transparent information about a firm's transactions, which makes supply chain management easier (20cube, 2018).

8. **Reduces waste**

   The reduction of waste is another advantage of sustainable logistics. Instead of maintaining paper files, the majority of businesses are centralizing and digitizing their documentation, records, and operational data within integrated web systems. As a result, the amount of paper waste generated during production is drastically reduced, and operations are streamlined by having customer insights, inventory information, and order management in one location (Champion, 2022).

9. **Heightens consumer awareness**

    Customers have demonstrated that they are aware of their carbon footprint. They want to know which brands best represent their beliefs and have the least negative effects on the environment. By incorporating green logistics into their operations, brands may boost customer awareness and provide them with advice on how to carry out their own sustainability activities (Champion, 2022).

    GSCM makes mention of the items' origins and packaging as a brand and offers guidelines so that customers can recycle materials at home as well. A yearly consumer report that highlights the accomplishment of ecofriendly objectives, such as the percentage of decreased gas emissions or a transition to renewable resources, might also be sent. These strategies increase the level of consumer involvement in the green logistics process (Champion, 2022).

10. **Builds brand reputation**

    Nowadays, information is easily accessible online, so having a green supply chain will help you develop your firm's brand reputation. Businesses which create technologically innovative, environmentally friendly items will be able to establish and maintain their brand identity (Shetty, 2020). Going green is a great way to show customers that the firm has embraced the green movement. Customers want to do business with companies that are concerned about the environment. Customers are reportedly willing to pay more for goods that guarantee ecofriendly shipping procedures and open supplier chains. Firms get a competitive edge in the market by implementing and publicizing concrete initiatives to improve green logistics in supply chain management. Customers are already willing to pay extra for goods from companies that use sustainable business strategies according to research. Being an ecoconscious retailer attracts favorable attention from new customers and is in line with what modern consumers want (Champion, 2022). Green logistics can be incorporated into any retail company model by lowering emissions, reducing paper and plastic waste, and raising consumer awareness. It is a good place to start that will have an effect on the environment both now and in the future. Making these programs a part of a continuous plan encourages customers to purchase ecofriendly products and promotes environmental change, which ultimately increases sales (Champion, 2022).

11. **Lowering gas emissions**

    Reduced greenhouse gas emissions are one benefit of green logistics. Following environmentally friendly best practices in logistics helps to lower the supply chain's carbon footprint. This covers everything, from cutting energy use to simplifying logistics processes for increased effectiveness (Champion, 2022).

12. **Cost cutting/reduction**

    By integrating digital technologies that promote sustainability, businesses can reduce costs. IT solutions that promote energy efficiency, resource substitution, and recycling can have a favorable effect on a company's financial statements (Shetty, 2020). Businesses that are pursuing green initiatives put a priority on lowering greenhouse gas emissions, which results in fewer shipments and shorter trips. Costs are reduced as a result of decreased fuel consumption and wear and tear on the vehicles. In order to increase margins by 0.25%, Nike, for example, modified the way it produced its new line of shoes. Labor expenses were cut by up to 50%, and material use was cut by 20%.

    Manufacturing with recycled materials can save costs. For instance, producers may now use recycled plastic to make 3D printing filament for less money than buying new plastic. Putting in the time and effort to guarantee that novel materials are safe and work as expected may be valuable nonetheless. Tossing out materials during production or shipping might be a missed opportunity; therefore, it is important to think outside the box on how to use the materials instead of wasting them. Recyclable materials can be put to new uses or even be turned into a source of income. Some factories that produce food, for instance, give their organic waste to local farmers so that it can be used as a fertilizer. The use of closed-loop recycling allows factories to repurpose substances like steel and glass into identical goods without compromising on quality. Thus, it may be possible to recycle manufacturing waste, such as excess materials or defective products, into usable forms.

If a firm is looking to save money and reduce waste, simplifying the firm's packing is a great place to start. A more space-efficient packaging design might also allow for more products to be shipped in the same amount of cargo space, which would cut down on transportation costs and carbon emissions. An end will be put on unsustainable methods eventually. If firms do not invest in long-term planning, they may be left high and dry if supply chain disruptions are brought on by environmental or socioeconomic factors. In order to be ready for a future in which a firm's current supply chain techniques will no longer be viable, it is a good idea to begin making plans now to adopt smarter and greener processes. Sustainable forestry practices, as opposed to clear-cutting trees, are a perfect illustration of this principle in action because they help maintain woodlands for continued use. Modifying even the smallest aspect of a firm's routine can have a significant impact on the firm's energy consumption and costs. Nike, for example, is well-known for employing a novel knitting method to lessen the need for human labor and natural resources while producing a sneaker that is both environmentally friendly and economically viable. Any increase in worker output, however slight, can have a significant impact on the amount of time machines spend running and, by extension, on their energy consumption.

13. Resource sustainability

A procedure or policy that enables reproduction and recycling at the same rate as product consumption should be in place across the supply chain if a company has implemented green practices there. Firms must have heard tales of how a hazardous product slipped through the cracks and entered the supply chain. Digital transformation aids in reducing risk. This is not only catastrophic for one individual but also for the entire business (Shetty, 2020). Such occurrences are extremely unlikely when there are digital security systems in place that guarantee transparency. Such solutions not only safeguard companies from dishonest partners but they also document and trace all labor and goods from point of origin to point of destination.

1.3.5 CHALLENGES OF CREATING A GREEN SUPPLY CHAIN

Globally, bigger companies are attempting to establish green supply chains to benefit the environment and enhance the image of their brands. Unfortunately, even the most prosperous companies in the world have a difficult time implementing green supply chains.

1. **Financial support is not available**

   According to Majumdar and Sinha (2019), one of the economic reasons that makes it challenging to deploy green initiatives to meet organizational goals is the lack of financial helpers. The use of GSCM is constrained due to a lack of initial funding, challenges locating organizations and lending funds, a shortage of loan capital for environmental development initiatives, and high recycling costs (Le et al., 2022).

2. **Lack of green industry professionals**

   Green industry expertise is needed in order to implement green practices. According to earlier studies, a major obstacle to green construction methods can be the lack of specialists in these domains.

3. **Inadequate backing from the senior executives**

   Lackadaisical top management does not provide the necessary motivation for GSCM practice implementation. GSCM activities within the organization can go a long way with the support and dedication of the senior management. Top management frequently becomes uneasy about GSCM procedures due to a lack of faith in them, a lack of knowledge of them, and the high initial expenses.

4. **The expensive implementation**

   For all stakeholders, the additional expenditures associated with putting green practices into effect present serious difficulties. It was also taken into account when researching how to use green methods in the building industry and other fields (Seuring and Muller, 2008; Liu et al., 2012; Zhang et al., 2011).

5. **Supplier adherence**

   The basis of green supply chains is good faith and trust. A business must obtain its raw materials from other green supply chains in order to adopt green supply chains (Shetty, 2020). However, it is typically next to impossible to get suppliers to follow ideals. Even top-tier vendors frequently flout laws governing green supply chains. Getting suppliers to support values will be challenging because most of them come from different nations. Every company, whether a buyer or a supplier, should attempt to join the green supply chain wave as one way to address this problem.

6. **Ignorance/lack of knowledge**

Global supply chains are incredibly intricate networks of buyers and sellers from all around the world. Knowing about lower-tier suppliers and other businesses that are involved in their supply chains is particularly challenging for businesses. For their business requirements, the majority of large corporations exclusively work with top-tier suppliers. Due to their ignorance and lack of information, many businesses are accused of using unfair methods. The existence of Nike's sweatshops in China serves as one such illustration. Even with the best of intentions, a corporation can only do a little.

7. **A lack of awareness and knowledge**

The lack of understanding and awareness of environmental initiatives and their advantages, according to earlier studies on green construction practices, is a key obstacle that prevents businesses from using green practices (Sourani and Sohail, 2011; Zhang et al., 2011). According to Bon-Gang (2018), a lack of knowledge on the indoor environment of sustainable and environmental buildings may be the result of insufficient research.

8. **Transport optimization**

There are many ways to reduce a firm's carbon footprint and save money by streamlining the firm's transportation logistics. For instance, load-planning software can help with logistics planning, improve cargo space utilization, and cut down on the number of trips needed to move a firm's goods. Additionally, switching from predominantly using air freight to another mode of shipment, like ocean freight, is more cost-effective and better for the environment.

9. **A dearth of green vendors**

Suppliers' green products are used by businesses to achieve green policies. If the material is not available through a standardized supplier and distribution network, businesses find it challenging to implement green practices. It is anticipated that working with suppliers who offer delivery guarantees, flexible payment plans, and competitive rates will boost green practices (Shi et al., 2013).

10. **Arbitrary and rigid stakeholder deadlines**

    Developers are expected to execute the project more quickly (from concept to delivery), particularly if it is predicted that demand for green practices will outpace the company's ability to meet it. The construction industry must go through a process and take more time than usual to implement green practices (Hwang and Tan, 2012). The timeframes that stakeholders assign to developers are frequently rigid and unforgiving. In order to compromise with all supply chain partners' green behaviors, a quick material supply method is necessary.

11. **Lack of collaboration or involvement with stakeholders**

    Stakeholders' propensity to protect their competitive advantage may discourage other stakeholders from getting involved at the conceptual stage to share ideas and best practices. According to Liu, Low, and He (2012), a major obstacle to implementing green practices is poor communication amongst stakeholders brought on by a lack of involvement (Handayani et al., 2021).

1.4   IMPLICATIONS

Supply chain leaders classify logistics capabilities as one of the pillars of organizational performance and economic development. Business leaders and policymakers identified the need to enforce and enhance sustainable logistics infrastructure and capabilities in developed countries, while the developing and underdeveloped countries' business leaders strive to implement policies to foster logistics performance domestically and internationally. Efficient and effective logistics connects organizations to the domestic and international markets through supply chain networks. Organizations identified as low logistics performance companies incur a higher cost because of transportation costs and unreliable supply chain networks; however, organizations with high logistics performance rankings enjoy low costs and a competitive advantage.

1.5 CONCLUSIONS

The chapter aimed to identify the benefits and challenges of GSCM. GSCM is an evolving concept and is still in its nascent stages. The study of the literature on GSCM and its benefits adds to a better understanding of the concept, while a study of the challenges that lay ahead for the field makes it very evident that there is still a long way to go before GSCM is fully embraced. With the above benefits, including better efficiency and cost savings, in the long run, green supply chains would become a prerequisite for business sustainability. Businesses too can transform a firm's supply chain into a green one by leveraging modern supply chain management technologies. However, as today's organizations increasingly become aware of their environmental footprint and the inherent financial benefit in moving toward 'greener' supply chains, the acceptance and implementation of GSCM practices as a key game changer is only going to rise.

KEYWORDS

- **green**
- **supply chain**
- **challenges**
- **benefits**
- **environment**

REFERENCES

Ananda, A. R. W.; Astuty, P.; Nugroho, Y. C. Role of Green Supply Chain Management in Embolden Competitiveness and Performance: Evidence from Indonesian Organizations. *Int. J. Supp. Chain Manag.* **2018**, *7*, 437–442.

Arora, K. Green Supply Chain Management: Need, Advantages and Challenges, 2020. https://www.linkedin.com/pulse/green-supply-chain-management-need-advantages-challenges-keshav-arora

Aziziankohan, A.; Jolai, F.; Khalilzadeh, M.; Soltani, R.; TavakkoliMoghaddam, R. Green Supply Chain Management Using the Queuing Theory to Handle Congestion and Reduce Energy Consumption and Emissions from Supply Chain Transportation Fleet. *J. Indust. Eng. Manag.* **2017**, *10*, 213–236. DOI: 10.3926/ jiem.2170

Aslam, H.; Rashid, K.; Wahla, A. R.; Tahira, U. Drivers of Green Supply Chain Management Practices and their Impact on Firm Performance: A Developing Country Perspective. *J. Quantit. Methods* **2018**, *2* (1), 87–113.

Asif, M. S.; Lau, H.; Nakandala, D. et al. Adoption of Green Supply Chain Management Practices Through Collaboration Approach in Developing Countries—From Literature Review to Conceptual Framework. *J. Clean Prod.* **2020**, *276*, 124191. https://doi.org/10.1016/j.jclepro. 2020.124191

20cube. Top 5 Benefits of Embracing Green Supply Chain, 2018. https://www.20cube.com/blog/5-benefits-of-green-supply-chain/

Bhateja, A.; Babbar, R.; Singh, S.; Sachdeva, A Study of Green Supply Chain Management in the Indian Manufacturing Industries: A Literature Review cum an Analytical Approach for the Measurement of Performance. *Int. J. Comput. Eng. Manag.* **2011**, *13*.

Champion, A. 4 Advantages of Green Logistics in Supply Chain Management & How to Apply Them. Flowspace, 24 Oct 2022. https://flow.space/blog/4-advantages-of-green-logistics-in-supply-chain-management-how-to-apply-them/

De, D.; Chowdhury, S.; Dey, P. K.; Ghosh, S. K. Impact of Lean and Sustainability Oriented Innovation on Sustainability Performance of Small and Medium Sized Enterprises: A Data Envelopment Analysis-Based Framework. *Int. J. Prod. Econ.* **2020**, *219*, 416–430. DOI: 10.1016/j.ijpe.2018.07.003

Diabat, A.; Govindan, K. An Analysis of the Drivers Affecting the Implementation of Green Supply Chain Management. *Resour. Conserv. Recycl.* **2011**, *55* (2011), 659–667.

Geffen, C.; Rothenberg, S. Suppliers and Environmental Innovation—The Automotive Paint Process. *Int. J. Operat. Prod. Manag.* **2000**, *20* (2) 166–186.

Gong, R.; Xue, J.; Zhao, L.; Zolotova, O.; Ji, X.; Xu, Y. A Bibliometric Analysis of Green Supply Chain Management Based on the Web of Science (WOS) Platform. *Sustainability* **2019**, *11*, 3459. DOI: 10.3390/su11123459

Ikram, A.; Su, Q.; Fiaz, M.; Rehman, R. U. Cluster Strategy and Supply Chain Management: The Road to Competitiveness for Emerging Economies. *Benchmarking* **2018**, *25*, 1302–1318. DOI: 10.1108/BIJ-06–2015–0059

Khan, S. A. R.; Jian, C.; Yu, Z.; Golpîra, H.; Kumar, A. Impact of Green Practices on Pakistani Manufacturing Firm Performance: A Path Analysis Using Structural Equation Modeling Computational Intelligence and Sustainable Systems. In: *Computational Intelligence and Sustainable Systems*; Springer, 2019; pp 87–97. DOI: 10.1007/978–3-030–02674–5_6

Le, T. T.; Vo, X. V.; Venkatesh, V. G. Role of Green Innovation and Supply Chain Management in Driving Sustainable Corporate Performance. *J. Clean. Prod.* **2022**, *374*, 133875.

Mathiyazhagan K.; Datta U.; Singla A.; Krishnamoorthi S. Identification and Prioritization of Motivational Factors for the Green Supply Chain Management Adoption: Case from Indian Construction Industries. *Opsearch* **2018**, *55*, 202–219.

Majumdar, A.; Sinha, S. K. Analyzing the Barriers of Green Textile Supply Chain Management in Southeast Asia Using Interpretive Structural Modeling. *Sustain. Prod. Consum.* **2019**.

Rao, P.; Holt, D Do Green Supply Chains Lead to Competitiveness and Economic Performance? *Int. J. Operat. Prod. Manag.* **2005**, *25* (9), 898–916.

Raman, P. Green Supply Chain Management in India—An Overview. *J. Supply Chain Manag. Syst.* **2014**, *3* (1).

Saada, R. *Green Transportation in Green Supply Chain Management*; Intechopen, 2021. https://www.intechopen.com/chapters/72772. DOI: 10.5772/intechopen.93113

Saade R.; Thoumy, M.; Sakr, O. Green Supply Chain Management Adoption in Lebanese Manufacturing Industries: An Exploratory Study. *Int. J. Logist. Syst. Manag.* **2019**, *32*, 520–547.

Shetty, J. What Is Green Supply Chain and Its Benefits? 29 Dec 2020. https://www.trademo.com/blog/2020/12/29/what-is-green-supply-chain-and-its-benefits/

Zhu, Q.; Sarkis, J. Relationships Between Operational Practices and Performance Among Early Adopters of Green Supply Chain Management Practices in Chinese Manufacturing Enterprises. *J. Operat. Manag.* **2004**, *22*, 265–289.

CHAPTER 2

Factors/Determinants of Green Supply Chain Management (GSCM) Practices

MOHAMMED ABDUL-BASIT FUSEINI[1], ALHASSAN SEIDU[2], SHANI SALIFU[3], and MOHAMMED MAJEED[4]

[1]Department of Marketing, Tamale Technical University, Tamale, Ghana

[2]Department of Secretaryship and Management, Tamale Technical University, Tamale, Ghana

[3]Chicago School of Professional Psychology, Chicago, USA

ABSTRACT

Organizational production and distribution models have undergone radical shifts as a result of climate change, carbon emissions, and the loss of natural resources. Within this framework, practitioners in many nations have begun to focus on "greening" their supply chains. Carbon taxes, for instance, are now legal in a number of countries. However, green supply chain management methods and the effect they have on business performance are still in the early stages of development. Therefore, this study set out to identify what drives the use of GSCM methods, often known as "green supply chain management". The main GSCM adoption factors found in the literature were mainly internal and external. These subfactors were as follows: stakeholder pressure, environmental factors, leadership commitment, technology and innovation, knowledge, cost, and brand image. Finally, the chapter discussed the trending issues in GSCM.

2.1 INTRODUCTION

Supply chain environmental management (SCEM), or "greening the supply chain," refers to the practice of selecting only environmentally responsible

---

Green Supply Chain Management. Mohammed Majeed, Kirti Agarwal, and Ahmed Tijani (Eds.)
© 2025 Apple Academic Press, Inc. Co-published with CRC Press (Taylor & Francis)

vendors to enter into contractual relationships with manufacturers. In addition, GSCM encompasses both reactive measures done in accordance with general national environmental initiatives and progressive practices implemented via a number of "R"s (Reduce, Reuse, Rework, Refurbish, Reclaim, Recycle, Remanufacture, and Reverse logistics). Green supply chain management emphasizes conserving nonrenewable natural resources, cutting down on pollution and waste, and limiting emissions. To ensure that a company's operations have no detrimental effects on the environment, it should implement green supply chain management (GSCM) techniques. Incorporating GSCM from the start of the SC processes all the way through to the finish and even after the products' shelf life has expired is done so that both the supply chain operations and the products produced by the company may perform better (Gilbert, 2017). In this early stage of going green, lowering energy use is the most important component. Producing enough energy to run everything from machinery and lights to climate control in a factory is no small task. Hydropower, wind energy, solar energy, and biofuels are just a few examples of alternative energy sources that might help you use less fossil fuels. Energy consumption can be drastically reduced by the use of modern manufacturing techniques and even little adjustments, such as the installation of light-emitting diode lighting. Green supply chain management has several benefits for companies that seek to implement environmental management efforts like green supply chain management, despite the fact that green supply chain management methods can cost more than a company's investment budget (Choi et al., 2017). Focusing on green supply chain management solutions will help businesses gain stakeholder support, credibility, and resources (Bu et al., 2020). Green supply chain management can be implemented by businesses in response to demand from consumers, management, government mandates, and competitive pressure (Choi et al., 2017). Green supply chain management strategies are now required by law and public concern, as stated by KIPPRA (2018) in the manufacturing sector. In order to stay ahead of the competition, a lot of businesses are constantly looking for ways to develop and enhance their return systems. Businesses are starting to investigate green supply chain management strategies as a means of increasing their profits (OECD, 2017).

When it comes to integrating sustainability into a company's operations, GSCM is a tried-and-true green strategy (Darnall et al., 2008). Factors that influence GSCM implementation and maintenance must be identified, though (Dhull and Narwal, 2016). Costing a lot of money and taking a lot of effort to maintain, GSCM is essential for the manufacturing processing industry (Faisal, 2015). Investigations found that industrial companies have not adopted green supply chain practices, and these were empirical studies. All of the aforementioned research was conducted in a variety of settings, each of which was affected in its own unique way by factors unique to the industries and geographic locations studied. In light of this context, the goal of this chapter is to conduct a literature study to identify the factors that influence the adoption of environmentally friendly supply chain management strategies. This research fills a gap in the existing literature on GSCM adoption.

2.2 LITERATURE

2.2.1 GSCM

When a company adopts "green" methods, it lessens their negative impact on the environment and climate while still achieving its stated goals (Kumar and Chandrakar, 2012). Going green, as described by Griskevicius et al. (2010), can be understood as a company's strategy to move from focusing on pollution control to proactively avoiding pollution. When compared to conventional supply chains, "Green Supply Chains address the environmental impacts of all processes of the supply chain, from the extraction of raw materials to the final disposal of commodities," as stated by Emmet and Sood (2010). As a result, there is a greater emphasis on total inventory costs, with increased transparency and information exchange among all supply chain participants. When compared to sustainable supply chain management, green supply chain management (GSCM) appears to be more narrowly oriented, with a concentration on the ecological component of sustainability while the social dimension is typically disregarded. One of the most common definitions of GSCM is proffered by Srivastava (2007), who says that it is the practice of incorporating ecological considerations into every stage of the supply chain, from initial concept to final disposal. This includes everything from product design and material selection to manufacturing and distribution. In their latest comprehensive literature study, Ahi and Searcy (2013) found 22 different definitions of GSCM. They discovered that the majority of the definitions they looked at emphasized the need of coordination and flows while also addressing environmental and economic concerns. Further, GSCM can be defined in a variety of ways, from the reactive monitoring of general environmental management programs to more proactive approaches and even environmental innovations (Zhu and Sarkis, 2004). Environmental methods such as "green" purchasing, "green" logistics, and "green" operations management are all part of what is known as "green supply chain management" (GSCM) (Zsidisin and Siferd, 2001). In GSCM, organizations within the same supply chain are required to work together to improve their environmental standards. By balancing marketing performance with environmental difficulties, green supply chains help lessen environmental challenges including pollution reduction and energy savings (Kumar and Chandrakar, 2012). As part of their commitment to environmental sustainability for the long term, most companies have incorporated GSCM principles and practices into their operations (Masudin, 2019). Adopting businesses gets an edge when GSCM is implemented because it achieves a balance between negative environmental consequences, social benefits, and profit-generating operations that generate value along the so-called triple bottom line (Tyagi et al., 2015). Greater Sustainable Community Management (GSCM) is an ecofriendly principle with a focus on improving community sustainability.

2.2.2 FACTORS FOR ADOPTING GSCM

When it comes to the future of our planet and the economy, green supply chain strategies are essential. Further, they contribute to competitiveness and economic performance through a variety of channels, including enhanced resource productivity, less waste, and satisfied consumer demand for environmentally friendly goods. However, the primary drivers of green supply chain practices adoption also impede their implementation if they are not handled effectively. Any number of internal and external factors can have a role.

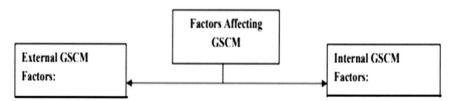

FIGURE 2.1 Determinants/factors for GSCM.

Source: Adapted from Kumar, R.; and Chandrakar, R. Overview of Green Supply Chain Management: Operation and Environmental Impact at Different Stages of the Supply Chain. *Int. J. Eng. Adv. Technol.* 2012, *1*, 3–4.

2.2.3 INTERNAL FACTORS (ELEMENT(S) INSIDE THE SYSTEM)

Like the internal factors identified by Kirchoff et al. (2016), these can be altered to improve the situation and raise GSCM awareness within an organization. When contrasted with external influences, the success rate and performance of green practices can be quickly improved by taking steps to control and solve these demotivating causes (Joseph, 2012). These include the high start-up costs of implementing GSCM and a lack of relevant expertise and experience in environmentally conscious activities.

2.2.4 EXTERNAL FACTORS (FORCES FROM OUTSIDE)

The term "external factors" refers to those elements of the environment outside of the company that might have a significant impact on internal endeavors like GSCM. The term "external motivating factors" refers to events and circumstances outside the company that the management has little to no control over. According to Sreejith and Vinaya's (2017) analysis, these external factors are roadblocks that are outside of the organization's control, and the most that upper management can do to improve corporate performance is to try to cope with them.

2.2.5 STAKEHOLDER INSISTENCE

Dubey et al. (2015) added that when upstream stakeholders in the supply chain are the ones who pay for the service or product, the pressure from these stakeholders will compel the linked firm to implement GSCM. As can be seen from the preceding remark, the upstream stakeholder holds the greater influence in determining the extent to which GSCM is applied to the entire supply chain.

2.2.6 ENVIRONMENTAL ASPECTS

Sustainable businesses take environmental considerations into account at every stage of production, consumption, and expansion. As a result, businesses are becoming increasingly conscious of the need to embrace environmentally friendly practices and processes in order to lessen their impact on the environment and boost sustainable output (Khan et al., 2019). When we talk about an organization's "environment," we are referring to its total responsibility for ensuring its own continued success. A company's environmental performance and green innovation may both benefit from increased emphasis on environmentally friendly practices throughout the whole GSCM

(Wang et al., 2021). Adopting GSCM methods reduces waste, boosts output, and promotes a more equitable relationship between the environment and the economy.

2.2.7 COMMITTED LEADERSHIP

When it comes to GSCM, top-down buy-in is essential for success. The success of GSCM efforts might be helped or hindered by the backing of upper management (Kumar and Chandrakar, 2012). The backing of upper management is a key factor in the success of GSCM programs because it inspires staff and links long-term business objectives with short-term sustainability objectives (Dhull and Narwal, 2016). A green supply chain plan can be developed more quickly and efficiently when there is widespread support from upper management. However, inconsistencies might emerge in the supply chain if decision makers cannot agree on what procedures to implement. Concerns about supply chain efficiency, quality assurance, and the overall success of green initiatives are all possible obstacles. Initial GSCM failure can be attributed to a lack of managerial backing, which in turn can demotivate staff (Kumar and Chandrakar, 2012).

2.2.8 TECHNOLOGIES AND NEW IDEAS

Through the use of a computer system and application software, IT applications to green supply chains in agriculture facilitate communication and collaboration between supply chain participants, ensuring that information is always up-to-date and that links between stages of the supply chain are solid (Shreejith, 2012). As a result, the integration of information systems is crucial to the success of green supply chains. Green supply chain management is bolstered by a number of applications and cutting-edge technologies. Warehouse management systems (WMS) that improve warehouse productivity are only one example; others include greener manufacturing processes that need less energy or fewer potentially harmful substances. Success typically follows when staff members acquire knowledge about and readily adopt the technology that makes possible green supply chains. It might be more challenging to achieve long-term improvements when there is resistance from employees or low adoption. Green innovation is the use of technological advancements to forward business objectives in a way that has a less negative effect on the environment (Xue et al., 2019). When it comes to green innovation, the main goals are to reduce costs and increase product differentiation (Sellitto et al., 2020). When applied in its entirety, green innovation can help organizations cut costs while also minimizing the negative effects of their goods, services, and internal operations on the environment (Khan and Johl, 2019). Green innovation that helps lower the cost of satisfying business needs can be triggered by the establishment of adequate environmental regulations and stringent environmental control (Li et al., 2017). GSCM was developed to integrate SCM and EM concepts. Sustainable supply chain and activity providers have a competitive advantage (Jum'a et al., 2021; Saade et al., 2019). That is why it is no secret that incorporating environmentally friendly technologies into daily operations has its benefits and that it can even alter the dynamics between a company's suppliers and customers (Lin et al., 2020). Adoption of GSCM has a substantial impact on the environmental, social, and financial performance of a business; hence, it has received a lot of attention from researchers and practitioners (Masudin, 2019).

2.2.9 CREATING A POSITIVE AND UNIQUE BRAND CULTURE

In general, implementing new green practices throughout a supply chain goes smoothly when doing so has good implications for the brand and the culture supports these changes. Additionally, great outcomes are driven by integrating your human resources staff in recruiting green supply chain professionals. Your company may not do as well if the green movement is not widely supported inside the company culture and if consumer demand is not high enough to force changes in the industry.

2.3 COST

To do logistics and to have the infrastructure, capability, or readiness to perform logistics during a given time period entails incurring logistics costs (Hälinen, 2015). In industrialized countries, logistics costs are expected to constitute at least 10% of corporate turnover, though this varies widely by method and industry (Engblom et al., 2012). Supply chain costs and logistics expenses are commonly used interchangeably, but their meanings are distinct. Supply chain costs cover all costs in the supply chain of the company, such as manufacturing and installation, whereas logistics costs often include expenditures connected to distribution and warehousing. The initial investment is always a concern when talking about environmentally friendly measures (Lindemann et al., 2012). Introducing green practices into an enterprise typically necessitates the investment in new machinery and tools. Employees need to be trained on the new machinery and equipment before they can be put to use. Also, the organization's staff needs training on GSCM's concepts, methods, and issues before they can begin using them. Establishing a sustainable supply chain may appear too expensive at first depending on the company and the industry. It can be intimidating to consider the cost of investing in a complete infrastructure and equipment upgrade. However, these are long-term investments with potential savings. Installing photovoltaic solar panels, for instance, on the roof of a green warehouse can help provide alternative energy, reducing the need for fossil fuels and the associated costs of keeping a business's facilities powered. A large amount of cash is required, but it will be more than paid back. There will be additional financial strain on the company as a result of the time and money spent on training. Low productivity from new machinery and tools will cut into a company's profit according to Baumers et al. (2016). These will drive up a business's operating expenses, making it harder for already struggling small and medium-sized firms to breakeven.

2.4 KNOWLEDGE

Knowledge participants have the potential to significantly improve supply chain efficiency at every stage. Organizations might benefit from consulting with green architects, consultants, and other supply chain professionals to help them maximize the value of their green initiatives. Consider how much easier sustainable distribution would be with Agility's help in creating a green logistics solution. Inversely, your plan may be less successful as a whole if you choose not to incorporate the advice of specialists.

2.5 TRENDS IN GSCM

Because they were developed in response to a real need, sustainable supply chain methods are gradually making their way into the mainstream lexicon. Overshooting nature's capacity to support its inhabitants is harmful, and now that most people and institutions realize this, the search for sustainable solutions has gathered steam. In response to this motivation, a number of environmentally friendly developments have been made in supply chains and related areas in recent times. According to a recent report by Agility (2021), businesses can improve their environmental performance and contribute to a more sustainable future by implementing the following supply chain trends and practices:

2.6　INNOVATIVE AND SHARED PREPARATION

Simple solutions exist for logistics providers and shippers to better manage timetable needs, such as including slow-steaming into the planning of international shipments. When marketing and sales personnel are involved in supply chain planning, they gain a deeper comprehension of the ebb and flow of customer and product demand.

2.7　REDUCING THE AMOUNT OF FLYING CARGO TO THE BAREST MINIMUM

When time is of the essence, air shipping is unparalleled in its efficiency. It is not exactly energy-efficient, unfortunately. More and more businesses are realizing the benefits of depending on ocean freight and rail transport for their long-term supply demands while employing air freight for short-term surges in demand. You can better meet customer demand and reduce your company's environmental impact if you carefully plan your freight and transportation options.

2.8　NEWLY FORMING MARKETS AND INFRASTRUCTURE

All around the developing world, ports, roads, and trains will see significant upgrades. Cleaner, more efficient trucking is on the rise in Southeast Asia because of improvements including upgraded infrastructure, faster shipping times, greater quality products, reduced environmental effects, and tighter regulations on truck fleets. In the Middle East, too, the trend is toward lower emission, more fuel-efficient vehicles.

2.9　CLEAN TRANSPORTATION ON RAILS AND IN THE AIR

More efficient rail systems will be implemented in developed areas like Europe and North America, while railways will improve in emerging markets, and electric rail will be increasingly used in logistics. Air freight will remain an important part of the overall transport mix, but shippers will continue to use it judiciously. For example, firms may transport small batches of new items by air to meet the initial expected demand, but most of the products travel by ocean to better control cost and environmental impact.

2.10 PUTTING MONEY INTO TRANSPORTATION SYSTEMS

Transportation efficiency is increasing as a result of investments in ports, trains, and roadways, particularly in developing regions like Southeast Asia. Reduced carbon output is a direct result of this. The construction of additional charging stations for large electric trucks is the next logical step. In North America, the West Coast Electric Highway offers a promising beginning with its network of fast-charging stations for electric vehicles across the states of California, Oregon, and Washington. However, experts agree that in order to keep up with the global demand for green trucks, this infrastructure must develop at a quicker rate in all regions.

2.11 ADDITIVE MANUFACTURING

From the aerospace sector to the production of medical equipment, 3D printing is finding more and more uses every day. Furthermore, when compared to other equipment and techniques used in manufacturing, 3D printing saves both time and money. Why? Three-dimensional printing has many advantages over traditional manufacturing methods. One is that they let firms to make goods only when they are needed, minimizing waste. Reduced energy use and waste from 3D printing contribute to reduced greenhouse gas emissions. By using a 3D printer, you can even create something fresh out of used materials.

2.12 LOGISTICS NETWORKS THAT RECYCLE THEIR OWN MATERIALS

The goal of circular supply networks is to reduce waste by reusing and recycling commodities. This strategy can take numerous forms, such as Apple's refurbishment and resale of previously sold iPhones or the recycling of components for use in the creation of brand-new goods. Unsurprisingly, the circular economy approach helps cut down on waste and conserves useful resources by diverting them from landfills. It has the potential to generate substantial revenue for businesses.

2.13 CONSTRAINTS THAT PROMOTE PROGRESS AND PROSPERITY

Clean and efficient transportation may take a giant leap ahead with the help of sensible legislation, which can be a driving force for change in developing and developed economies equally if implemented correctly. The logistics industry can help create and pass laws that are good for business and the environment by focusing on streamlining and standardizing processes and minimizing waste in the supply chain.

2.14 STOCKPILING CARBON EMISSIONS FOR TRADING

Carbon trading refers to the international trade of "carbon credits" with the aim of reducing CO_2 emissions in each participating country. The amount of carbon dioxide (CO_2) emissions that each country is permitted to produce is capped. Carbon credits allow countries with greater emissions to pay those with lower emissions for the "right" to emit additional CO_2 into the environment. Trading is not limited to large corporations. The theory behind this setup is that there are many 'hidden costs' associated with using fossil fuels, such as damage to the natural world and the increased demand for medical attention caused by poor air quality. By assigning a monetary value to the privilege of emitting carbon, governments and businesses will have a financial reason to cut back on their emissions. In fact, the number of carbon trading systems in operation around the world is increasing.

2.15 TECHNOLOGY DEVELOPMENTS THAT ARE IMPACTING GREEN SUPPLY CHAIN PRACTICES

Greener outcomes are now more accessible than ever thanks to advancements in supply chain technology that optimize efficiency at each stage of a product's journey (Agility, 2021).

2.15.1 INTERNET OF THINGS (IOT)

With the help of IoT, businesses can track vitals like energy consumption, inventory levels, and machine uptime in real-time. Sensors can monitor a warehouse's temperature and illumination, for instance, allowing for remote regulation of those two factors. Energy waste, overstocking, and other mistakes are brought to light, raising awareness within organizations. As a result, it is easier to see where the supply chain as a whole requires improvement.

Increased supply chain efficiency and automation of procedures, such as stock reordering and optimizing warehouse picking patterns, are made feasible by the digitalization of the supply chain. This aids supply chain managers in reducing wasteful overordering and expedited shipment errors (like air freight). As a result, less trash and energy are produced thanks to these upgrades.

2.15.2 ARTIFICIAL INTELLIGENCE (AI)

Artificial intelligence (AI) facilitates automation, which in turn increases efficiency and reduces the possibility of human error. These skills are applicable at every stage of the supply chain, from reducing inefficiencies in production to predicting future demand for a product to optimizing the time and cost of transporting that product to the customer. Artificial intelligence reduces wastage because it makes humans more productive. Assume, for the sake of argument, that AI-enabled route optimization technologies save a few minutes per truck trip. That has the potential to significantly cut annual fuel costs and carbon dioxide emissions.

2.15.3 ROBOTICS

Automation with robots has the ability to improve logistics and other processes throughout the whole supply chain. Drones, for instance, may one day be more cost-effective than trucks for transporting packages of a modest size. Further, autonomous trucks might automate traffic choices, improving efficiency across the board, from delivery routes to fuel usage.

2.16 SCIENTIFIC STUDY OF MATERIALS

Greener and more efficient production and packaging have resulted from developments in materials engineering in recent years. For instance, cutting-edge methods have made it less difficult to create lightweight yet sturdy materials out of recycled resources. In addition, businesses may optimize their products for years to come with the use of life cycle planning software (Agility, 2021).

2.17 DISCUSSION

There is now a heightened understanding, on a worldwide scale, of the contributions that businesses may make to address the world's most pressing environmental problems. The result has been a shift in consumer preferences toward environmentally friendly goods. Stakeholders have also stepped up their pressure on businesses to adopt greener business practices, making GSCM adoption all the more crucial (Sarkis, 2017). Social responsibility and environmental criteria and guidelines, such as the Kyoto Protocol, have also been established as a result of the pressure placed on organizations to develop environmental policies and strategies (Wu and Pagell, 2017). For the purpose of gauging SC efficiency, businesses can look into a variety of metrics. Considerations including turnaround time, product quality, client satisfaction, and repeat business are just a few. All of the organization's current assets—its current resources, capabilities, devices, equipment, systems, instructions, and infrastructure—must be taken into account as part of a thorough and thorough preparation for the adoption of GSCM. Third, organizations' suppliers should be recognized as critical enablers for GSCM to be effectively implemented. Possible steps in this manner include forming strategic alliances and/or partnerships. Finally, the interconnections between GSCM and other new concepts like CSR, the global business environment, green marketing, and green technology need to be investigated in greater depth in future studies. These aspects can be found at both the micro- and macro organizational levels. The results of this research will aid GSCM practitioners, authorities, and stakeholders in the supply chain of the construction industry in gaining insight into crucial components of GSCM. Because the government acts as a moderator to monitor and supervise the environmental performance of organizations while they produce products and provide services to customers, environmental regulations and policies enacted by the government are a major external element (Huang et al., 2015). In addition, it is crucial to pay attention to the recognized external aspect of customer happiness, which is placed second, as well as the market's new opportunities and the pressure from competitors, which is ranked third. As Jayaram and Avittathur (2015) have pointed out, a strong selling point is required to attract more clients who are interested in ecofriendly methods. According to Sumeet et al. (2015), there is a glaring deficiency in green expertise in the business world. Since going green is the new normal, more and more companies will need to hire consultants with this skill set in order to comply with governmental regulations and industry standards when constructing new buildings.

2.18 CONCLUSIONS

It is clear from the literature that incorporating environmental practices into organizational activities is now a must for long-term viability and stakeholder satisfaction. The innovation necessary to get a market advantage is greening the SCs. Time, skill, dedication, and capital are all necessities for GSCM procedures. However, businesses will often start doing things a certain way if they can profit from it. In the literature, certain factors are generally classified as internal and external (Zailani et al., 2012). The purpose of this research is to examine the moderating effect of firm size on the relationship between GSCM adoption and other characteristics in Jordanian manufacturing enterprises. As a result, the research added to the body of knowledge in a number of ways. To give just one example, the study provides a comprehensive framework to academics and decision makers that illustrates the elements influencing supply chain managers' adoption intentions of GSCM methods. The research shows that four of the seven factors—supplier commitment, environmental sustainability, customer satisfaction, and cost factors—are the most important in convincing managers to embrace GSCM. In particular, these are what supply chain managers consider to be the most influential elements in relation to their plans to implement GSCM. We also learnt that the customer factor is the most important, followed by the cost factor, the environmental element, and the supplier factor. The results of this investigation will illuminate the weight and importance of many aspects in GSCM planning.

2.19 RECOMMENDATIONS

In order to boost performance, the study suggested that manufacturing companies adopt green supply chain management strategies. More studies should be conducted at other academic institutions to confirm these findings. The adoption of GSCM is mostly determined by organizational factors.

Because of its positive effects on corporate social responsibility and worker productivity, it can help spread awareness and interest in GSCM and CIT. The government is also crucial in this. To enable the green transformation of businesses, the government should strengthen assistance for SMEs by providing the necessary funding and technology, as well as drafting suitable legislation and regulations. Enhancing product offerings and design, decreasing operating expenses, and generating an enterprise green brand image can all play a role in the successful implementation of a company's green transformation strategy.

KEYWORDS

- **factors**
- **green**
- **supply chain management**
- **GSCM**

REFERENCES

Agility. Guide to Sustainable and Green Supply Chain Practices, 28 Apr 2021. https://www.agility.com/en/blog/what-are-green-supply-chain-practices-your-guide-to-supply-chain-sustainability/

Ahmed, W.; Najmi, A.; Khan, F. Examining the Impact of Institutional Pressures and Green Supply Chain Management Practices on Firm Performance. *Manag. Environ. Qual.* **2019**, *31* (5), 1261–1283. http://dx.doi.org/10.1108/MEQ-06–2019–0115

Ahi, P.; Searcy, C. A Comparative Literature Analysis of Definitions for Green and Sustainable Supply Chain Management. *J. Clean. Prod.* **2013**, *52*, 329–341.

Corsi, K.; Arru, B. Role and Implementation of Sustainability Management Control Tools: Critical Aspects in the Italian Context. *Account., Audit. Account. J.* **2021**, *34* (9), 29–56. http://dx.doi.org/10.1108/AAAJ-02–2019–3887

Darwish, S.; Shah, S.; Ahmed, U. The Role of Green Supply Chain Management Practices on Environmental Performance in the Hydrocarbon Industry of Bahrain: Testing the Moderation of Green Innovation. *Uncert. Supply Chain Manag.* **2021**, *9*, 265–276. DOI: 10.5267/j.uscm.2021.3.006

Dubey, R.; Gunasekaranb, A.; Papadopoulos, T.; Childe, S. J. Green Supply Chain Management Enablers: Mixed Methods Research. *Sustain. Prod. Consump.* **2015**, *4*, 72–88.

Dhull, S.; Narwal, M. Drivers and Barriers in Green Supply Chain Management Adaptation: A State-of-Art Review. *Uncertain Supply Chain Manag.* **2016**, *4* (1), 61–76.

Engblom, J.; Solakivi, T.; Töyli, J.; Ojala. Multiple-Method Analysis of Logistics Costs. *Int. J. Prod. Econ.* **2012**, *137* (1), 29–35.

Emmet, S.; Sood, V. *Green Supply Chains : An Action Manifesto*; Wiley: Chichester, 2010.

Hälinen, H.-M. *Understanding the Concept of Logistics Cost in Manufacturing*; Publications of Turku School of Economics: Turku, 2015; pp A-1:2015.

Jum'a, L.; Zimon, D.; Ikram, M. A Relationship Between Supply Chain Practices, Environmental Sustainability and Financial Performance: Evidence from Manufacturing Companies in Jordan. *Sustainability* **2021**, *13*, 2152.

Jayaram, J.; Avittathur, B. Green Supply Chains: A Perspective from an Emerging Economy. *Int. J. Prod. Econ.* **2015**, *164*, 234–244.

Khan, S. A. R.; Chen, J.; Zhang, Y.; Golpîra, H. Effect of Green Purchasing, Green Logistics, and Ecological Design on Organizational Performance: A Path Analysis Using Structural Equation Modeling. *Inf. Technol. Intel. Transp. Syst.* **2019**, *314*, 183–190. DOI: 10.3233/978-1-61499-939-3-183

Khan, P. A.; Johl, S. K. Nexus of Comprehensive Green Innovation, Environmental Management System-14001-2015 and Firm Performance: A Conceptual Framework. *Cogent Bus. Manag.* **2019**, *6* (1), 1691833. http://dx.doi.org/10.1080/23311975.2019.1691833.

Kumar, R.; Chandrakar, R Overview of Green Supply Chain Management: Operation and Environmental Impact at Different Stages of the Supply Chain. *Int. J. Eng. Adv. Technol.* **2012**, *1*, 1–6.

Laari, S.; Töyli, J.; Solakivi, T.; Ojala, L. Firm Performance and Customer-Driven Green Supply Chain Management. *J. Clean. Prod.* **2016**, *112*, 1960–1970. http://dx.doi.org/10.1016/j.jclepro.2015.06.150

Lin, C.-Y.; Alam, S. S.; Ho, Y.-H.; al-Shaikh, M. E.; Sultan, P. Adoption of Green Supply Chain Management Among SMEs in Malaysia. *Sustainability* **2020**, *12*, 6454.

Masudin, I. A Literature Review on Green Supply Chain Management Adoption Drivers. *J. Ilm. Tek. Ind.* **2019**, *18*, 103–115.

Shreejith, B. Examining Green Production and Its Role within the Competitive Strategy of Manufacturing. *J. Ind. Eng. Manag.* **2012**, *5* (1), 53–87.

Srivastava, S. K. Green Supply-Chain Management: A State-of-the-Art Literature Review. *Int. J. Manag. Rev.* **2007**, *9* (1), 53–80.

Tyagi, M.; Kumar, P.; Kumar, D. Analysis of Interactions Among the Drivers of Green Supply Chain Management. *Int. J. Bus. Perform. Supply Chain Model.* **2015**, *7*, 92–108.

Zhu, Q.; Sarkis, J. Relationships Between Operational Practices and Performance Among Early Adopters of Green Supply Chain Management Practices in Chinese Manufacturing Enterprises. *J. Operat. Manag.* **2004**, *22* (3), 265–289.

Zhao, Y.; Zhang, L.; Chen, X.; Cao, C. Impact of Quality Management on Green Innovation. *J. Clean. Prod.* **2017**, *13* (8), 462–470.

United Nations Global Compact. Using Bus: Better Word. from https://www.unglobalcompact.org/sdgs/about (accessed on 29 Mar 2022).

CHAPTER 3

Key Green Supply Chain Management Practices Today

SHANI SALIFU[1], ALHASSAN SEIDU[2], and
MOHAMMED ABDUL-BASIT FUSEINI[3]

[1]Chicago School of Professional Psychology, Chicago, USA

[2]Department of Secretaryship and Management, Tamale Technical University, Tamale, Ghana

[3]Department of Marketing, Tamale Technical University, Tamale, Ghana

ABSTRACT

Climate change and depletion of the ozone layer are two key pollution challenges that have emerged as a top priority in recent decades. The construction industry is a major contributor to environmental pollution. Green purchasing, production, delivery, packing, promoting, education about the environment, internal resource stewardship, and recouping investments are all initiatives that business leaders should pursue. Providing GSCM tactics to gain a competitive edge and informing company managers on strategies that optimize environmental conservation and minimize unfavorable environmental impacts, such as global warming, are two examples of how this research could lead to beneficial social change. Environmentally responsible procedures were advocated for use by manufacturing companies along the whole supply chain, from the sourcing of raw materials to the final disposal of finished goods. The findings can be used by regulators to encourage more businesses to adopt GSCM practices by making it mandatory for them to do so and providing rewards to those who have.

3.1 INTRODUCTION

The degradation of the natural world as a result of increasing human and industrial activity is a proven truth. In today's world, environmental pollution is the most pressing issue, and if it isn't fixed soon, it could spell the end of human civilization. Air pollution is the most urgent environmental crisis at the moment. The rise in atmospheric concentrations of greenhouse gases, which is causing global warming, is currently the greatest threat to human civilization. Before the industrial revolution, atmospheric carbon dioxide concentrations were estimated to be around 280 ppm; now, they have risen to an alarming 380 ppm and are continuing to grow rapidly. It is impossible to separate the function and evolution of the industrial environment in achieving long-term sustainability from the many attempts to mitigate the threats of global warming, regulate pollution, and enhance eco-friendly practices (United Nations Global Compact, 2020). Companies in the developed world must incorporate social effectiveness as a resource for openness from sustainability awareness, which is then anticipated to serve as a pivotal factor in the management's decision-making regarding the company's success (Corsi and Arru, 2021). The purpose of green supply chains is to reduce environmental impacts such as air, water, and waste pollution by employing ecologically responsible and socially just techniques at every step of the process. Managers are under increasing pressure from governments and customers to adopt GSCM processes, with an emphasis on coordinating with external suppliers, in order to remain competitive in the global market (Yan et al., 2016). As the world economy has grown increasingly interconnected and unstable, GSCM has emerged as a crucial competitive strategy for businesses operating in the global marketplace (Gandhi et al., 2015). The authors (Martín-de Castro et al., 2016) of a study found that environmentally responsible practices led to increased success for businesses. Although previous studies have concentrated on traditional metrics of supply chain performance, such as cost, time, and accuracy, customers and governments are increasingly pressuring businesses to comply with environmental and social responsibilities due to environmental corrosion (Mathiyazhagan et al., 2014). Businesses have been driven to reduce their impact on the environment as a result of governmental legislation and consumer awareness (Zhu et al., 2016). However, company leaders have had a hard time pinpointing the obstacles that stand in the way of GSCM's widespread adoption (Govindan and Soleimani, 2017). Environmental performance, waste reduction, financial savings, and a competitive edge can all benefit from GSCM initiatives implemented by business management (Daddi et al., 2016).

Some business executives in the industrial sector are ignoring the proven effectiveness of GSCM in boosting bottom-line results (ater et al., 2018). About 70% of business executives said they do not include GSCM strategies in their operational operations, even though industry leaders have raised awareness of GSCM in developing markets (Geng et al., 2017). Studies on the effects of green production, green procurement, green logistics, green design, and green distribution on sustainable performance have been undertaken on numerous multinational corporations and major businesses and are widely available in the literature (Ananda et al., 2018). The goal of this chapter is to review the literature on GSCM practices that are core to a firm's success.

3.2 GSCM

GSCM is the practice of incorporating environmental considerations into conventional supply chain management, such as through material reuse, material reduction, and material recycling (Yan et al., 2016). The integration of supply chain management has evolved as a result of the introduction of new technology and the rise of a competitive marketplace. Immediate feedback at every stage of the supply chain speeds up the shipment of products ordered by customers (MacCarthy et al., 2016). Natural resources are threatened by reckless consumption, and wasteful practices have negative effects on the ecosystem (Montabon et al., 2016). A manager can use a variety of resources to assist them develop and execute effective GSCM plans. Multinational companies can reap many financial benefits from obtaining ISO 14001 certification, including operational effectiveness and efficiency, product/brand awareness on a global scale, marketing opportunities, increased competitiveness, and lower waste management costs (Cherrafi et al., 2016). Depending on the company's business and location, cost savings and improved productivity may be the most compelling reasons to implement ISO 14001 (Treacy et al., 2018). When an organization adopts ISO 14001 and subsequently becomes certified, it reaps environmental, financial, and managerial benefits (Iatridis and Kesidou, 2018). Managers can use the BSC model to evaluate the environmental impact of their supply chains (Ferreira et al., 2016).

3.3 GSCM PRACTICES

FIGURE 3.1 GSCM practices.
Source: Author's creation.

3.4 GREEN DESIGN

What we mean when we talk about "green design" is the procedure of creating goods and services that are gentler on the planet. "Green design" is synonymous with eco-design, design for the environment, and life-cycle design. Sustainable, reusable, and easily repairable items are the backbone of green design. Green design is used by top executives in the supply chain to cut down on waste, expenses, and environmental damage by reusing and recycling materials. The term "green design" refers to the process of creating products that are safer for the environment by reducing their reliance on toxic substances and energy usage (Diab et al., 2015). World Business Council for Sustainable Development pioneered the idea of eco-design, and it has since had an impact across the board in the manufacturing process (Fernando, 2017). Products are made, packaged, and disseminated with eco-design principles in mind. The organization's long-term viability stands out among the many benefits. Eco-design provides a better environmental commitment and is, thus, a groundbreaking approach to green supply chain management, all of which contribute to the company's sustainability performance. A large portion of the GSCM literature is dedicated to the topic of "green design," or the process of creating products while keeping environmental factors in mind. As a result of the advancements in modern society and the evolution of the corporate world, packaging is now considered an integral part of our daily lives. Packaging is the process of encapsulating a product for distribution or sale. It includes securing, labeling, and packaging things in order to protect them during travel and storage. Packaging is an integral part of the branding process because it plays a role in communicating the image and identity of a company. Packaging is defined by Saliba (2017) as the act of containing, protecting, and presenting the contents through the long chain of production, handling, and transportation to their destinations in the same condition as they were at the time of production. Green design, as described by Fiksel (1996), is the practice of giving due consideration to environmental health and safety concerns across a product's whole life cycle, from inception to disposal. Environmental risk management, product safety, pollution prevention, resource conservation, and waste management are just some of the many disciplines that contribute to the success of a green design (Srivastava 2007). It appears that there is now a substantial body of work in the field of green design. Two major environmental techniques—life cycle assessment (LCA) and environmentally aware design—provide frameworks for organizing this research.

Companies that prioritize profits over the environment evaluate designs by weighing the benefits of going green against the costs of doing so (Hong and Guo, 2018). One of the benefits of green design, as proposed by Li et al. (2015), is the development of long-term competitive advantages. The costs of environmentally friendly design must be weighed against revenue streams, as pointed out by Hong and Guo (2018). By providing more affordable, environmentally friendly goods and services, a company can set itself apart from the competition through its green design initiatives.

3.5 ENVIRONMENT-FRIENDLY DATA PROCESSING SYSTEM

Adapted information systems that keep tabs on environmental impacts are called "green information systems" (Esty and Winston, 2006). Data on the organization's manufacturing, purchasing, selling, and logistics activities' contributions to and consequences of environmental sustainability is crucial to the effective application of GSCM principles (Preuss, 2002). This information can then be used to increase environmental sustainability throughout the supply chain through informed decision-making based on evaluated data (Preuss, 2002). By supporting the company's internal environmental management systems and catering to the reporting demands of many stakeholders, green information systems effectively serve as the backbone of environmental management activities (El-Gayar and Fritz, 2006). Coordinating with clients on eco-design, production, packing, and shipping is made easier with the data provided by green information systems. In terms of cohesiveness and cohesion, SCM is greatly aided by the dissemination of data via environmentally friendly information technologies (Chandra et al., 2007). According to Frohlich and Westbrook (2001), logistical integration refers to the degree to which all parties involved in the supply chain work together to manage the flow of basic information and physical goods. Hamprecht et al. (2005) use a case study of the food sector to argue for the necessity of integrating environmental controls with other quality controls inside the information system that spans the entire food supply chain. Decisions about eco-design (in terms of material and energy consumption, reuse, recycling, and recovery of materials) will be supported by data from green information systems. Overstock, junk, and unused capital equipment can all be recouped, thanks to the data provided by green IT systems.

3.6 ECO-FRIENDLY PROCUREMENT

As part of green supply chain management, "green purchasing" is also a crucial technique. In "green purchasing," only "goods and services that are less harmful to the environment" are selected. The term "green supply chain" describes a process that includes green purchasing, environmental management of manufacturing resources, environmental circulation marketing, and reverse logistics (RL) (Yunis et al., 2016). Green purchasing is often regarded as an efficient strategy for promoting products and services that have a low environmental impact. Furthermore, it aids in raising shoppers' awareness of environmental issues. The use of environmentally responsible purchasing practices is critical to the success of environmental initiatives. Having an appreciation for the natural environment and its inhabitants is crucial for many reasons, including the conservation of scarce resources and the protection of endangered species. Increasing people's understanding of the economic, aesthetic, and biological value of protecting natural resources and lessening or eliminating the negative effects of human modification is the primary function of environmental education. The practice incorporates ecological considerations into the buying process. Buying in a sustainable manner is known as "green procurement," and it involves activities such as material reduction, reuse, and recycling (Salam, 2008). Green procurement refers to the PLC-wide practice of acquiring goods and services that are better for the environment and cause less harm (Lacroix, 2008). Buying recycled paper is one good example (Arora, 2020). Saving money through waste prevention is typically more effective earlier in the supply chain rather than later. Since waste reduction must first begin with purchasing decisions, recycling and reuse rates at a company are important indicators of green purchasing success. Hokey and Galle (2001) argued that cutting down on emissions such as those from cars and factories was crucial to the growth of the green procurement movement. Both the technology, equipment, and facilities of waste separation and the purchasing practices of companies can be affected by the types of resources available to them. Recent studies on purchasing habits show that it is also deeply linked with environmental management, which has been overlooked in recent years as purchasing has been seen as a bottom-line financial consideration. Improvements in organizational performance, as well as monetary and ecological considerations, have been found to be positively impacted by environmentally conscious purchasing practices (Liobikiene et al., 2016). Organizations can reduce their environmental impact through any number of green purchasing practices. Each tactic is unique in its design and its effect on the ecological habits of service providers. It emphasizes items with greener features. Customers who value sustainability are likely to reward the company with higher market share if given the option between conventional and eco-friendly options (Khoiruman and Haryanto, 2017). To minimize waste and its negative effects on the environment, many businesses are adopting a practice known as "green purchasing" (Song, 2017). Integrating internal and external resources is what makes proactive supplier collaboration beneficial to sustainable success (Hong and Guo, 2018). Green supply chain activities percolate down via suppliers via collaborative contractual agreements, thereby solidifying green purchasing habits. Efficient workflows and ethical leadership are essential to the long-term viability of a process-based approach to green purchasing (Song, 2017). The procurement of materials, components, and services all play significant roles in ensuring the viability of supply chains (Islam et al., 2017). The ability to make green purchases benefits both the environment and the economy (Yook et al., 2017). Investments in green purchasing activities give a favorable return on investments, which may boost profitability, as agreed upon by Islam et al. (2017) and Yook et al. (2017). Socially responsible performance metrics can be developed through green purchasing methods made possible by supply chain managers employing a collaborative supply chain strategy.

3.7 REVERSE LOGISTICS

RL refers to the process of bringing unwanted items back into a business in order to be used or discarded. Planning, incorporating, and attempting to control the efficacious, cost-effective raw material flow in process inventory, finished goods, and related information from the point of consumption back to the point of origin, with the goal of recapturing value or proper disposal, is what is known as RL. When a product is returned to a manufacturer, the logistics behind the product's subsequent disposal, removal, recycling, reprocessing, or repair are referred to as "RL" (Wright et al., 2011). Organizing, implementing, and regulating the cost-effective flow of raw materials in process inventory, finished items, and related information from the point of consumption back to the point of origin, with the goal of recapturing value or correct disposal, is what is known as RL. Indicative of the discussion of whether there is a monetary benefit to RLs, it adds to the goal of creating business and environmental value from RLs procedures. RLs do not cover the disposal process, although it is nevertheless a possible endpoint for a flow of materials (Bensalem and Vichara 2019). Effective RL networks have been proven to yield substantial economic benefits and boost organizational competitiveness, thus their growing recognition as a strategic factor in GSCM is not surprising. As Sung (2019) points out, the numerous environmental protection requirements and the pressure on businesses to comply with them have shifted focus to RLs. In most sectors, the maker must bear responsibility for the product well beyond the point at which it is sold or the product's useful life ends. Supply chain hubs can gain insight into both their upstream and downstream operations by considering RL activities (Lau and Wang, 2009).

Value is captured in the process of investment recovery and re-manufacturing by reselling and recycling previously used components. Businesses can handle product obsolescence better and recover lost investments with the aid of RL strategies. Efforts to recover lost data are a strategic use of resources, and as such, they need to be coordinated intricately with parties upstream and (Kirchoff et al., 2016). The relevance of recycling has increased in the modern industrialized world, and recycling has become the norm rather than the exception for many products. If the product can be recycled, the sale to the final consumer could not mark the end of the business's operations. RL is "the process of planning, implementing, and controlling the efficient, cost-effective flow of raw materials, in-process inventory, finished goods, and related information from the point of consumption to the point of origin for the purpose of recapturing value or proper disposal" (Rogers and Tibben-Limbke, 1998). Collection, transport, inspection/sorting, storage, reprocessing (including recycling, reusing, repairing/refurbishing, etc.), and disposal are all examples of RL operations that are common regardless of the product or business. On the basis of Thierry et al.'s (1995) categorization of the main recovery options and Fleischmann et al.'s (1997) categorization of return-objects, Lu and Bostel (2007) proposed four types of basic RL networks: the directly reusable network (DRN), the remanufacturing network (RMN), the repair service network (RSN), and the recycling network (RN). Customers are more likely to remain loyal to businesses that take steps to reduce their environmental impact, such as recycling products or using eco-friendly materials and methods in product packaging and design (Wu et al., 2012). For instance, pharmaceuticals contain high-value compounds that necessitate careful RL management, particularly for stale and recalled inventory (Narayana et al., 2014). Because of the severe environmental damage that can result from pharmaceutical compounds leaching into water sources such as rivers, this is a major concern (Jones et al., 2001). Due to its high waste-to-product ratio, the pharmaceutical industry is in need of effective RL solutions (Narayana et al., 2014). The negative effects of trash and expired drugs on the natural world can be lessened by the application of RLs.

3.8 INTERNAL ENVIRONMENTAL MANAGEMENT

Environmental management from the inside out entails making "green supply chain management" a strategic objective for the company, with buy-in and backing from upper- and lower-level management (Papanas et al., 2019). Green purchasing, customer collaboration, eco-design, and investment recovery are GSCM activities that can be used once environmental sustainability has been recognized as a strategic objective and has the commitment and support of top and middle-level management. For the practices to be effective, the imperative must first be included in the organization's overarching plan (Hadi, 2019). Innovations, such as technological advances, initiatives, and activities, rely heavily on the backing of higher authorities in order to be successfully adopted and implemented. Green supply chain management aids businesses in the supply chain in achieving superior environmental performance in three primary areas: internal environmental management, green purchasing, and customer environmental collaboration. When properly implemented, internal environmental management procedures significantly improve an organization's environmental performance (Chetthamrongchai et al., 2019). In addition, the environmental performance of the entire supply chain is determined by the internal environmental management practices of particular enterprises, as these practices make it feasible to integrate eco-friendly knowledge and information, eco-friendly resources, techniques, and procedures. Similarly, "green shopping," also known as "environmentally preferred purchasing," refers to the practice of buying goods and services that produce less adverse environmental effects throughout their whole lifecycle (Nataraj et al., 2019).

3.9 GREEN MANUFACTURING (ECO-FRIENDLY PRODUCTION)

The term "green manufacturing" refers to a production method that is both efficient and gentle on the environment by using renewable resources and other eco-friendly materials. Worker and machine safety are at the heart of green manufacturing practice, whereas process and system-level techniques emphasize control and planning, respectively (Govindan et al., 2015). The manufacturers whose products and services are not environmentally friendly are losing business partnerships and customers, according to recent polls and research (Gupta, 2019). There has been a significant uptick in the prevalence of this method among both manufacturers and their clients. Green production is related with the long-term success of businesses, beyond the obvious benefits to market share and sales. Manufacturing that is more environmentally friendly uses fewer nonrenewable resources, produces less waste, and releases fewer greenhouse gases. At this point in time, decreasing energy use is the single-most important aspect of greening a firm's operations. Managers will need a lot of power to run the firm's factory's heating and cooling systems, light fixtures, and other machinery. Hydropower, wind energy, solar energy, and biofuels are just a few examples of alternative energy sources that might help managers use less fossil fuels. Energy consumption can be drastically reduced by the use of modern manufacturing techniques and even little adjustments, such as the installation of light-emitting diode lighting. Waste is typically categorized into five categories in lean production—production that exceeds customer needs or adds no value; processing that takes too long; excess storage of raw materials, components, or finished goods; inventory that sits idle; and motion that is too slow or unnecessary all contribute to waste. Every step of the manufacturing process should be analyzed to find the wasteful ones.

Green manufacturing refers to production techniques that make minimal-to-no waste or pollution of any kind, make use of inputs with minimal environmental implications, and are extremely efficient. The use of green manufacturing practices can save money on raw materials, boost production efficiency, minimize the cost of ensuring worker and environmental safety, and boost a company's public profile. Remanufacturing is an industrial process in which used products are returned to like-new condition; whereas, green manufacturing tries to lessen the environmental impact of production by making use of sustainable materials and technologies. Green manufacturing entails the use of manufacturing tools that are quick, dependable, and low-energy-consuming. The energy-saving light bulb is one illustration. These lights consume nearly half the energy of regular bulbs while still giving off a respectable quantity of light. Machine manufacturers are adapting their designs based on this trend. A firm's manufacturing company can gain from green manufacturing in several ways. In addition to helping the planet, this move will also please the firm's clientele, their investors, and improve the public's impression of its business. The positive effects on the natural world are the first advantage of green production. Factories that take environmental precautions may receive preferential insurance rates. To encourage green production, the government is also providing tax incentives. Green production also saves money, which is a nice bonus. Manufacturers can search for environmentally friendly manufacturing equipment. Companies can save tens of thousands of rupees by switching to wind and solar power. Realistically, if managers can reduce a firm's energy expenditures, they can lower the selling prices of their products that is charged from clients. Furthermore, managers can keep prices stable and still make a healthy return on firm's items, which is wonderful for firm's shareholders.

Production in accordance with green manufacturing principles requires that certain conditions not be breached, including those related to worker and user health and safety, product and environmental contamination, and waste management (Gong et al., 2019). Energy consumption, greenhouse gas emissions, and waste disposal can all be reduced with careful green production planning and management. Reduced municipal waste is achieved through green manufacturing's increased focus on efficiency (Aziziankohan et al., 2017); reduced or eliminated air, water, and land pollution is the ultimate goal of green production (Johansson and Winroth, 2009). Further, they claimed that by switching to green production methods, the danger to people and other living things in the environment would be greatly diminished. Adopting green manufacturing practices can improve production and energy costs, raw material costs, worker safety, and environmental costs.

3.10 GREEN PACKAGING

Hellström and Nilsson (2011) state that packaging is "a crucial characteristic of making preparations goods for transfer, distribution, storage, sales, and end-use." Its primary objective is to maximize sales and profits by minimizing delivery costs while ensuring that products reach consumers in good condition at the lowest possible price. Eco-friendly packaging gives thought to the package at every stage of its existence. Everything from where firm's vendor gets their raw materials to how people recycle the packaging must be considered. A good first step is to use boxes and packing materials made from post-consumer recycled materials. Biodegradable packing peanuts are another viable alternative. This material, which can be made from anything from corn to mushrooms, can be broken down quickly in the gardens of consumers or in a landfill. Which brings up an additional issue: consumers need to be taught how to properly recycle packaging. Both the protection of goods in transit and the dissemination of information about those goods to the target market are important functions of packaging (Arboretti and Bordignon 2016). Packaging is essential for the safety of products and the general welfare of the consumer market. Packaging is simply one contributor to a product's environmental footprint, thus efforts to lessen that footprint have been, and continue to be, a primary focus of innovation in the packaging business. About a fifth of the domestic waste stream and between a tenth and a twentieth of the commercial and industrial waste stream is devoted to this highly visible utilization of resources. Because of this, consumers and policymakers alike should be concerned about packaging.

3.11 GREEN WAREHOUSING

Green warehousing is concerned with making warehouses more eco-friendly by cutting down on waste and energy consumption. The rapid pace at which warehouses become obsolete is a significant obstacle. With the support of green infrastructure, the auto industry has become more environmentally responsible. To determine if green marketing and storage was effective and how it is connected to business performance, Yan and Yazdanifard (2021) conducted an empirical study. Researchers found through surveys, questionnaires, and secondary sources that most businesses agreed that "green" practices would improve society, and that businesses that adopted these policies saw gains in productivity. Older warehouses have a higher rate of CO_2 emissions since they are less energy efficient. In a fortunate turn of events, warehouses can become more environmentally friendly through refurbishment. Among the many possible enhancements to a building are the installation of installation, the use of alternative energy sources such as hydro and wind power, and the installation of windows to optimize natural light. The utilization of third-party managed warehouses in advantageous locations is another reason why many businesses now contract with such firms. Warehouses save businesses money on transportation costs the closer they are to major distribution centers.

3.12 GREEN TRANSPORTATION

Green transportation is often known as transportation that is gentler on the environment than conventional modes of transport (Ubeda et al., 2011). High levels of noise and air pollution are a result of the overuse of road freight (Demir et al., 2014). Entrepreneurs may save money and reduce their impact on the environment by reducing wasteful practices in transportation and packing. Reusable shipping containers cut down on garbage and save money (Yusuf et al., 2017). Warehouses that are both well-designed and secure have a positive impact on productivity because they facilitate the storing, retrieval, and distribution of goods (Cosimato and Troisi, 2015). Restructuring shipments to reduce the number of air cargo deliveries or truck journeys is one strategy to reduce the environmental impact of transportation. Alternatively, managers can purchase trucks that operate on alternate fuels or are electric. In recent years, advancements have made these methods practical even for transcontinental journeys. Don't discount rail travel either; it's a viable option that's easy on the environment. Trains are superior to vehicles in terms of cargo capacity, fuel efficiency per ton-mile, and overall cost. Finally, select a freight forwarder that places a premium on environmentally friendly shipping practices. Green transport and distribution initiatives can be defined as the shift toward ecologically friendly fuels and other more efficient transport technologies (Demir et al., 2014). The environmental performance of businesses and their products can be enhanced by the use of green transportation and distribution practices (Zhang et al., 2011).

3.13 LIFE CYCLE MANAGEMENT

The entire product's lifespan is taken into account throughout the design phase of a green product. Say, for instance, managers are in the business of creating playground sets for kids to use in their backyards. If the playground equipment is made of durable enough materials, firm's customer can give it to another child when their own child outgrows it. In addition, if the playground is made of recyclable materials such as wood, it may be reused after its initial use as something else, such as mulch, paper, or even outdoor furniture. The notion of LCA can be thought of as a subset of "green" design. The results of LCA are put to good use in the development of eco-friendly merchandise. LCA is a method for determining how a product will affect the environment, workers' health, and available resources at every stage of its production, distribution, use, remanufacturing, recycling, and disposal. Along with informing the creation of laws and regulations meant to protect the environment, LCA's findings can be used to design goods that cause as little harm as possible to the natural world.

3.14 GREEN DISTRIBUTION

When referring to logistics, "green distribution" describes actions taken to reduce negative effects on the natural world. Greener options may be made at every stage of the supply chain, from warehousing to order fulfillment to packaging to last-mile delivery. If firm's company is looking to lessen its impact on the environment, green logistics is the way to go. Energy efficiency is a top priority in green distribution processes. The goal may be to maximize fuel efficiency in ground transportation, which could involve anything from more efficiently packing trucks or shipping containers to minimizing time spent in transit. Equipment idle time can be reduced if and only if firm's team works efficiently together to complete tasks. The sum of these benefits is a large decrease in energy consumption and carbon emissions. Mwaura et al. (2016) analyzed the effects of environmentally friendly distribution methods on Kenyan food producers. Construct validity was examined using survey and factor analysis in this cross-sectional study, and criterion validity was evaluated with a linear regression model. The findings revealed that the organization's distribution operations were significantly influenced by technology, with the Internet being one of the distribution channels utilized. When asked about their commitment to greener distribution practices, suppliers expressed strong support for those that reduce environmental impact.

3.15 GREEN/SUSTAINABLE LOGISTICS

Understanding how green logistics is a crucial part of environmentally friendly supply chain methods requires looking at the optimal flow of data and goods in a way that decreases the impact on the environment. The term "green logistics" refers to the practice of arranging for the smooth transport of goods and data from their initial place of consumption to their final destination, whether that be for reuse or recycling (Cosimato and Troisi, 2015). While traditional logistics deals with the forward flow of raw materials, RLs is concerned with the management of their backwards flows. To put it more simply, RLs entails transporting items from their final destination after usage back to the point of origin for further processing, refilling, repairs, recycling, or disposal (Arora, 2020). Successful business executives balance the environmental goals of recyclable materials with the financial costs of shipping and RLs (Yang et al., 2019). Pollutants and harmful gases that harm the environment and people's health primarily come from the transportation sector (Asrawi et al., 2017).

3.16 DISCUSSION

This study comes to the conclusion that adopting GSCM techniques in their entirety results in increased financial and marketing performance, which in turn enhances organizational performance (Green et al., 2012). As a result, manufacturing companies should adopt environmentally friendly methods throughout the whole supply chain, from the acquisition of raw materials and suppliers to the design, production, packaging, distribution, and end-of-life disposal of their products. They will probably do better financially and in the market as a result. More eco-friendly products are being demanded by consumers. Therefore, items must include eco-friendly features to suit customer desire. Producers are better able to understand the environmental demands of their customers because to client collaboration. Manufacturers and consumers should work together to adapt to changing client demands for eco-friendly products. When observing clients' behavior, changes in their requirements will automatically become apparent (Stevens and Johnson, 2016). Numerous other aspects of an organization may be affected, either directly or indirectly, by the needs of the client. In order to reduce waste and remove product environmental harm, product designers and suppliers may cooperate in response to consumer needs (Laari et al., 2016). Customers' requirements may have an impact on a product's features, supplier adaptability, internal service quality, green design, green procurement, ISO 14000, internal environmental manufacturing plan, cleaner fabrication, suppliers' requirements, number of patents, and level of innovativeness in green product research and development (Laari et al., 2016). As the "loop" is closed and a product's lifespan is concluded, RLs are essential to GSCM (Zhu et al., 2008). The focus of RLs is on the destruction and retrieval of raw materials, work-in-progress, finished goods, and information (Jumadi and Zailani, 2010, p. 262). For procedures such as recycling, refurbishing, reusing, and remanufacturing, RLs is crucial (Choudhary and Seth, 2011).

RLs is one of the GSCM practices that is most frequently disregarded. Previous studies have shown that recovering goods and packaging that have passed their prime greatly lowers the environmental footprints created by the business' operations (Lee et al., 2012; Mitra and Datta, 2013; Laosirihongthong et al., 2013). This is because it reduces the need for disposal and extra consumption, improves the company's reputation, and ultimately increases profitability. Therefore, the regulatory structure that can enable product recovery should be reviewed by the government. Consumers should be made aware of the benefits of collecting and recovering used goods and packaging, according to the government and industry. As a result, the market for remanufactured and reconditioned goods would grow, which would lower the nation's import costs. All parties involved, including the company, the consumer, the government, and most significantly the environment, win out in the end.

3.17 IMPLICATIONS

Wu et al. (2012) advocate for studies that educate managers on the specific requirements of GSCM methods. For this reason, this chapter makes an effort to highlight the managerial implications of GSCM practice design for businesses. It also aims to understand the ramifications of these strategies from the perspectives of both the customer and the supplier, shedding light on the various techniques organizations take to raise the environmental compliance of their suppliers. In this way, the study contributes to the growing body of evidence linking GSCM practices and organizational success and alleviates some of the doubt that has emerged as a result of conflicting results in previous research.

Academic research should close knowledge gaps in the literature and add to the existing body of managerial and research expertise. Findings from this study contribute to the growing body of knowledge about GSCM practices and the factors that influence their adoption. Better results for gas manufacturing companies can be achieved through increased use of green product design, which clarifies eco-branding and labeling methods and guarantees a constant level of quality in the products delivered. The same holds true for including suppliers early on so that eco-friendly product design techniques can be developed. Manufacturers of natural gas should constantly keep some of their capital aside for remanufacturing and recycling, two processes that use up a lot of their overall capital. This is due to the fact that it is in this context where crucial decisions affecting sustainability will be made. Companies should put more money into green distribution to save money on procurement by avoiding costly mistakes caused by rescheduling and rerouting shipments. Partnerships, training, and capacity building should all be carried out in a uniform fashion. Electric vehicle difficulties are included in this category. Because it considers the GSCM concept as a whole, this research contributes significantly to the current body of literature.

3.18 CONCLUSION

The purpose of this section was to analyze what factors lead to environmentally friendly supply chain management. The goal of environmentally responsible design is to create goods and processes that are safe for the environment without compromising on quality, cost, or performance. Awareness and understanding on the part of top management authorities in organizations have been linked to the implementation of GSCM techniques inside an establishment. Senior management's environmental advocacy leads to the development of a company-wide environmental vision and mission voyage. The review found that gas manufacturing companies that used green product design, distribution, warehousing, and RLs saw improved financial results. In particular, it delves into the environmental, operational, economic, and social effects of the four core green supply chain management strategies mentioned earlier: eco-design, green purchasing, environmental collaboration, and RLs. Therefore, this thesis contributes to the practice of the industry by elucidating which aspects of GCSM procedures have a positive or direct impact on performance and how these positive impacts can be achieved inside an organization. The findings of this study indicate that better financial and marketing results can be achieved by using GSCM practices across the board. In light of this, it is imperative that manufacturing companies adopt environmentally friendly procedures throughout the whole supply chain, from the sourcing of raw materials and suppliers through the last stages of product disposal. As a result, they should see improved market and financial results.

3.19 RECOMMENDATIONS

This research provides a deeper knowledge of GSCM and a framework for analyzing the regulators' and SC managers' current GSCM adoption capacities and activities, both of which are helpful in gauging the green practice levels in intra- and inter-firm SC. Verification of internal variables' mediation role in reaction to external influence on environmental concerns also aids managers in comprehending the implementation of a green SC. When implementing environmental strategies at the corporate strategy and throughout the business, managers should create a comprehensive framework that includes policies, processes, and role descriptions that apply to all employees within the company. Management should use GSCM processes throughout the supply chain, encompassing staff, suppliers, and consumers, to gain a competitive edge. Green purchasing, production, distribution, branding, marketing, educating, internal operations, and recouping investments are all areas that need attention from managers. The purpose of an environmentally proactive policy is to increase value creation and competitive advantage through the systemic and persistent enhancement of green performance. In addition, organizations are more likely to gain a competitive advantage and reap more financial benefits if CEOs take a proactive approach to environmental management by evaluating the green strategies in their companies' SC and enforcing the green strategy. In order to comply with international regulations concerning the reduction of discharges, waste, resource use, and general environmental protection, managers should implement ISO 14001 environmental norms. To achieve a healthy balance between short-term performance (as evaluated by financial parameters) and long-term success (as measured by nonfinancial elements), managers should use the BSC model to transform competitive strategies into key performance indicators (KPIs). Environmentally responsible procedures were advocated for use by manufacturing companies along the whole supply chain, from the sourcing of raw materials to the final disposal of finished goods. The findings can be used by regulators to increase the prevalence of GSCM activities through tougher enforcement of environmental regulations and incentives for businesses that have already adopted such practices.

KEYWORDS

- green
- SCM practices
- environment
- customer
- design
- manufacturing
- procurement

REFERENCES

Čater, B.; Čater, T.; Prašnikar, J.; Ivašković, I. Environmental Strategy and Its Implementation: What's in It for Companies and Does It Pay Off in a Post-Transition Context? *J. East Eur. Manag. Stud.* **2018,** *23*, 55–83. https://doi.org/10.5771/0949-6181-2018-1-55

Cherrafi, A.; Elfezazi, S.; Govindan, K.; Garza-Reyes, J. A.; Benhida, K.; Mokhlis, A. A Framework for the Integration of Green and Lean Six Sigma for Superior Sustainability Performance. *Int. J. Prod. Res.* **2016,** *55* (15), 1–35. https://doi.org/10.1080/00207543.2016.1266406

Chetthamrongchai, P.; Jermsittiparsert, K.; Saengchai, S. The Mediating Role of Pharmacy Engagement on the Relationship of Perceived Service Quality, Customer Perception, Price Strategy with Pharmacy Customer Devotion. *System. Rev. Pharm.* **2019,** *10* (2), 120–129

Daddi, T.; Testa, F.; Frey, M.; Iraldo, F. Exploring the Link Between Institutional Pressures and Environmental Management Systems Effectiveness: An Empirical Study. *J. Environ. Manag.* **2016,** *183*, 647–656. https://doi.org/10.1016/j.jenvman.2016.09.025

Fiksel, Ed. *Design for Environment: Creating Eco-Efficient Products and Processes*; McGraw Hill: New York, 1996.

Geng, R.; Mansouri, S. A.; Aktas, E. The Relationship Between Green Supply Chain Management and Performance: A Meta-Analysis of Empirical Evidences in Asian Emerging Economies. *Int. J. Prod. Econ.* **2017,** *183*, 245–258. https://doi.org/10.1016/j.ijpe.2016.10.008

Genovese, A.; Acquaye, A. A.; Figueroa, A.; Koh, S. L. Sustainable Supply Chain Management and the Transition Towards a Circular Economy: Evidence and Some Applications. *Omega* **2017,** *66*, 344–357. https://doi.org/10.1016/j.omega.2015.05.015

Govindan, K.; Diabat, A.; Shankar, K. M. Analyzing the Drivers of Green Manufacturing with Fuzzy Approach. *J. Clean. Prod.* **2015,** *96*, 182–193. https://doi.org/10.1016/j.jclepro.2014.02.054

Govindan, K.; Soleimani, H. A Review of Reverse Logistics and Closed-Loop Supply Chains: A Journal of Cleaner Production Focus. *J. Clean. Prod.* **2017,** *142*, 371–384. https://doi.org/10.1016/j.jclepro.2016.03.126

Green K. W.; Zelbst, P. J.; Meacham, J.; Bhadauria, V. S. Green Supply Chain Management Practices: Impact on Performance. *Supply Chain Manag.: Int. J.* **2012**, *17* (3), 290–305.

Hadi, N. R. et al. The Impact of Atorvastatin Reload in Patients Undergoing Percutaneous Coronary Intervention and its Correlation with the Toll-like Receptors. *Syst. Rev. Pharm.* **2019**. https://doi.org/10.5530/srp.2019.2.10

Hong, Z.; Guo, X. Green Product Supply Chain Contracts Considering Environmental Responsibilities. *Omega* **2018**. DOI: 10.1016/j.omega.2018.02.010

Iatridis, K.; Kesidou, E. What Drives Substantive Versus Symbolic Implementation of ISO 14001 in a Time of Economic Crisis? Insights from Greek Manufacturing Companies. *J. Bus. Ethics* **2018**, *148*, 859–877. https://doi.org/10.1007/s10551-016-3019-8

Islam, S.; Karia, N.; Fauzi, F. B. A.; Soliman, M. A Review on Green Supply Chain Aspects and Practices. *Manag. Market.* **2017**, *12* (1), 12–36. DOI: 10.1515/mmcks-2017-0002

ISO (n.d.). https://www.iso.org/standard/60856.html

Jones, O. A. H.; Voulvoulis, N.; Lester, J. N. Human Pharmaceuticals in the Aquatic Environment a Review. *Environ. Technol.* **2001**, *22* (12), 1383–**1394**.

Khor, K. S.; Udin, Z. M.; Ramayah, T.; Hazen, B. T. Reverse Logistics in Malaysia: The Contingent Role of Institutional Pressure. *Int. J. Prod. Econ.* **2019**, *175*, 96–108. DOI: 10.1016/j.ijpe.2016.01.020

Kumar, R.; Chandrakar, R. Overview of Green Supply Chain Management: Operation and Environmental Impact at Different Stages of the Supply Chain. *Int. J. Eng. Adv. Technol.* **2012**, *1*, 1–6.

Laari, S.; Töyli, J.; Solakivi, T.; Ojala, L. Firm Performance and Customer Driven Green Supply Chain Management. *J. Clean. Prod.* **2016**, *112*, 1960–1970. https://doi.org/10.1016/j.jclepro.2015.06.150

Laosirihongthong, T.; Adebanjo, D.; Tan, K. C. Green Supply Chain Management Practices and Performance. *Ind. Manag. Data Syst.* **2013**, *113* (8), 1088–1109.

Lee, S. M.; Kim, S. T.; Choi, D. Green Supply Chain Management and Organizational Performance. *Ind. Manag. Data Syst.* **2012**, *112* (8), 1148–1180.

Lee, S. Y.; Klassen, R. D. Drivers and Enablers That Foster Environmental Management Capabilities in Small-and Medium-Sized Suppliers in Supply Chains. *Prod. Oper. Manag.* **2008**, *17* (6), 573–586.

Liu, Y.; Zhu, Q.; Seuring, S. Linking Capabilities to Green Operations Strategies: The Moderating Role of Corporate Environmental Proactivity. *Int. J. Prod. Econ.* **2017**, *187*, 182–195. DOI: 10.1016/j.ijpe.2017.03.007

MacCarthy, B. L.; Blome, C.; Olhager, J.; Srai, S.; Zhao, X. Supply Chain Evolution–Theory, Concepts and Science. *Int. J. Operat. Prod. Manag.* **2016**, *36*, 1696–1718. https://doi.org/10.1108/IJOPM-02- 2016-0080

Madani, S. R.; Rasti-Barzoki, M. Sustainable Supply Chain Management with Pricing, Greening and Governmental Tariffs Determining Strategies: A Game Theoretic Approach. *Comput. Ind. Eng.* **2017**, *105*, 287–298.

Martín-de Castro, G.; Amores-Salvadó, J.; Navas-López, J. E. Environmental Management Systems and Firm Performance: Improving Firm Environmental Policy Through Stakeholder Engagement. *Corp. Soc. Respons. Environ. Manag.* **2016**, *23*, 243–256. https://doi.org/10.1002/csr.1377

Mathiyazhagan, K.; Govindan, K.; Noorul Haq, A. Pressure Analysis for Green Supply Chain Management Implementation in Indian Industries Using Analytic Hierarchy Process. *Int. J. Prod. Res.* **2014**, *52*, 188–202. https://doi.org/10.1080/00207543.2013.831190

Min, H.; Galle, W. Green Purchasing Practices of US Firms International. *J. Operat. Prod. Manag.* **2001,** *21* (9), 1222–1238.

Mitra, S.; Datta, P. P. Adoption of Green Supply Chain Management Practices and Their Impact on Performance: An Exploratory Study of Indian Manufacturing Firms. *Int. J. Prod. Res.* **2013,** (ahead-of-print), 1–23.

Montabon, F.; Pagell, M.; Wu, Z. Making Sustainability Sustainable. *J. Supply Chain Manag.* **2016,** *52*, 11–27. https://doi.org/10.1111/jscm.12103

Narayana, A. S.; Elias, A.; Pati, K. R. Reverse Logistics in the Pharmaceuticals Industry: A Systemic Analysis. *Int. J. Logist. Manag.* **2014,** *25* (2), 379–398.

Nataraj, M.; Maiya, A. G.; Karkada, G.; Hande, M.; Rodrigues, G. S.; Shenoy, R.; Prasad, S. S. Application of Topical Oxygen Therapy in Healing Dynamics of Diabetic Foot ulcers—A Systematic Review. *Rev. Diab. Stud.* **2019,** *15*, 74–82.

Papanas, N.; Pafili, K.; Demetriou, M.; Chatzikosma, G.; Papachristou, S.; Papazoglou, D. Automated Measurement of Sural Nerve Conduction is a Useful Screening Tool for Peripheral Neuropathy in Type 1 Diabetes Mellitus. *Rev. Diab. Stud.* **2019,** *15* (1).

Rogers, D. S.; Tibben-Limbke, R. S. Going Backwards: Reverse Logistics Trends and Practices. Reverse Logistics Executive Council, 1998. http://www.rlec.org/reverse.pdf (accessed 23 Nov 2007).

Salam, M. Green Procurement Adoption in Manufacturing Supply Chain. Paper presented at the Proceedings of the 9th Asia Pacific Industrial Engineering & Management Systems Conference, 2008.

Sarkis, J.; Gonzale-Toree, P.; Belarmino-Diaz. Satakeholder Pressure and the Adoption of Environmental Practices: The Mediating Effect of Training. *J. Operat. Manag.* **2010,** 163–176.

Stevens, G. C.; Johnson, M. Integrating the Supply Chain… 25 Years on. *Int. J. Phys. Distrib. Logist. Manag.* **2016,** *46*, 19–42. https://doi.org/10.1108/IJPDLM-07-2015-0175

Treacy, R.; Humphreys, P.; McIvor, R.; Lo, C. ISO14001 Certification and Operating Performance: A Practice-Based View. *Int. J. Prod. Econ.* **2018,** *208*, 319–328. https://doi.org/10.1016/j.ijpe.2018.12.012

Wu, J.; Dunn, S.; Forman, H. A Study on Green Supply Chain Management Practices Among Large Global Corporations. *J. Supply Chain Operat. Manag.* **2012,** *10* (1), 182–194.

Yang, J.; Ma, J.; Zhao, H.; Cater, J.; Arnold, M. Family Involvement, Environmental Turbulence, and R&D Investment: Evidence from Listed Chinese SMEs. *Small Bus. Econ.* **2019,** *53* (4), 1017–1032. https://doi.org/10.1007/s11187-018-0113-6

CHAPTER 4

Key Drivers of Green Supply Chain Management

SHANI SALIFU[1], ALHASSAN SEIDU[2], and IBRAHIM SULEMANA[3]

[1]Chicago School of Professional Psychology, Chicago, USA

[2]Department of Secretaryship and Management, Tamale Technical University, Tamale, Ghana

[3]Department of Marketing, Tamale Technical University, Tamale, Ghana

ABSTRACT

The purpose of green supply chain management (GSCM), also known as an environmentally innovative supply chain, is to factor in environmental factors when planning and executing supply chain operations. When it comes to long-term environmental stewardship, most companies now see GSCM as a must. They now realize that the entire supply chain, from supplier to consumer, stands to benefit greatly from implementing the principle of green elements in their adopted technology (end customers). Considerable difficulties will be encountered by the management of the company under study as a result of the drivers engaged in the adoption of sustainable supply chain management. Deploying GSCM is seen as thankless work that raises total product cost due to the complexity of GSCM procedures, customer and cost constraints, state intervention, engagement with stakeholders, and regulation uncertainty.

4.1 INTRODUCTION

For a distribution network to be ecologically sustainable, it must incorporate green supply chain management (GSCM), which is the practice of using eco-friendly materials throughout the production process and then repurposing those materials into new products at the end of their useful lives (Balaji et al., 2014, p. 423). Sustainable development would benefit greatly from this, since more resources may be protected for future generations while also safeguarding our natural environment. Ecological, competitive, and monetary benefits have been attributed to the adoption and implementation of GSCM projects inside a firm. Suppliers, manufacturers, distributors, wholesalers, retailers, and consumers are all integral cogs in the wheel of a supply chain. Both upstream and downstream redistribution chains include these actors, who play various roles in the creation and distribution of final goods. To address issues in the industrial sector that contribute to environmental contamination, GSCM integrates environmental considerations with supply chain management principles. Wastes, including emissions, energy, solid waste, and harmful chemicals, are the primary focus of GSCM, which aims to minimize or eliminate them. GSCM also aims to have an impact on things like product design, manufacturing method, material choice, and raw material and final product transportation options. Surprisingly, ever since the notion of GSCM was introduced, no one has come up with a single description of it. However, there are recurring themes in the many definitions, such as "environmental management," "green procurement," and "sustainability" (Tseng et al., 2019). For the purposes of sustainability, GSCM can be characterized as the incorporation of environmental consideration into organizational operations while also taking reverse logistics into account. Sustainable practices are integrated into product development, production, supply chain management, and disposal as part of GSCM (Wibowo et al., 2018). So, GSCM is the method that places a premium on incorporating environmental principles throughout a product's lifespan in order to improve environmental performance, manage risks, satisfy consumers' demands, etc. (Malviya et al., 2015). Supply chain risk and expense can be reduced over time, allowing the company to have less of an effect on public and environmental health. Management of the supply chain in a sustainable manner is a modern idea. However, in the contemporary context, environmental sustainability and health of all businesses are of paramount importance. There are not many individuals interested in GCSM because of two main problems that businesses confront. The absence of self-regulation is the first issue, and the standardization of methods is the second (Rupa and Saif, 2022). By addressing key customers' worries about potential negative effects on the environment and human health, GSCM strategies help businesses increase profits (Shekarian et al., 2022). In addition, by adopting GSCM, companies can influence future company management in terms of cutting costs and increasing the prevalence of environmentally friendly goods (Darwish et al., 2021). Yet, studies on the drivers of implementing GSCM are few and requires more scholarly works. Hence, the purpose of the study is to evaluate the drivers of GSCM.

4.2 LITERATURE

4.2.1 GREEN SUPPLY CHAIN MANAGEMENT

Planning, evaluating, and scheduling all of the steps in the supply chain, from sourcing and procurement through conversion and logistics, fall within the purview of logistics (Jaggernath and Khan, 2015). The term "GSCM" refers to the incorporation of eco-friendly practices throughout the whole supply chain, from raw material procurement through product creation and distribution to product disposal (Malviya and Kant, 2015). Manufacturing companies have been early adopters of GSCM, a kind of corporate environmental management. Its goal is to lessen destructive effects on the environment. Green supply chain management (GSCM) is the practice of incorporating environmental considerations into all stages of the supply chain, from initial ideation through product disposal. This includes everything from the selection of suppliers to the production of environmentally friendly goods. GSCM comprises of the manufacturing process that reduces waste and pollution (Ohieng, 2016). End-of-life management is a crucial part of this process, which begins with the creation of a product's initial concept and continues through its development, production, and distribution to customers. Green supply chain management (GSCM) places an emphasis on environmental considerations throughout the whole supply chain and necessitates strategic, long-term partnerships between all participants. Strategic competitiveness is boosted by GSCM techniques in a way that benefits the environment and the bottom line. By working together, GSCM techniques lessen their negative effects on the planet without compromising other important factors, such as price, dependability, performance, or energy efficiency (Wei et al., 2016). Leaders in the supply chain can improve their company's economic and social standing by implementing GSCM procedures, which include the proper disposal of products that have outlived their usefulness. To sum up, GSCM improves business outcomes (Shafique et al., 2017). Cost savings, environmental, and social benefits are all attributed to GSCM methods, as hypothesized by Wei et al. (2016) and Shafique et al. (2017).

4.2.2 GREEN SUPPLY CHAIN MANAGEMENT DRIVERS

Competition intensity, shifting government policies, and a more educated consumer base are just a few of the drivers that have woken businesses up to the relevance of GSCM (Hsu et al., 2013). Just a few key drivers, including those stated earlier, have been highlighted. Jain and Sharma (2014) identified 14 reasons for the adoption of GSCM, of which customer pressure, legislation, and competitiveness are the primary ones. It was confirmed by Rao and Holt (2005) that there is a strong correlation between green supply chain drivers, economic performance, and competitiveness.

4.2.3 DRIVERS (COERCIVE, NORMATIVE, AND MIMETIC OR COGNITIVE DRIVERS) (DIMAGGIO AND POWELL, 1985)

1. **Coercive Drivers**

   When formal and informal pressures, including those exerted by government institutions and internal controls, combine, they give rise to coercive drives. Governments can use political coercion by, for instance, imposing tariffs, fines, and other economic sanctions (Aslam et al., 2018). When people in authority get their way, they exert coercive pressures (Zhu and Sarkis, 2007). For instance, governments exert control over businesses by passing regulations that must be followed (Rivera, 2004). Companies take preventative environmental action because they are afraid of the costs of not complying. According to Darnall et al. (2008), regulatory mandates for businesses to adopt GSCM processes can sometimes result in advantageous market openings. As a result, domestic businesses catering to international customers have been compelled to implement stringent environmental regulations (Ochieng, 2016).

2. **Normative Drivers**

   Normative drivers (forces of conformity) are ethically motivated and propose a justifiable action in view of what is generally accepted in a given field, profession, or academic setting. This helps businesses improve their goals and refine their methods. Stakeholders outside the company with an interest in the company's success often exert normative pressures (Ochieng, 2016). Customers, community members, investors, and vendors are all examples of stakeholders. Companies that cave to these pressures are seen as more credible by the general public. The customer is the primary normative pressure for manufacturers to adopt GSCM methods, as stated by Sarkis et al. (2011). By organizing protests and boycotts, environmental and community groups bring attention to the ways in which businesses' operations harm the environment. In addition, labor unions exert pressure on these businesses to prevent environmental incidents that could hurt union members. The importance of trade associations in overseeing the environmental practices of their members has also grown in recent years (Darnall et al., 2008). Institutional pressure may also come from shareholders (Ochieng, 2016). If a company has a solid track record when it comes to protecting the environment, it will be easier to recruit investors. Suppliers with a concern for the environment may avoid doing business with companies that don't share their values, as pointed out by Henriques and Sadorsky (1999).

3. **Cognitive or Mimetic Drivers**

As a result of environmental uncertainty and a lack of technological understanding, cognitive and mimetic processes emerge. When this happens, companies start behaving like others who are similar to them (DiMaggio and Powell, 1983). This happens when problems experienced by several businesses in a comparable setting tend to be similar. Thus, they try to deal with the unknown and lessen the risks by ensuring they don't fall to the bottom of the barrel compared to other businesses in the same industry. Mimetic pressures arise when a company begins to adopt the practices of its more innovative rivals (Ochieng, 2016). One of the key motivating factors for businesses to adopt GSCM processes is the threat of imitation. Globalization has opened the door for businesses in developing nations to gain knowledge about environmental management techniques from their more advanced counterparts in industrialized nations through self-regulation (Christmann and Taylor, 2001).

4.2.4 EXTERNAL DRIVERS

1. **Customer Drivers/Customer Requirements**

The needs of the customer play a significant role in SC design and specifications, and most suppliers will adhere to those needs. Firms are under increasing pressure from their communities and customers to adopt environmentally friendly policies and procedures (Zhu et al., 2008). Furthermore, the client plays a significant role in the growth and success of the business (Feng et al., 2018). In recent years, improving customer satisfaction has become an integral part of business strategy due to the correlation between satisfied customers and future revenue growth. The impact of green consumers on green innovation in businesses was investigated by Lv and Li (2021). That's why GSCM relies heavily on input from satisfied customers. Cooperation from customers has been shown to boost output, consumption, and business growth in previous studies. The owner of the building or unit is the ultimate consumer. In this industry, customers never interact with any third party except the programmers. Firms should only consult the developer about this metric. However, there is a dearth of literature that investigates the extent to which green building practices are a result of consumer pressure on developers. It was a key factor in encouraging environmentally friendly practices in other industries, such as manufacturing (Handayani et al., 2021). Customers, especially large customers, can influence suppliers to implement green practices by adopting an environmentally conscious mindset. The demand has a domino effect on the supply chain as a whole. In addition, customers can alter product characteristics and advertisement material characteristics in accordance with environmental requirements if they work with industrial organizations to do so. In addition, customers can work with businesses to ensure that products and services are disposed of in an environmentally responsible manner, and they can work with businesses to introduce eco-friendly marketing channels that are safe for the public's health and the country's natural resources. This cooperation from customers is crucial in ensuring that businesses can fulfill the environmental standards set by the public, customers, and government regulators (Large and Thomsen, 2011). Customer environmental cooperation is one of the main green supply chain approaches that plays a key part in reducing the environmental consequences of businesses in the hydrocarbon industry in Bahrain, a country where this sector plays a more prominent economic role. Suppliers can succeed in this endeavor with the aid of their most important clients by working together on the creation of new products and improvements to existing ones. The level of customer knowledge plays an important role in green purchasing decisions, as does the motivation behind purchases. "Eco-literacy" is another term for this concept. An individual's view of a product and the company as a whole will remain bad so long as they are aware of the product's detrimental effects on the environment (Ayodele et al., 2017). To that end, it has been proposed that educating buyers would be an effective strategy for preserving dependability in terms of ecological sensitivity. Consumers' willingness to pay more for eco-friendly goods is consistently correlated with their level of environmental consciousness. Therefore, the raised consciousness contributes to a better quality of life for individuals and their immediate surroundings.

2. **Global Market Entry**

Green practices are propelled in large part by the prospect of expanding into international markets. The business uses eco-friendly methods to satisfy the low-carbon regulatory requirements of overseas governments, as well as the needs of overseas clients and the knowledge of overseas partners in the environmental sector (HM Government, 2013).

3. **Statutes, Rules, and Regulations of Government**

By enacting laws and regulations and then exercising oversight over businesses to ensure that they are followed, governments, national standard institutes, industrial development bureaus, and municipal authorities can have a significant impact on various sectors of the economy. All around the world, governments have passed laws to limit the damage that development can do to the natural world. Countries are required to adopt GSCM practices by international organizations, such as the United Nations and the European Union. A society that adopts a set of excellent, just, and fair laws upon which the society and its government are based is said to be ruled by the Rule of Law. Companies have to satisfy regional, national, and international regulations while also meeting the needs of their customers, which are all established by government legislation (Luthra et al. 2011:234). It has been stated that regulatory pressures are a major factor in the rise of green supply chains. Green supply chains can be propelled by regulatory mandates from the government. There are three ways in which governments can serve as drivers in the adoption of green supply chains:

The government needs to do three things to create a greener and cleaner world: (1) engage in open and honest environmental regulations; (2) promote green innovations in the most important areas of GSCM; and (3) engage in activities that educate regular people on the importance of doing their part to make the world a better place.

Organizations are prompted to reduce their impact on the environment by reducing their consumption of nonrenewable resources and their release of greenhouse gases as a result of government regulations and legislation. As governments increasingly keep tabs on how we dispose of and repurpose things at the end of their useful lives, they have a profound effect on the reverse logistics stage of any given company's supply chain (Sheu et al., 2005). As a result of rules and regulations, environmental responsibility is no longer optional but mandatory (Diabat and Govindan, 2011). Small, medium, and big firms are encouraged by government regulations to adopt GSCM projects (Lee and Klassen, 2008). Emissions-specific environmental policies are the single-most critical part of an efficient environmental policy approach. More severe penalties for noncompliance are now in place as a result of regulations. When businesses fail to adopt eco-friendly procedures, they are hit with fines and other regulatory penalties, which, according to Bhool and Narwal (2013), drives up the cost to the business. The focus of environmental regulations around the world has switched from pollution prevention in factories to the products' complete use cycles. As a result, more government agencies will be able to join green supply chain efforts. Organizations can be prompted by governments to create environmentally friendly buildings through tax breaks and new infrastructure. Programs that encourage increased performance indicators while also meeting the requirements of environmental laws and regulations go under the umbrella term of "repair, recycle, and dispose" (Khor et al., 2016). Organizations should recognize environmental concerns and learn how green supply chain solutions can give them an edge, as argued by Madani and Rasti-Barzoki (2017) and Khor et al. (2016). Proactive environmental management by business leaders may result in the development of unique capabilities that give their company an edge in the marketplace. Leaders in organizations that integrate environmental sustainability into their supply chains go from a reactive to a proactive mindset, one that prioritizes not only meeting legal requirements but exceeding them through proactive regulatory compliance and value-seeking. Companies with a positive environmental outlook are more likely to invest in green initiatives (Liu et al., 2012).

4. **Environmental Commitment**

   The firm's dedication to environmental protection has been shown to inspire green practices on numerous occasions. For most businesses, being green is more of a moral need than a legal requirement because of the positive impact it may have on the environment and the local community (Hsu and Hu, 2008; Hsu et al., 2013).

5. **Positive Impact on the Economy**

   The capacity to reduce the manufacturing costs of manufacturing goods or services provided without diminishing the product's planned usage or quality might be an economic gain that motivates GSCM (Bhool and Narwal 2013). It's crucial to remember that lowering prices shouldn't mean sacrificing product quality (Handayani et al., 2021). Savings can be realized by excluding non-essential features from items. Using less resources (such as energy, water, and raw materials) in the manufacturing process has monetary benefits as well, because it helps to maintain the quality of the environment and reduces the overall cost of production.

6. **Pressures from Stakeholders**

   Green practices from other supply chain participants might be encouraged by the specific demands and expectations of stakeholders. According to research conducted by Robin and Poon (2009), this pressure is hierarchical and is typically exerted by the developer upon the provider. To attract more bidders, developers are moving away from traditional cost-based delivery systems and placing greater emphasis on contractors' ability to implement environmentally friendly techniques (Handayani et al., 2021). Public attention to environmental issues has risen in recent years as the quality of the planet has declined. Products made by the business have been in high demand from the public because of the company's green business practices. Most businesses are reviewing their environmental supply chain strategies because of public pressure. Businesses may be able to attract new consumers who are concerned about the environment as a result of the pressure or disruption public environmental awareness may generate. Targets for the organization's financial and ecological performance are shaped by the aims and objectives of management. The company may reap the benefits of green supply chain initiatives by better utilizing its resources and capabilities (Liu et al., 2012). Concerns from stakeholders can have a beneficial effect on public perceptions of environmental issues (Liston-heyes and Vazquez Brust, 2016). Sustainable limitations that represent stakeholders' environmental concerns and the financial viability of green investments are intertwined in supply chain environmental decisions. According to Zhu and He (2017), businesses should prioritize increasing their offerings' environmental friendliness through pricing competitiveness in the marketplace. Companies' adherence to market needs and environmental requirements might benefit from the stakeholder collaboration that results from open communication between the company and its various stakeholder groups.

7. **Non-Governmental Organizations and Environmental Activists**

   These collectives have the potential to increase environmental consciousness in both public and private sectors. To begin, they can advocate for the purchase of eco-friendly goods over their conventional counterparts. Environmental activists and non-governmental organizations (NGOs) can influence companies despite their little technical knowledge by raising public awareness about the importance of going green and mandating that businesses follow suit. How NGOs might work with businesses to increase environmental consciousness was investigated by Kong et al. (2002). It was discussed how customers should have the agency to affect change through their purchases and how they should be able to better their own lives as a result.

8. **Sustainability as a Source of Competitive Advantage**

   A "greening image" of the end-use environment is provided by green image, a driver of GSCM. What's more, when a company has a "green image," it means that its customers view it favorably since it uses eco-friendly practices in their manufacturing. The application of GSCM has the potential to boost the company's reputation and brand at the same time. In addition to luring customers with the correct green image, a business can also gain access to perks like easier loan approval, lower tax rates, and more opportunities to win government contracts. Target costing is influenced by market competitiveness and unpredictability (Pathak et al., 2020). The only way to ensure long-term success in an ever-changing market is to maximize profits while cutting expenses as much as possible.

9. **Improve One's Standing in the Market**

In order to attract more investors and customers, a company's reputation is expected to play a significant role in the decision to implement eco-friendly practices. According to Zhang et al. (2011), developers in China who have a solid track record of embracing eco-friendly policies have drawn affluent buyers and commanded higher prices. In a similar vein, Shi et al. (2013) noted how contractors are becoming increasingly eager to use environmentally friendly methods of building in an effort to boost the industry's image.

4.2.5 INTERNAL DRIVERS

1. **Cost Drivers (Factors that Affect Prices)**

Green building approaches have been recognized by the construction industry as a means to cut expenses. However, this calls for a substantial outlay of cash for eco-friendly machinery and technologies. A contractor can save money on things like fuel, manpower, materials, and disposal by making some smart choices (Carris et al., 2012). Making money is a company's primary motivation. Reduced production costs and higher profits are the results of implementing GSCM. Saving money involves reducing the consumption of resources like fuel, water, and other manufactured goods. Saving money and bettering the environment is a worthwhile goal. In addition, earlier studies have shown that using GSCM can help you save money.

2. **Organizational Green Awareness**

Another crucial endeavor for businesses to create GSCM practices is to consider the financial effects of repurposing used goods for new purposes such as repair, reuse, reassembly, refurbishment, and recycling. Texas Instruments (TI), for instance, launched 223 new initiatives to protect natural resources between 2005 and 2006. As a result of the original $9.7 million investment producing annual savings of $7.7 million, the payback period is a mere 15 months.

These initiatives improve TI's resource efficiency, particularly with regard to water and fossil fuels, and lessen the company's negative effects on the natural environment (Texas Instruments 2007).

3. **Facilities**

The facilities in a supply chain network are the locations where raw materials are processed into intermediate products and final products are produced from their component parts. The responsiveness and effectiveness of the supply chain are in large part determined by the facilities and their capacities to carry out their functions. Centralizing production and inventory, for instance, can lead to greater efficiency thanks to economies of scale. Location, capacity, and adaptability of the facilities all play a role in the supply chain's effectiveness. The first category is a production facility, whereas the second is a warehouse or other storage facility (Trivedi, 2022). Stores, assembly lines, and manufacturing halls are all examples of facilities. Improved supply chain performance is a direct result of better management of these facilities' functions, locations, capacities, and adaptability. In the field of facilities management, one organization has distinguished itself as either more responsive or more efficient, but not both. An auto parts wholesaler, for instance, would likely have multiple distribution centers strategically placed near its clientele to facilitate speedy and convenient product delivery. Decisions about location, and the capacity and capabilities of that site, are thought to have substantial positive and negative effects on supply chain performance. To better serve their clients, fast food chains often cluster their shops in densely populated areas. Efficiency can be improved by reducing the number of locations used and consolidating operations in high-traffic zones. Take the example of online retailers serving their massive customer base from a few of strategically placed hubs. However, responsiveness may suffer as a result of the cost savings because many of the company's clients may be located distant from the production plant. The inverse is also correct. By putting facilities in close proximity to consumers, we're increasing the number of facilities we'll need and decreasing our overall effectiveness. However, this facility contributes to the achievement of the company's competitive strategy objectives if the client requires and is prepared to pay for the responsiveness that having multiple sites offers.

4. **Inventory**

   Transport facilities in the form of several modes (multimodal) and routes, each with its unique technical specifications, have been utilized to transfer stock from one location in the supply chain to another. The selection of transport modes and routes has a major impact on the supply chain's responsiveness and efficiency (affecting the speed and cost of transportation). All sorts of components and completed goods can be found in a GSC stockpile. The administration generates both internal and external asset inventory reports (Trivedi, 2022). Changing inventory policies is considered highly sensitive because it can have a major impact on the efficiency and traceability of the supply chain. As opposed to stocking a large selection of products, many retailers are focusing on meeting the evolving demands of their customers and getting their orders to them quickly. To better respond to customer needs, a clothing store, for instance, could stock up on supplies and use them to satisfy current demands.

5. **Transportation**

   Transporters are responsible for physically moving goods from one location in the supply chain to another. Different types of transportation—full truck, courier, portion load, rapid mode—have different efficiency standards. The goal of GSCM is efficient transport. According to Wang et al. (2015), a business leader's capacity to generate a sustained competitive advantage depends in large part on the efficiency with which information and resources are transported. It is safe to say that the transportation of goods is the backbone of logistical operations across all spheres of society and industry (Amaral and Aghezzaf, 2015). Transportation is used by business, government, and social leaders to distribute and deliver goods to consumers (Cascetta et al., 2015). We can improve our response time by using a quick transportation service, but the high cost and increased risk of damage reduce the service's efficiency (Sunil and Meindl, 2007). Joint route planning is a more efficient method of transportation for manufacturing companies. The idea behind this is that manufacturing companies can improve their productivity and adaptability by maintaining their transportation function in tandem with the external environment. The two most common methods for achieving this goal—outsourcing transportation functions and horizontal cooperation with other transportation service providers—are discussed. Together, these ideas allow for distribution costs to be reduced, which is how economies of scale are realized. Decisions on how to move goods around the supply chain have major effects on their traceability and efficiency (Trivedi, 2022). For instance, if a logistics firm cared about providing the best possible service, they may rush to deliver a shipment. One such example is increasing the responsiveness of the product supply chain; nevertheless, this is not considered efficient because the rapid mode is costly. Supply chain managers still face difficulties with shipping goods despite the assistance of reliable transportation service providers (Jie et al., 2015). According to Kaewunruen et al. (2016), the adaptive and sustainable integration of transportation and transit systems into their natural and constructed contexts presents considerable problems at the convergence of social, technological, and economic systems. According to Kaewunruen et al., company executives should prioritize customer satisfaction in the transportation and transit system all over the world in order to meet economic, social, and corporate needs.

6. **Pricing**

   Trivedi (2022) argues that the pricing of a company's goods and services in the supply chain is determined by the pricing as a driver. Consumers' responses to prices can affect demand and supply chain effectiveness. For instance, if the price of a shipment changes depending on how much notice the customer gives, customers who are concerned with cost will place their orders as soon as possible, while those who can wait will do so as soon as possible before the deadline. Customers who place a high value on accountability have that reflected in their prices, while others who place a lower value on accountability can save money (Trivedi, 2022). In the relevant literature, there are two distinct methods of pricing discussed: the linear pricing approach and the strategy matrix pricing approach. Following the five steps of the linear pricing model is the industry standard. For example, (a) a company's pricing strategy may aim to maximize profits, increase sales, increase market share, increase return on investment, or simply ensure the company's continued existence. When it comes to (b) pricing policies, businesses have a number of options, including (but not limited to): skimming pricing, penetration pricing, life cycle pricing, above/at/below competitors' prices, and customer value. (c) Establish retail prices by implementing the aforementioned methods. Methods based on cost, competition, or consumer desire can be used to compile this list. (d) Allowances for distribution channels to carry out services and discounts based on quantity, season, credit, special sales, and other factors. To account for variations in cost between regions, (e) final pricing will be subject to adjustments. It's the disparity between "normal" prices and "shipping zone" costs. Price determination occurs post-adjustment. The pricing strategy matrix method takes into account customer traits when establishing prices. This method involves contrasting the company's goals with the existing competitive landscape and assessing the resulting options (Duke, 1994).

7. **Information**

The information gathered along the supply chain comprises of facts and figures about stock, storage areas (size, location, etc.), shipping routes, and clients. The more a provider knows about its customers and their preferences, the more responsive and efficient it can be in meeting those needs (Sunil Chopra and Meindl, 2007). Analysis is performed on information gathered from all points in the supply chain, including storage areas, distribution centers, shipping terminals, costs, prices, and end users. Information plays a crucial part in the supply chain's success and is the most important factor in determining its efficiency. Due to the potential knock-on effects on all other drivers if it fails to perform properly (Trivedi, 2022). Knowledge helps supply chains function more smoothly and quickly to meet demand. The availability of data allows management to boost sensitivity and efficiency across the board, not just in the GSCM (Trivedi, 2022). One example is the improved access to data that has helped many companies strike a better balance between supply and demand, as well as manufacturing and distribution. The manager of the Swedish postal service initiated a consumer participation program in the creation of new transportation services in January of 2000. It was at this time that the corporation realized it needed to better understand its clients in order to retain them. In order to tailor their offerings to their clients' specific needs, the company's management has decided to hold regular face-to-face meetings with them. To accomplish this, the company and the client share relevant data. After gauging consumer interest, they launched a transportation service using a single vehicle instead of five, which cut down on both costs and pollution (Lundkvist and Yakhlef, 2004). The only way for a company to save money in this way is if the company and the client share information directly.

However, supply chain managers aren't always aware of how GSCM might help bolster their company's edge in the market (Govindan et al., 2014). Information acquisition can help supply chain managers maintain an edge in today's ever-evolving economic climate (Su et al., 2014). Holsapple et al. (2015) argue that information is one of the most important sources of long-term competitive advantage. Therefore, it is crucial for supply chain managers to learn about GSCM tactics.

8. **Sourcing**

The source is the original establishment from which a product was acquired. Sourcing refers to the whole collection of organizational activities needed to acquire products and services. Sourcing refers to the process of locating and acquiring needed goods and services from reliable vendors at competitive prices and in adequate time frames. Supply chain management activities like manufacturing, warehousing, and transport cannot be completed without efficient sourcing. A company's accountability and efficiency in its supply chain are affected by the choices it makes at the strategic sourcing level (Trivedi, 2022). The company should make manufacturing facilities in high-cost areas highly sensitive while maintaining their efficiency. Know that sourcing expenses are reflected. Accounts payable also tracks payments made to suppliers (Trivedi, 2022).

4.3 DISCUSSION

Enhancing brand reputation, adherence to management, lowering environmental risk, and governmental restrictions are just some of the many motivations that push businesses toward greening their supply chain. Green practices may be adopted by some businesses so that they can present an image of being conscientious of the environment. Customer demand is a major motivator for firms to make changes to their supply chains that are more environmentally friendly. Environmental performance, waste reduction, financial savings, and a competitive edge are just some of the benefits that management teams may reap from implementing GSCM techniques (Daddi et al., 2016). Consumer and NGO activism led to strict new environmental laws. Leadership within the organization demonstrates an interest in sustainability. The study's most important contribution may be the exposure of green supply chain managers' tactics for boosting their companies' competitive edge. Without having to be an expert in environmental sustainability models or methods, GSCM allows managers to learn about the potential economic and social effects of their decisions (Pryshlakivsky and Searcy, 2015).

4.4 CONCLUSION

The purpose of this research was to determine what factors encourage or discourage the construction industry from adopting GSCM. Interactions between facility inventory, transportation, sourcing data, and pricing are key determinants in determining GSCM performance. Businesses can tailor how they create and oversee these drivers to strike the best possible balance between responsiveness and efficiency in light of their own unique strategic and financial goals. As a result, keeping this equilibrium requires monitoring the supply chain's drivers' performance, as this is the only way to know exactly when and how the strategic alignment has been reached.

This chapter adds to the current body of knowledge and can serve as a guide for policymakers as they consider innovative approaches to supply chain management that may be more environmentally friendly. Internal environmental management procedures that are more efficiently and effectively executed lead to better environmental performance. Similarly, the study findings demonstrate the beneficial effects of green purchasing on the environmental performance of industrial businesses. Improving environmental performance can be aided by purchasing products and services in a more sustainable manner. The study also elaborates on the favorable correlation between environmental performance and customer cooperation on the part of both consumers and businesses. To a greater extent, customers help businesses with environmental initiatives, the better those businesses perform environmentally. In addition, the study suggests that green innovation acts as a significant moderator between internal environmental management and environmental performance, as when a business organization prioritizes green innovation, it is more likely to implement environmentally friendly supply chain management practices, which in turn has a more positive effect on environmental performance. In addition, the research finds that green innovation works well as a moderator between green purchasing and environmental performance.

KEYWORDS

- **GSCM**
- **drivers**
- **customer**
- **environmental**
- **green**
- **SC**
- **SCM**

REFERENCES

Adeniyi, O.; Ojo, L. D.; Idowu, O. A.; Kolawole, S. B. Compliance with the Stipulated Procurement Process in Local Governments: A Case from a Developing Nation. *Int. J. Procurement Manag.* **2020,** *13* (5), 678–700.

Agan, Y. Acar, M. F.; Borodin, A. Drivers of Environmental Processes and Their Impact on Performance: A Study of Turkish SMEs. *J. Clean. Prod.* **2013,** *51*, 23–33.

Amaral, R. R.; Aghezzaf, E. H. City Logistics and Traffic Management: Modelling the Inner and Outer Urban Transport Flows in a Two-Tiered System. *Transp. Res. Procedia* **2015,** *6*, 297–312. DOI: 10.1016/j.trpro.2015.03.023

Cascetta, E.; Carteni, A.; Pagliara, F.; Montanino, M. A New Look at Planning and Designing Transportation Systems: A Decision-Making Model Based on Cognitive Rationality, Stakeholder Engagement and Quantitative Methods. *Transp. Policy* **2015,** *38*, 27–39. DOI: 10.1016/j.tranpol.2014.11.005

Christmann, P.; Taylor, G. Globalization and the Environment: Determinants of Firm Self-Regulation in China. *J. Int. Bus. Stud.* **2001,** *32* (3), 439–458.

Christopher, M. *Logistics and Supply Chain Management: Creating Value-Added Networks*; Pearson Education, 2005.

Darnall, N.; Henriques, I.; Sadorsky, P. Do Environmental Management Systems Improve Business Performance in an International Setting? *J. Int. Manag.* **2008,** *14* (4), 364–376.

Darwish, S.; Shah, S.; Ahmed, U. The Role of Green Supply Chain Management Practices on Environmental Performance in the Hydrocarbon Industry of Bahrain: Testing the Moderation of Green Innovation. *Uncert. Supply Chain Manag.* **2021,** *9*, 265–276. DOI: 10.5267/j.uscm.2021.3.006

Diabat, A.; Govindan, K. An Analysis of the Drivers Affecting the Implementation of Green Supply Chain Management. *Resour. Conserv. Recycl.* **2011,** *55* (6), 659–667.

DiMaggio, P. I.; Powell, W. W. The Iron Cage Revisited: Institutional Isomorphism and Collective Rationality, Organizational Fields. *Am. Sociol. Rev.* **1983**, *48*, 147–160.

Duke, C. R. Matching Appropriate Pricing Strategy with Markets and Objectives. *J. Product Brand Manag.* **1994**, *3* (2), 15–27.

Feng, M. Y.; Yu, W. T.; Wang, X. Y.; Wong, C. Y.; Xu, M. Z.; Xiao, Z. Green Supply Chain Management and Financial Performance: The Mediating Roles of Operational and Environmental Performance. *Bus. Strateg. Environ.* **2018**, *27*, 811–824. DOI: 10.1002/bse.2033

Handayani, N. U.; Wibowo, M. A.; Dyah Ika Rinawati, D. I.; Gabriella, T. Drivers and Barriers in the Adoption of Green Supply Chain Management in Construction Projects: A Case of Indonesia **2021**, *11* (2). https://ijcscm.com/menu-script/index.php/ijcscm/article/view/73/65m.

Henriques, I.; Sadorsky, P. The Relationship Between Environmental Commitment and Managerial Perceptions of Stakeholder Importance. *Acad. Manag. J.* **1999**, *42* (1), 87–99.

Jie, Y. U.; Subramanian, N.; Ning, K.; Edwards, D. Product Delivery Provider Selection and Customer Satisfaction in the Era of the Internet of Things: A Chinese E-Retailers' Perspective. *Int. J. Prod. Econ.* **2015**, *159*, 104–116. DOI: 10.1016/j.ijpe.2014.09.031

Kaewunruen, S.; Sussman, J. M.; Matsumoto, A. Grand Challenges in Transportation and Transit Systems. *Front. Built Environ.* **2016**, *2* (4), 1–5. DOI: 10.3389/fbuil.2016.00004

Kumar, A. S.; Suresh, N. *Operations Management*; New Age International Ltd Publishers: New Delhi, 2009; pp 30–251.

Kumar, P.; Wagle, S. *Greening the Supply Chain*, 2014; Viewed 10 August 2016.

Kumar, R.; Chandrakar, R. Overview of Green Supply Chain Management: Operation and Environmental Impact at Different Stages of the Supply Chain. *Int. J. Eng. Adv. Technol.* **2012**, *1*, 1–6.

Lee, S. Y.; Klassen, R. D. Drivers and Enablers That Foster Environmental Management Capabilities in Small-and Medium-Sized Suppliers in Supply Chains. *Prod. Operat. Manag.* **2008**, *17* (6), 573–586.

Liu, X.; Yang, J.; Qu, S.; Wang, L.; Shishme, T.; Bao, C. Sustainable Production: Practices and Determinant Factors of Green Supply Chain Management of Chinese Companies. *Bus. Strategy Environ.* **2012**, *21*, 1–16.

Lundkvist, A.; Yakhlef, A. Customer Involvement in New Service Development: A Conversational Approach. *Manag. Serv. Qual.* **2004**, *14* (2/3), 249–257.

Lv, H. J.; Li, D. D. Impacts of Heterogeneous Green Consumers on Green Innovation in Electric Vehicle and Charging Pile Firms. *Sustain. Produc. Consum.* **2021**, *28*, 1216–1231. DOI: 10.1016/j.spc.2021.08.002

Ochieng, O. S. Green Supply Chain Management Practices and Performance of ISO 14001 Certified Manufacturing Firms in East Africa. Unpublished PhD Thesis. University of Nairobi, 2016. http://erepository.uonbi.ac.ke/bitstream/handle/11295/97198/Odock_

Ofori, G.; Gang, G.; Briffett, C. Impact of ISO 14000 on Construction Enterprises in Singapore. *Constr. Manag. Econ.* **2000**, *18*, 935–947. https://doi.org/10.1080/014461900446894

Pathak, D. K.; Verma, A.; Kumar, V. Performance Variables of GSCM for Sustainability in Indian Automobile Organizations Using TOPSIS Method. *Bus. Strateg. Dev.* **2020**, *3*, 590–602.

Pryshlakivsky, J.; Searcy, C. A Heuristic Model for Establishing Trade-Offs in Corporate Sustainability Performance Measurement Systems. *J. Bus. Ethics* **2015**, *144* (2), 1–20. https://doi.org/10.1007/s10551–015–2806-y

Rivera, J. Institutional Pressures and Voluntary Environmental Behavior in Developing Countries: Evidence from the Costa Rican Hotel Industry. *Soc. Nat. Resour.* **2004,** *17* (9), 779–797.

Robin, C.; Poon, C. Cultural Shift Towards Sustainability in the Construction Industry of Hong Kong. *J. Environ. Manag.* **2009,** *90,* 3616–3628. https://doi.org/10.1016/j.jenvman.2009.06.017

Rupa, R. A.; Saif, A. N. M. Impact of Green Supply Chain Management (GSCM) on Business Performance and Environmental Sustainability: Case of a Developing Country. *Bus. Perspect. Res.* **2022,** *10,* 140–163. DOI: 10.1177/2278533720983089

Shafique, M.; Asghar, M.; Rahman, H. The Impact of Green Supply Chain Management Practices on Performance: Moderating Role of Institutional Pressure with Mediating Effect of Green Innovation. *Bus., Manag. Educ.* **2017,** *15* (1), 91–108. DOI: 10.3846/bme.2017.354

Shekarian, E.; Ijadi, B.; Zare, A.; Majava, J. Sustainable Supply Chain Management: A Comprehensive Systematic Review of Industrial Practices. *Sustainability* **2022,** *14,* 7892. DOI: 10.3390/su14137892

Sheu, J. B.; Chou, Y. H.; Hu, C. C. An Integrated Logistics Operational Model for Green-Supply Chain Management. *Transp. Res. Part E: Logist. Transp. Rev.* **2005,** *41* (4), 287–313.

Shi, Q.; Zuo, J.; Huang, R.; Huang, J.; Pullen, S. Identifying the Critical Factors for Green Construction—An Empirical Study in China. *Habitat Int.* **2013,** *40,* 1–8. https://doi.org/10.1016/j.habitatint.2013.01.003

Srivastava. Green Supply-Chain Management: A State-of-the-Art Literature Review. *Int. J. Manag. Rev.* **2007,** *9,* 53–80.

Sunil C. S.; Meindl, P. *Supply Chain Management: Strategy, Planning, and Operations*, 3rd ed.; Prentice-Hall: Englewood Cliffs, 2007; CH. 3, pp 48 and 49.

Trivedi, S. Six Important Supply Chain Drivers. Management Enthusiast, 10 Aug 2022. https://managemententhusiast.com/six-important-supply-chain-drivers/

Wang, M.; Jie, F.; Abareshi, A. Evaluating Logistics Capability for Mitigation of Supply Chain Uncertainty and Risk in the Australian Courier Firms. *Asia-Pac. J. Market. Logist.* **2015,** *27,* 486–498. DOI: 10.1108/APJML-11–2014-0157

Wei, H. L.; Ju, P. H.; Angkasa, Y. A. Implementing Green Supply Chain Management to Achieve Competitive Advantage. In: *2016 5th IIAI International Congress on Advanced Applied Informatics (IIAI-AAI)*, 2016. DOI: 10.1109/iiaiaai.2016.242

Zhang, X.; Shen, L.; Wu, Y. Green Strategy for Gaining Competitive Advantage in Housing Development: A China Study. *J. Clean. Prod.* **2011,** *19* (2–3), 157–167. https://doi.org/10.1016/j.jclepro.2010.08.005

Zhu, Q.; Sarkis, J. The Moderating Effects of Institutional Pressures on Emergent Green Supply Chain Practices and Performance. *Int. J. Prod. Res.* **2007,** *45* (18–19), 4333–4355.

Zhu. Q.; Sarkis, J.; Lai, K.H Confirmation of a Measurement Model for Green Supply Chain Management Practices Implementation. *Int. J. Prod. Econ.* **2008,** *111* (2), 261–273.

Zsidisin, G. A.; Siferd, S. P. Environmental Purchasing: A Framework for Theory Development. *Eur. J. Purchasing Supply Manag.* **2001,** *7* (1), 61–73.

CHAPTER 5

Green Distribution for Green Supply Chain Management

ALHASSAN SEIDU[1], SHANI SALIFU[2], and MOHAMMED ABDUL-BASIT FUSEINI[3]

[1]Department of Secretaryship and Management, Tamale Technical University, USA

[2]Chicago School of Professional Psychology, USA

[3]Department of Marketing, Tamale Technical University, USA

ABSTRACT

This chapter examined green distribution practices. The study employed a secondary data research design. The literature pointed out that green distribution practices are green marketing, packaging, warehousing, storage, and transportation. Packaging, advertising, shipping, warehousing, selling, and transporting goods in an environmentally friendly manner are all part of a well-oiled green distribution machine. Based on the outcome of the review, "green distribution" is an essential factor in lowering operating expenses and improving productivity across a wide range of industries. When green distribution is done right, it boosts profits, improves product quality, lowers expenses, and helps the environment.

5.1 INTRODUCTION

Many of the forces that have emerged in the 21st century have made it difficult for firms to maintain their previous levels of success and profitability.

Green Supply Chain Management. Mohammed Majeed, Kirti Agarwal, and Ahmed Tijani (Eds.)
© 2025 Apple Academic Press, Inc. Co-published with CRC Press (Taylor & Francis)

Businesses in the present era need to be more diversified and well managed to enhance performance and compete in the global market. This is due to several factors, including advances in technology, more competition, globalization, heightened awareness, and a wider range of cultures (Panya et al., 2021). The supply chain is one of the most important activities in a contemporary company and deserves careful management to achieve optimal efficiency and productivity. The need for a sustainable supply chain to halt global warming and other environmentally harmful practices has been underlined in countries all over the world. A sustainable approach to the environment is one that conserves natural resources and ensures the preservation of a high standard of living for future generations (Gillaspy, 2018). The challenge lies in striking a balance between supplying necessities and protecting natural resources. Companies that care about the environment and their impact on future generations must include environmental preservation into their everyday operations and commercial endeavors. It stressed taking into account the needs of both people and the natural world by integrating economic considerations with environmental safeguards. In other words, it mandates that businesses act in a way that increases their financial standing while also protecting future generations' ability to live in a habitable environment (Little et al., 2016). This entails what is known as "green distribution," or the incorporation of environmental concerns into the distribution process. Distribution is the link in the supply chain that transports goods from the manufacturing phase to the final consumer. Distribution is the most important factor in a company's bottom line since it influences both supply chain expenses and consumer satisfaction. As concerns about global warming have grown, many businesses have begun using environmentally friendly delivery methods. These methods cover everything from giving more thought to the environment during distribution to decreasing the amount of fossil fuels and greenhouse emissions utilized in production and shipping.

According to Toke et al. (2010), "green supply chain management" (GSCM) is the practice of incorporating environmental considerations into all stages of the supply chain, from initial product conception to final disposal. This includes everything from the selection of raw materials to the methods used to create the finished product. Supply chain management that takes environmental considerations into account throughout the various links in the chain is called "green distribution." In addition to this primary meaning, it can also be seen as the equitable and environmentally sound distribution of products and services (Nwura et al., 2016). Most of the research on SSCM practices has concentrated on GSCM techniques, according to a literature study (Kumar and Rajeev, 2016; Kumar et al., 2020; Mati and Thomas, 2019; Imbambi et al., 2017; Mitullah et al., 2017; Sarhaye and Marendi, 2017). Little is known about how packaging GSCM practices affect the success of businesses. The role of green distribution in GSCM had not been established by prior studies. As a fundamental part of GSCM, green distribution will be the focus of this chapter.

5.2 LITERATURE

5.2.1 *GREEN DISTRIBUTION*

Sustainable shipping is also known as "green distribution," and it refers to the process of carrying goods without negatively impacting the environment. The term "green distribution" is used to describe the practice of transporting goods and services from their point of origin through an environmentally friendly channel to the end user (Mwaura et al, 2016). Murphy (2012) claims that the manufacturing sector is coming under growing pressure to adopt environmentally friendly measures. Many nations have implemented initiatives to reduce packaging waste and its associated environmental impacts (Nwura et al., 2015). As a result, many governing structures have adopted environmental policies and regulatory frameworks. This has led to a rise in sustainable distribution practices and the incorporation of environmental design into a wide range of sectors (Murphy, 2012). As a result, producers need to understand the norms and check that their goods are legal. Green logistics begins with green distribution, which creates a blueprint of the distribution setting and the primary procedures involved. Organizations should focus on supplier management to lessen the possibility of external environmental impact when developing and evaluating a sustainable distribution plan (Mashkova, 2022).

The goal of every company's distribution function should be to improve the company's standing in the eyes of its clientele. For example, all markets must be made aware of the items' capabilities, specifications, and availability. The manufactured goods also need to make it to the market without delay. Distribution networks that are up to the task are required. For the sake of the planet, it is crucial that people have access to eco-friendly goods distributed via eco-friendly methods of production and consumption. Green packaging, transportation (Dheeraj and Vishal, 2012), and storage are all key components of a successful green distribution strategy. Manufacturers must understand the standards and guarantee their products conform to environmental issues, as well as control and access their distribution patterns, for businesses to fully adopt and achieve the potential rewards of green distribution. Distribution is crucial to a company's success because it facilitates the transportation, delivery, and bulk handling of products; safeguards those products from the harmful effects of the environment and other potential sources of contamination; and shapes consumer behavior with respect to environmentally friendly choices (Dellis 2016).

5.2.2 AREAS OF GREEN DISTRIBUTION

Packaging, advertising, shipping, warehousing, selling, and transporting goods in an environmentally friendly manner are all part of a well-oiled green distribution machine.

5.2.3 GREEN SOURCING/PROCUREMENT

Each year, more and more scholarly works are released on the topic of sourcing (Giuniperoa, et al., 2019). However, it is vital to first comprehend the basics to appreciate the context of the analyzed cases, the latest breakthroughs in the sourcing field, and to be able to make a novel contribution. Green procurement, as defined by Min and Choi (2019), is "an environmentally conscious purchasing process that lowers or eliminates waste sources and promotes the sustainability (e.g., recycling and reclamation) of purchased materials without detracting from performance requirements." In the context of more sustainable supply chains, "green sourcing" refers to the practice of acquiring raw materials in an eco-friendly and resource-efficient manner (Mashkova, 2022). When we talk about "green sourcing," we are referring to the practice of acquiring goods and services in a manner that has the least possible negative effect on the environment.

5.2.4 GREEN STORAGE (ECO-FRIENDLY STORAGE)

For the sake of a more sustainable planet, green storage is an indispensable instrument (Hutomo et al., 2018). One of the most important parts of a green distribution system is green storage. Green storage refers to a method of storing data that takes environmental concerns into account (Alshura and Awawdeh, 2016). Green storage, as defined by Dheeraj and Vishal (2012), is incorporating environmental consideration into an organization's storage activities without sacrificing the goals that storage must achieve. To summarize, green storage is the practice of storing items in a warehouse that is also beneficial to the environment. According to Zhang and Zheng in Mwaura et al. (2016), businesses with a strong commitment to enhancing their environmental image can integrate sustainability issues into their storage activities by designing and constructing a warehouse or storage facility to meet the criteria of non-polluting environment, while also strengthening and maintaining good humidity, corrosion, waterproofing, and other factors. Redesigning and inventing the storage facility to incorporate environmental protection and simplifying the process to reduce energy consumption and greenhouse gas emission are both essential parts of incorporating a green element into their storage process (Ravet, 2013).

5.2.5 GREEN WAREHOUSING

The term "green warehousing" refers to a specific method of stocktaking and warehousing that makes use of environmentally friendly storage facilities in urban areas. Because of this, distribution centers only employ environmentally friendly transportation methods and use eco-friendly packaging (Mashkova, 2022). In conventional warehousing, consideration is given to logistics such as transit times, inventory levels, and packaging supplies. Anything that helps the center stay on schedule while processing orders is fine with us. The concept of green warehousing is based on the assumption that distribution centers can reduce their negative impact on the environment. Any distribution center can lessen its impact on the environment by implementing certain measures. Incorporating environmentally friendly practices into storage facilities can yield a positive return on investment (ROI) almost immediately, as well as worldwide improvements over the long term that will please stakeholders. Heating, cooling, and lighting systems in warehouses are the primary sources of pollution in worldwide supply chains. The larger the warehouse, the greater the impact on the environment. Key performance indicators such as emissions, natural resource use, and waste and recycling amounts provide warehouse managers with a means of gauging the environmental impact of their operations. Even though the term has not yet been formally defined, "green warehousing" has recently been included by certain authors among the ecologically sustainable processes of a supply chain (Bartolini et al., 2019). As stakeholders increase their pressure on companies to lessen their carbon footprints, green practices in environmentally friendly warehouses become more vital. To succeed, businesses need to keep up with ever-changing rules and regulations from the government, fulfill the needs of their customers, and remain financially stable through insurance (Agility, 2023).

5.2.6   GREEN TRANSPORTATION

Methods of transportation that reduce their environmental impact. Using green modes of transportation could help Nigeria achieve environmental sustainability. One of the most important roles of a green distribution system is green transportation. Green transportation, as described by Ottman (2018), is the practice of incorporating environmental considerations into the transportation system. According to Erdogan and Miller-Hooks (2012), "green transportation" is any mode of transportation that does not use or rely on fossil fuels, but instead makes use of renewable or regenerated energy sources like solar or electricity. The goal of "green" transportation is to find the most efficient path for vehicles to take to reduce pollution and fuel consumption (Pelletier et al., 2014).

5.2.7   GREEN MARKETING

Green marketing, social marketing, environmental marketing, and sustainable marketing are all other names for ecological marketing. In the context of GSCM, "green marketing" refers to efforts made to meet consumer demands while minimizing negative effects on the environment (Onurlubaş, 2017). This also helps businesses thrive in highly competitive domestic and global marketplaces (Rostamzadeh et al., 2015). There are several green marketing strategies that may be put into effect to make sure that all available raw ingredients and mineral wealth are put to good use. Among these methods are "green" product design, "green" product advertising, "green" pricing, "green" market targeting, and "green" product positioning (Sutduean et al., 2019).

5.2.8   GREEN PACKAGING

Eco-friendly packaging (using environmentally friendly packaging) is a key component of green distribution. Because of their impact on the product's transportability, packaging characteristics such as size and materials utilized affect distribution. A green package, also known as an ecological package or an environmentally friendly package, is one that is constructed entirely from plants, is biodegradable, promotes sustainable development, and poses no threat to human or animal health at any point in the packaging's lifecycle. Green packaging, in a nutshell, is suitable packaging that may be reused, recycled, or deteriorated and corrupted without causing pollution in humans or the environment throughout the product's life cycle. Green packaging, as defined by Ninlawan et al. (2010), includes both the reduction of packing size and the adoption of environmentally friendly materials. Additionally, they stress the importance of working together with suppliers to standardize packaging, encourage and embrace returnable packing solutions, and promote recycling and reuse of packaging materials. Better packaging and reorganized loading patterns have been shown to decrease material use and increase warehouse and trailer utilization, according to research by Amemba et al. (2013). In addition to reducing the need for handling, this also saves time. According to both sets of research, one way to increase warehouse efficiency through green packaging is to package commodities in smaller units. According to Hutomo et al. (2018), a company's distribution system should give environmental marketing near-top priority. They went on to say that green distribution can help achieve environmental sustainability since it is an effective distribution system that has a low impact on people's quality of life. According to the further data supplied by Ninlawan et al. (2012), green packaging can be implemented further by expanding the usage of green packaging materials, encouraging reuse and recycling programs, or adopting standardized packaging methods. Yet, the system evaluator indicators are used to control and manage the packaging system.

In a time when customers are more aware of environmental issues, Dellis (2016) affirmed that green packaging can help achieve environmental sustainability. The implementation of environmentally friendly modes of transportation, however, necessitates careful thought on several issues. Eco-friendly packaging sometimes involves clever wrapping to lessen environmental impact. Green packaging conveys the appearance of inherent and transferrable monetary concerns for the environment to the consumer. Positive associations can be made between a company's care for the environment and the care it shows its customers by sending green mail (Ottman, 2018). Companies can reap the same benefits as their customers by offering bundles. For example, the outside of bundling fills in as a correspondence stage for a wide range of data. Information of interest to potential purchasers would go under this category and would include things such as item components, cost, and application details. In addition, it is used as a tool in marketing strategies to increase consumer interest in products, hence reducing inventory waste. Additionally, packaging regulates the size and quantity of a product (Ottman, 2018).

Green Packaging
- Recyclable materials
- Size of packaging material
- Reusable materials

Green Transportation
- Fuel efficiency
- Vehicle emissions control
- Route Planning

Green Storage
- Storage facility flexibility
- Mode of powering storage facility
- Design and construction of storage facilities

Eco-Labeling
- Danger symbols
- Disposal labels
- Declaration of contents

FIGURE 5.1 Areas of green distribution.
Source: Authors.

5.2.9 BENEFITS OF GREEN DISTRIBUTION

Distribution methods that are friendly to the environment place a premium on saving resources and reducing energy waste. That could imply anything from maximizing fuel economy in land transportation to more efficiently packing trucks or shipping containers. Sometimes, how little equipment sits idle depends on how well your team works together to complete the task at hand (Agility, 2023). The sum of these benefits is a large decrease in energy consumption and carbon emissions. In addition, a well-oiled enterprise is more likely to have a contented staff, more satisfied customers, and fewer wasted materials. Since maximizing productivity is a priority for most organizations, firms, and the people both stand to benefit from this. Many different types of risk can be mitigated by adopting more eco-friendly distribution practices. To start, distribution centers that adopt greener techniques are healthier for the health of both their personnel and the local ecosystem. After all, the company could be held responsible for problems caused by harmful practices, such as failing to follow rules for the emissions of greenhouse gases from commercial trucks. In today's market, consumers look for companies that care about the environment (Agility, 2023). A firm's reputation can take a hit if it engages in irresponsible acts, such as producing too much trash or failing to implement eco-friendly measures.

5.3 IMPLICATIONS

In several ways, this article could encourage green distribution practices among manufacturers of sachet and bottled water. It is hoped that sachet and bottle water manufacturers would gain new insight from the study into the ways in which green logistics, including green transportation, green storage, green packaging, and reverse logistics, can contribute to environmental sustainability. This research will be useful for bottle and sachet water distributors since it will inspire them to create systems to collect empty plastic water bottles from their customers. The research will also raise awareness among managers and marketers of the benefits of utilizing renewable energy sources like solar power to maintain product quality in warehouses. Because of this, they will be able to cut back on their reliance on polluting fossil fuels, which will in turn lower their levels of carbon dioxide and other gas emissions. This research will educate entrepreneurs and financiers on the importance of green distribution for the future of the bottled and sachet water industry. This research will inform them of the need to use environmentally responsible distribution methods in the fight for global environmental sustainability. Most importantly, this study will serve as a valuable resource for students, academics, and researchers who are interested in learning more about this issue or a similar one. Considering the current economic climate, warehouse managers who are interested in green warehousing should be aware of how to track progress and where to discover the most efficient goods and procedures currently on the market. As a result of the availability of information online, consumers are suddenly aware of how their purchases affect the planet. Those who are concerned about their environmental impact look for businesses that emphasized green practices at every stage of production. Individuals who care about the environment are willing to pay a premium for environmentally friendly goods and services.

5.4 CONCLUSIONS

Therefore, to be inventive, effective, competitive, and efficient in today's ever-changing dynamic marketing environment, management should be devoted to green distribution practices. Based on the outcome of the review, Green Distribution is an essential factor in lowering operating expenses and improving productivity across a wide range of industries. When green distribution is done right, it boosts profits, improves product quality, lowers expenses, and helps the environment.

5.5 SUGGESTIONS FOR FUTURE RESEARCH

The findings of this study call for more investigation into the relationship between GSCM practices and the success of service providers, manufacturers, and retailers.

KEYWORDS

- **green distribution**
- **green marketing**
- **packaging**
- **warehousing**
- **storage**
- **transportation**

REFERENCES

Agility. What is Green Distribution and Sustainable Logistics?, 2023 https://www.agility.com/en/blog/what-is-green-distribution-and-sustainable-logistics/

Bartolini, M.; Bottani, E.; Grosse, E. H. Green Warehousing: Systematic Literature Review and Bibliometric Analysis. *J. Clean. Prod.* **2019**, *226*, 242–258. https://doi.org/10.1016/j.jclepro.2019.04.055

Dellis, G. *Green Packaging*; M.Sc. Thesis, International Hellenic University, Thessaloniki, Greece, 2016.

Eberle, U.; von Helmolt, R. Sustainable Transportation Based on Electric Vehicle Concepts: A Brief Overview. *Energy Environ. Sci.* **2010**, *3* (6), 689–699.

Erdogan, S.; Miller-Hooks, E. A Green Vehicle Routing Problem: Transportation Research Part E. *Logist. Transp. Rev.* **2012**, *48* (1), 100–114.

Giuniperoa, L. C.; Bittnerc, S.; Shanksa, I.; Cho, M. H. Analyzing the Sourcing Literature: Over Two Decades of Research. *J. Purchas. Supply Management* **2019**, *25* (5).

Hutomo, A.; Haizam, M.; Sinaga, O. The Mediating Role of Organizational Learning Capability on Green Distribution and Green Packaging Towards Sustainability Performance as a Function of Environmental Dynamism: Indonesia and Malaysia Fishery Industries. In: *2nd International Conference on Energy and Environmental Science: Conference Series: Earth and Environmental Science*, Vol. 164, 2018.

Imbambi, M. et al. Influence of Material Capability on Competitive Advantage of Sugar Companies in Western Kenya. *Int. J. Acad. Res. Bus. Soc. Sci.* **2017**, *7* (2). DOI: 10.6007/IJARBSS/v7-i2/2632

Kumar, A. et al. Behavioral Factors on the Adoption of Sustainable Supply Chain Practices. *Int. J. Resour. Conserv. Recycl.* **2020**, *158*. doi.org/10.1016/j.resconrec.2020.104818

Kumar, D.; Rajeev, P. V. Value Chain: A Conceptual Framework. *Int. J. Eng. Manag. Sci.* **2016**, *7* (1), 74–77.

Mashkova, Y. Green Logistics for Greener Supply Chain Management, 9 Sept 2022. https://www.track-pod.com/blog/green-logistics-guide/

Min, H.; Choi, S.-B. Sourcing Practices in Korea. *Manag. Res. Rev.* **2019**, *43* (1), 1–18.

Muma, B. O.; Nyaoga, R. B.; Matwere, R. B.; Nyambega, E. Green Supply Chain Management and Environmental Performance among Tea Processing Firms in Kericho County, Kenya. *Int. J. Econ. Finance Manag. Sci.* **2014**, *2* (5), 270–276.

Murphy, E. Key Success Factors for Achieving Green Supply Chain Performance; A Study of UK ISO 14001 Certified Manufacturers. PhD thesis, The University of Hull, 2012.

Mwaura, A. W.; Letting, N.; Ithinji, G.; Orwa, B. H. Green Distribution Practices and Competitiveness of Food Manufacturing Firms in Kenya. *Int. J. Econ. Comm. Manag.* **2016**, *4* (3), 189–207.

Mwaura, A.; Letting, N.; Ithinji, G.; Orwa, H. B. Reverse Logistics Practices and Their Effect on Competitiveness of Food Manufacturing Firms in Kenya. *Int. J. Econ. Finance Manag. Sci.* **2015**, *3* (6), 678–684.

Ninlawan, C.; Seksan, P.; Tossapol, K.; Pilada, W. The Implementation of Green Supply Chain Management Practices in Electronics Industry. In: *World Congress on Engineering 2012*; 4–6 July 2012; Vol. 2182; International Association of Engineers: London, 2010; pp 1563–1568.

Onurlubaş E. Knowledge Levels of the Consumers About Eco-Friendly Products. *J. Int. Sci. Res.* **2017**, *2* (7), 10–18. DOI: 10.23834/isrjournal.343742

Panya, K. O.; Ochiri, G.; Achuora, J.; Gakure, R. W. Effects of Green Distribution on the Organizational Performance of Sugar Sub-Sector in Kenya. *Strategic J. Bus. Change Manag.* **2021,** *8* (3), 939–952.

Pelletier, S.; Jabali, O.; Laporte, G. Good Distribution with Electric Vehicles: Review and Research Perspectives. Interuniversity Research Centre on Enterprise Networks, Logistics and Transportation, 2014. www.cirrelt.com (assessed 23 July 2018).

Ravet, D. Delivering Sustainability Through Supply Chain Distribution Network Redesign. *Central Eur. Bus. Rev. Res. Papers* **2013,** *2* (3), 22–29.

Rostamzadeh, R.; Govindan, K.; Esmaeili, A.; Sabaghi, M. Application of Fuzzy VIKOR for Evaluation of Green Supply Chain Management Practices. *Ecol. Indicators* **2015,** *49*,188–203.

Sutduean, J.; Joemsittiprasert, W.; Jermsittiparsert, K. Supply Chain Management and Organizational Performance: Exploring Green Marketing as Mediator. *Int. J. Innov. Creativity Change* **2019,** *5* (2), 266–283.

Toke, L. K.; Gupta, R. C.; Dandekar, M. Green Supply Chain Management; Critical Research and Practices. In: *2010 International Conference on Industrial Engineering and Operations Management*; Dhaka, Bangladesh, 2010.

Zhang, Y.; Liu, J. The Establishment of Green Logistics System Model. In: *Proceedings of 2009 International Conference on Management Science and Engineering*, 2009; pp 892–897.

CHAPTER 6

Benefits of Green Transportation

IBRAHIM SULEMANA[1], SHANI SALIFU[2], and ALHASSAN SEIDU[3]

[1]Department of Secretaryship and Management, Tamale Technical University, Tamale, Ghana

[2]Chicago School of Professional Psychology, Chicago, USA

[3]Department of Marketing, Tamale Technical University, Tamale, Ghana

ABSTRACT

The purpose of the study is to review literature on the benefits of green transportation. The various modes of green transportation, such as bicycle, public transportation, electric automobiles, pedal power, and walking, are the most significant ways of travel. Local sustainable development may move more quickly as a result of the many social and economic advantages of sustainable mobility. Investments in bicycle riding, pedestrian walkways, and nonpedestrian pathways can improve commuter safety, assist create jobs, and make it easier and more economical to access social and career opportunities. Also, it offers a genuine opportunity to cut costs for both the general public and the government.

6.1 INTRODUCTION

The corporate relationships with consumers and suppliers that are beneficial in integrating green practices, green transportation, and reverse logistics are just a few of the many diverse aspects of green supply chain management methods (Sun and Zhu, 2018). Yasin et al. (2022). Sustainable transportation is a means of travel that is both safe and has little impact on the environment. It has been used for quite some time. Sustainable transportation is also referred

---

Green Supply Chain Management. Mohammed Majeed, Kirti Agarwal, and Ahmed Tijani (Eds.)
© 2025 Apple Academic Press, Inc. Co-published with CRC Press (Taylor & Francis)

to as "green transportation." It is crucial to realize that environmentally damaging fossil fuels like coal, oil, and other types of fuels are avoided by sustainable transportation, which relies on renewable energy. On the contrary, because it makes use of renewable energy sources, sustainable transportation is secure. All ecologically friendly forms of transportation are included in electric buses. A company's measures to make sure that its cars and other forms of transportation are ecologically friendly are referred to as "green transportation." Together with other electric modes of transportation, green transportation also includes trolley buses, tram cars, light rail, and subway systems. Green transportation, which precisely refers to the convenient, secure, effective, low-pollution, humanized, and diverse urban transportation system, is a novel concept and a practice objective. It coordinates with ecological environment and urban development, adjusts to trends in habitat environment development, and is driven by public transportation. Along with the idea of sustainable development, which is the shift from a "vehicle-oriented" to a "people-oriented" society, the notion of green transportation is put forth (Zhang et al., 2010). Green transportation promotes a reduction in the use of personal vehicles, an increase in walking, bicycling, and using public transit, as well as the use of clean energies and vehicles. Many types of travelers can use this low-cost, pollution-free, and land resource- and space-saving transportation system. Moreover, environmentally friendly, ecological, and low-carbon transportation all continue under the umbrella of green transportation. It represents quick, safe, and comfortable transportation and offers benefits such as high effectiveness, minimal pollution, and low energy usage (Li et al., 2018). A set of assessment indices is required to assess the green traffic of the city development because the development of the city's social and economic systems depends on it. Yet, green transportation is a novel idea and a useful objective when it relates to an urban transportation system that is convenient, safe, efficient, low-polluting, humanized, and diverse. By coordinating with the ecological environment and urban growth, it is adjusting tendencies in the habitat environment that are being driven by public transportation. It benefits the economy as well as the ecological environment. The economy has improved significantly since going green. More time could be spent on other issues of our world, and the threat of our world collapsing would no longer be a concern. Agriculture could be produced much more, more materials could be created for the production of other objects, the polluted oceans could have time to recover, the ozone layer could be less polluted and the effects of the holes in it could lessen until scientists have found a new way to completely erase the exposure. With the employment of green (sustainable) transportation methods, there will be fewer instances where oil leaks into the water, fewer nonrenewable resources will be consumed, and marine life might relax and spend some time without anything unnaturally interfering with the natural order of things. It is really a huge problem to preserve this world that Green Transportation goes above and beyond what was intended and explores how individuals who are merely idly idling might contribute. With today's energy-saving light bulbs, recycling system, usage of biofuel in their vehicles, and other practices that can benefit our ecosystems. A better ecology leads to a healthier planet, which affects our economy in addition to the physical sense. Therefore, the purpose of the study is to review literature on the benefits of green transportation.

6.2 LITERATURE

6.2.1 *GREEN TRANSPORTATION*

Transport that does not deplete natural resources, such as fossil fuels, is referred to as green or sustainable transportation. These types of transportation rely on renewable energy. They also have a very low environmental impact because these modes emit little to no greenhouse gases (Adhikari et al., 2016). Any mode of transportation that has a minimal negative environmental impact is considered green. Public transportation or private means of transportation, such as a quick e-bike (such as an electric city bus). Walking is regarded as a green form of transportation. The fact that green mobility is ecological unifies it across the board. Sustainable transportation uses resources that would not run out after being used, making it possible for future generations to utilize them (Keego, 2021). Using resources wisely and effectively, changing the way that transportation is organized, and choosing healthier modes of transportation are all key to green transportation. The management of privately owned automobiles, innovation, and production of vehicles that use renewable sources of energy such as wind, sun, biofuels, and hydroelectricity are all necessary for this to have any chance of success.

Green transportation image by Paul Krueger

6.3 MODE OF GREEN TRANSPORT

6.3.1 *PUBLIC/MASS TRANSPORTATION*

In most cases, using public transportation is similar to carpooling. To reduce traffic and pollution, many nations are concentrating on creating public transit, such as electric buses or metro systems. Although there are fewer parking spaces in cities, the vast majority of people choose public transportation since it can save them time and money.

6.3.2 HYBRIDIZED VEHICLES

To generate power, hybrid vehicles combine an internal combustion engine with one or more electric motors that use battery energy. Hybrid vehicles are also powered by electricity. Most hybrid vehicles are engineered to automatically recharge their batteries while braking by transferring energy. The hybrid vehicle's battery cannot be recharged by a wall outlet. Instead, the battery is charged by the internal combustion motor and regenerative braking. Some of the most inventive green buses on the market today are already available. The Mercedes-Benz Ciatro G Green-Tec Hybrid Bus, which makes use of four electrical wheel hub motors and automotive lithium-ion batteries, is a prime example.

6.4 THE ELECTRIC CAR

Businesses can save a lot of money by using electric cars and trucks, especially fleet vehicles that frequently drive up to 100 miles each day. Even though they are more expensive to buy than identical gasoline or diesel vehicles, electric vehicles offer much lower running costs. Electric cars, motorbikes, trucks, trains, boats, and scooters are a few famous examples. Even though power plants that generate energy may also release poisonous emissions, electric vehicles that are powered by electricity do not produce any harmful gasses. Even so, renewable energy sources including geothermal, hydroelectric, solar, and wind turbines can be used to generate power. Less expensive maintenance is another advantage for electric vehicle owners. For companies that operate sizable fleets with significant fuel and maintenance expenses, these long-term savings grow enormously.

6.5 GREEN TRAIN

Trains are becoming more environmentally friendly thanks to hybrid locomotives and other cutting-edge green technologies as the majority of governments throughout the world are now more committed than ever to promoting green transportation. Similar technologies used in hybrid autos are also employed by cutting-edge hybrid locomotives.

6.5.1 VEHICLES WITH SEVERAL OCCUPANTS

Carpooling, another name for multioccupant vehicles, helps to minimize pollution levels by reducing the number of vehicles on the road. Vehicles with several occupants are a very beneficial and environmentally friendly form of transportation. When frequently traveling in the same direction, groups of friends and coworkers can share one vehicle.

6.5.2 *PEDESTRIANS/WALKING*

It is preferable to walk to work, school, the grocery store, and other destinations. Walking is free, it emits no greenhouse gases, and it is also a fantastic type of physical training for the body. Almost anyplace they wish to go, they can run, jog, or walk. They can travel further by using a scooter, skateboard, or other device with wheels. All of this is accomplished by using only one's own legs and feet. There are countless health advantages to walking, and experts concur that including it in everyday activities can significantly enhance people's physical and emotional well-being (Marwah, 2022). Walking's positive effects on the environment and economy, including better space utilization, free transportation, and quieter and more pleasant surroundings, provide the justification for why it could actually save the planet.

6.6 BICYCLE/PEDAL POWERED

The use of bicycles as a means of transportation is also another fantastic way to reduce pollution and carbon emissions. It is cheaper than walking, more efficient than walking, and good for your health. Bicycles are much more affordable than cars, both to buy and maintain. However, cycling has been a neglected means of transportation by city planners in many locations throughout the years (Bradshaw, 2014). Greenhouse gas emissions can be reduced significantly when people choose to ride bicycles instead of cars. Pedal power, like foot power, allows people to get some exercise while getting around town without using petrol or contributing to pollution. Despite the environmental benefits of walking, the many advantages of riding a bike cannot be overstated. Bicycles are now accessible to the general public at affordable prices.

6.7 SOLAR POWERED

There is a wide variety of solar-powered vehicles available. To recharge their batteries, certain electric cars can utilize solar energy despite not needing fossil fuels such as gasoline or diesel (Marwah, 2022). Then there are hybrids, which run on a mix of electricity and gasoline. To reduce their environmental impact, owners need to just recharge their automobiles with renewable energy, such as solar energy, the energy from the sun, which uses energy captured from the sun, is even better.

6.8 MONORAIL

Transportation on a monorail is fast and easy. It uses an electric locomotive and travels along a single track. Monorails come in two varieties—suspended and straddle—but both operate on a single track, require frequent inspections of the rails, and have substantial operating costs, all while moving at a maximum of 60 km/h (Purohit, 2016). Due to its raised nature and simplicity of construction, they require a small horizontal and vertical footprint. Not only their timetables do not change due to traffic but also they depart and arrive at the same time every day. When compared to other transportation modes, such as cars or buses, monorail systems have a negligible effect on the environment. This includes factors such as noise and air pollution, as well as traffic congestion and toxic emissions. With their electric or battery power, they are one of the least polluting choices for public transportation (Marwah, 2022).

6.9 ELECTRIC MOTORCYCLES

Electric motorcycles are emission-free in the same way that other electric vehicles are. As a rule, they run on batteries. To be sure, the production of grid electricity used to charge electric bike batteries may contribute to pollution. However, electric bikes are really expensive.

6.9.1 BIOFUEL POWERED

Public transportation, including some cars, buses, and airlines, has made the transition to biofuels. Biofuels can be produced from a wide range of materials, including biomass, vegetable oil, microalgae, maize, sugar beet, soybean, miscanthus, nicotine, biogas, and many forms of trash (Marwah, 2022).

6.9.2 BENEFITS OF SUSTAINABLE TRANSPORTATION

Sustainable and socially acceptable strategies that address ecological, economic, and societal inequalities are essential to successful green transportation and supply chain management. It's good for everyone involved, from passengers to the planet to the transportation industry.

6.10 FOSTERS PHYSICAL AND MENTAL WELL-BEING

Greener modes of transportation are better for public health since they produce less harmful emissions. Particulate matter released by vehicles' exhaust can be detrimental to people's lungs and hearts (Marwah, 2022). Fossil fuels including coal, oil, and natural gas produce harmful byproducts during energy production that have been linked to an increase in cancer and other cardiovascular disorders. Emissions and air pollution can be reduced when people choose sustainable modes of transportation, which benefits public health. People would be able to breathe easier and live longer if more individuals made use of public transit or environmentally friendly vehicles for their daily commutes (Patel, 2022). Also, eco-friendly modes of transportation boost citizens' health and happiness. Walking and riding a bike are excellent methods of exercise and health maintenance.

6.11 REDUCES POLLUTION OUTPUT

Almost 30% of America's greenhouse gas emissions come from the transportation sector. Still, over 82% of those pollutants originate from private automobiles (Marsh, 2020). Transportation by bus or train is significantly more environmentally friendly than driving a car or truck although it is only accounting for 6% of all trips. Also, many public transportation systems are going electric, which will further decrease pollution. Transporters who are unable to make the transition to electric or low-emission cars may find a viable alternative in clean diesel (Marsh, 2020).

6.12 DECREASED FUEL USE

There are two main strategies employed by environmentally friendly modes of transportation to address the issue of excessive and hazardous fuel use: (1) Complete cessation of fuel use: More people using nonmotorized modes of transportation including walking, skateboarding, biking, and scootering will reduce the demand for fossil fuels. (2) Substituting more environmentally friendly fuels for conventional ones. Biofuels, hydrogen, and electricity are all viable alternatives to traditional fossil fuels. Together with measures to encourage walking and cycling, they can help a city meet the transportation needs of its diverse population, regardless of income or location. Either way, a community can take a major step toward sustainability by lowering its reliance on fossil fuels.

6.12.1 CLEAN UP THE AIR

As transportation accounts for 29% of global greenhouse gas emissions, shifting people away from these polluting modes of transportation is already a primary priority for cities and organizations around the world. To ensure that future generations have enough clean air to breathe, city planners should encourage walking, cycling, and other eco-friendly transportation alternatives.

6.12.2 REDUCES TRAFFIC

Congestion naturally diminishes when more individuals opt for environmentally friendly modes of transportation rather than driving themselves. Those who continue to utilize roads in the city will have shorter commutes and less stress on the roads. Also, people who opt for public transportation typically arrive at their destination faster. To go from one place to another even more quickly, trains and some trolleybuses do not have to stop at signals and junctions (Marsh, 2020).

We need to create an economy that can last.

More employment in transportation will be created as public transit infrastructure is built, cleaner alternatives to diesel-fueled automobiles are developed, and these new modes of transportation are staffed (Patel, 2022). The current transportation infrastructure will be upgraded concurrently with the production and marketing of environmentally friendly vehicles. More jobs in transportation will be created as a result, helping to reduce economic inequality and lay the groundwork for long-term economic growth. It will also reduce the need for expensive fossil fuels.

6.12.3 SHORTER TRAVEL TIMES

Reduced traffic congestion and accident rates as a result of widespread eco-friendly commuting would mean less time spent in the car overall. In addition, there are many more ways to get from A to B than there are with a car or other large vehicle, making walking, biking, scooters, and skateboards viable alternatives. In this way, a cyclist can save a significant amount of time by utilizing a route that a motorist would have to avoid.

6.13 MAINTAINS OPEN SPACE

As a bonus, compact growth is encouraged by sustainable transportation, cutting down on commute times. The urban core may have more paved areas, whereas the suburbs and rural areas outside of cities have fewer. Parks, agriculture, and other forms of green space now have greater capacity to expand. There would be less runoff from the land and the wildlife it supports if there were fewer roads in rural regions (Marsh, 2020).

6.14 COSTS LESS

The use of environmentally friendly forms of transportation, such as bicycles, multioccupant automobiles, and electric motorcycles, can help businesses and individuals save a significant amount of money on the high cost of gasoline (Patel, 2022). In the early phases of development, investing in sustainable transit may be costly due to the need to construct roads, buy buses, and set up the necessary infrastructure for transportation networks (Marwah, 2022). However, the payoff in terms of financial and time savings is usually worthwhile. Also, public transportation system maintenance is less expensive than road maintenance. The United States invested $177 billion in roads in 2017, whereas just $70 billion in public transportation and $5 billion in rail (Marsh, 2020).

6.15 CONSUMER DEVOTION/LOYALTY

The demand for eco-friendly goods and services has increased as consumers have become more concerned of global warming. Due to the environmental impact that huge organizations have, consumers also expect those corporations to make strides toward lowering their carbon footprint. So, they give their money to environmentally conscious companies rather than those who do little to mitigate global warming (Patel, 2022).

6.16 THE FOSTERING OF EMPLOYMENT OPPORTUNITIES

Putting money into environmentally friendly modes of transportation usually results in greater employment opportunities. Those in need of employment can find it in the public transportation industry, which includes infrastructure construction, the creation of environmentally friendly alternatives to diesel-fueled cars, and the hiring of people to operate various modes of transportation. Public transportation's multiplicative effect on job creation is 2.5 times greater in areas with high unemployment than in areas with low unemployment (Marsh, 2020). Since it requires the expertise of so many different people (designers, innovators, builders, maintainers, etc.), creating sustainable modes of transportation is also incredibly diverse and open (Marwah, 2022).

6.17 REDUCES WASTED TIME

By automating business processes and automatically discovering ways to lessen an organization's environmental effects, routing software aids in making businesses more environmentally responsible. Certain systems, known as ESG-driven ones, evaluate businesses on their social and ecological footprints (Patel, 2022).

6.18 ENHANCES ROAD SAFETY

Environmentally friendly bus rides are ten times safer per mile than driving your car into the city (Marsh, 2020). However, taking the bus or train instead of driving can cut a commuter's risk of getting in an accident by more than 90%. People in urban regions typically drive to their places of employment, education, and other errands if walking is not an option or is too far (Marwah, 2022).

6.19 HONESTY GOALS

A positive effect on society is a crucial part of sustainable transportation. Everyone, regardless of means, social standing, or physical ability, has access to and can benefit from public transportation and nonmotorized modes of mobility (Marwah, 2022).

6.20 SAVES ENERGY

Reduced energy consumption is another benefit of easing traffic congestion. Cars are unable to move forward due to congestion waste fuel and increased pollution levels due to frequent starts and stops. Although overall energy consumption is higher for a transit vehicle, it is lower per passenger for a private vehicle. Hence, taking the bus, train, or subway, or even just walking or riding a bike, promotes environmental responsibility (Marsh, 2020).

6.21 DISCUSSION

The goal of this research was to examine existing research on the subject of green transportation's advantages. Furthermore, green mobility is not only a low-carbon and environmental means of travel but also a return to a healthy and leisurely way of life (Li, 2016). Building a green transportation system is beneficial for a number of reasons, including the reduction of carbon emissions to mitigate the greenhouse effect, the improvement of air quality and the health of city residents, the conservation of energy, and the reduction of exhaust emissions to ease traffic congestion. As a result, the development of urban green transportation is a crucial step toward conserving energy, as it can cut down on carbon and particulate matter 2.5 (PM2.5) emissions while also enhancing the quality of the environment (Cao et al., 2015). However, there are a few features of green transportation that might pique a user's interest and draw them in. Advantages over competing products in terms of perceived value to consumers, ease of use, and enhanced levels of happiness or social status are all factors in how quickly a new product or service is adopted (Lane and Potter, 2007). Consumers are more inclined to adopt products that are straightforward and convenient to use, and green transportation fits this profile. In addition, green transportation can help you save money on gas by reducing driving and commuting (Ozaki and Sevastyanova, 2011). At the same time, environmentally friendly modes of transportation are quickly replacing private automobiles as people's preferred mode of travel. Hence, green modes of transportation are highly beneficial to the environment as they are both practical and beneficial to human health. Green transportation is something that should be developed and implemented so that people would be drawn to it in order to make life better for future generations.

6.22 CONCLUSION

The goal of this research is to examine previous work concerning the positive aspects of environmentally friendly modes of transportation. Sustainable transportation is defined as the maintenance of a desirable, healthy, and dynamic equilibrium between human beings, vehicles, and environmental systems. It is a way of talking about transportation that is easy on the planet, uses little fuel, and satisfies both human and environmental needs. If you're looking for environmentally friendly options for transportation, this is one of them. Now more than ever, tomorrow's transportation must be environmentally friendly and cost effective. There are several reasons why we should switch to environmentally friendly public transportation. Green transportation is the future because it can reduce pollution, save people money, and reduce traffic on congested highways. I suggest you get on board now. Transportation is significantly responsible for environmental degradation due to the prevalence of vehicles and the use of unsustainable transport. The transportation industry is the leading contributor to global warming because it relies on fossil fuels and the emissions produced when these fuels are used. Access to safe transport systems, which aim to reduce traffic accidents, injuries, and deaths, and to increase road and pedestrian safety, is one of the benefits of sustainable urban mobility and transportation. Two, transportation options should be reasonably priced and available to people of all socioeconomic backgrounds and physical capacities. Third, we have transportation options, which can be represented by the following three words: possible routes and how often they occur. Using green transportation means limiting waste and emissions to what the world can handle, cutting down on land consumption and noise pollution, and making efficient use of renewable and nonrenewable resources at or below their generation and replacement rates, respectively. Promoting links between environmental protection, economic efficiency, and social growth in transportation networks is essential for sustainable development. The environmental dimension seeks to understand the symbiotic relationship between the natural world and industrial processes and to make sure that environmental issues are addressed across the board in the transportation industry.

The environment is also an important factor to consider when thinking about sustainability, as it must be preserved in its natural state, unspoiled by human development. Reducing travel or development limitations is not necessarily the answer to a more sustainable transportation industry. Instead, companies should work to reduce waste in all aspects of their operations, from the workplace to the delivery of finished items. How cities of the future are laid out will be influenced by the need to accommodate a variety of transportation options, including improved bicycle and pedestrian infrastructure. To successfully lessen the carbon impact of the transportation sector, changes in development standards, land use planning, and community efforts will be necessary.

KEYWORDS

- green
- transport
- bicycle
- public transportation
- electric automobiles
- pedal power
- walking

REFERENCES

Adhikari, A.; Biswas, I.; Avittathur, B. Green Retailing a New Paradigm in Supply Chain Management. In: *Handbook of Research on Strategic Supply Chain Management in the Retail Industry*, 2016. DOI: 10.4018/978-1-4666-9894-9.ch016

Bradshaw, C. The Green Transportation Hierarchy: A Guide for Personal & Public Decision Making, 2014. http://vault.sierraclub.org/sprawl/articles/trips.asp (accessed 04 Nov 2015).

Keego. What Is Green Transportation? 31 Jan 2021. https://keegomobility.com/blog/what-is-green-transportation/

Marsh, J. 8 Main Benefits of Sustainable Transportation, 13 May 2020. https://environment.co/benefits-of-sustainable-transportation/

Marwah, S. S. Benefits of Sustainable Transportation, 2022. https://bleedgreenfoundation.com/benefits-of-sustainable-transportation-2022-updated/#Advantages_of_Sustainable_Transportation

Patel, R. What Is Green Transportation and its Significance? 2 Dec 2022. https://www.upperinc.com/guides/green-transportation/

Purohit, A. What Is the Difference Between Light Metro, Metro, and Monorail? 2016. https://www.quora.com/What-is-the-difference-betweenlight-metro-metro-and-monorail

Sun, J.; Zhu, Q. Organizational Green Supply Chain Management Capability Assessment: A Hybrid Group Decision Making Model Application. *IEEE Eng. Manag. Rev. 2018*, *46* (1), 117–127. DOI: 10.1109/emr.2018.2809907

Yassin, A. M. M.; Hassan, M. A.; Elmesmary, H. M. Key Elements of Green Supply Chain Management Drivers and Barriers Empirical Study of Solar Energy Companies in South Egypt. *Int. J. Energy Sector Manag.* **2022**, *16* (3), 564–584. https://doi.org/10.1108/IJESM-10-2020-0014

Zhang, R. P.; Zhou, C. S.; Ming, L. B. Compact City and Green Transportation System Construction, 2010.

CHAPTER 7

Green Marketing Aspect of Green Supply Chain Management

ALHASSAN SEIDU[1], SHANI SALIFU[2], and IBRAHIM SULEMANA[3]

[1]Department of Secretaryship and Management, Tamale Technical University, Tamale, Ghana

[2]Chicago School of Professional Psychology, Chicago, USA

[3]Department of Marketing, Tamale Technical University, Tamale, Ghana

ABSTRACT

As a result of environmental concerns rising to the forefront of public consciousness, numerous companies worldwide have incorporated eco-friendly practices into their standard operating procedures. In today's commercial world, "green marketing" has become a major focus. Many buyers are beginning to alter their purchasing habits and approaches to advertising since they are concerned about the environment. The purpose of the chapter to examine the meaning, challenges, and benefits of green marketing (GM) as well as GM mix. From the review, it was realized that green design, packaging, advertising, etc. are GM practices. Therefore, it is evident that GM has certain positive benefits. Advertising that a company is environmentally conscious is a great way to gain new customers. While businesses see the benefits of being green, they also know there are obstacles to implementing these measures.

7.1 INTRODUCTION

Concerns about the environmental effects of current patterns of consumption and production gave rise to the green marketing (GM) concept in the

1960s and 1970s (Konar and Cohen, 2001). However, as interest in environmentally friendly products grew in the late 1980s, green marketing became a focal point of the marketing world (Mishra and Sharma, 2010). This is undeniably the case when considering the eco-friendliness and responsible business practices of the companies they patronize. For this reason, many of the most profitable and well-known corporations in the world are investing in GM campaigns. Business practices that aim to reduce waste by using eco-friendly commodities, conserving energy, and promoting environmental wellness and sustainability were called "green marketing" by Rahman et al. (2012). Commercializing and advertising goods and services that are eco-friendly so that the world or its environment is not harmed is all about "green marketing"! (Boada, 2021). Today, you can hear the term "green marketing" bandied about in boardrooms, capitols, and philanthropies alike. Environmentalists' rules and government regulations have been cited as reasons for the subject's recent spotlight (Mukonza et al., 2021). Changes in product design, production methods, packaging, and labeling, as well as promotional tactics, are all part of the broad scope of GM (Podvorica and Ukaj, 2020). GM, which is a form of corporate social responsibility (CSR) communication, may increase brand affinity among specific demographics. As a result, communication must be tailored to specific demographic subsets, which can be further subdivided into generations of consumers (Maniatis, 2016). In the previous few decades, there has been a significant uptick in environmental concerns and understanding, particularly in industrialized countries, and as a result, the demand for green products has skyrocketed. In spite of this, this need has been largely unmet, which has opened the door for businesses in developing nations to fill this void (Kumar and Ghodeswar, 2015). Researching the green marketing strategies of companies in emerging markets can shed light on how they seek to gain an advantage over more established rivals. According to Majeed (2022) and Tiwari et al. (2015), GM is still in its infancy and requires more study. This research set out to answer the question, "How can green marketing methods affect customer response?" Therefore, the purpose of this research is to gain a better comprehension of GM's processes and challenges. This chapter is a helpful resource for green marketers, as it offers advice on how to create effective strategies based on GM (green packaging, advertising, eco-labels, etc.), and encourage a more positive attitude toward green product purchases, both of which are necessary for increasing green product purchase behavior. The purpose of the chapter to examine the meaning, challenges, and benefits of GM as well as GM mix.

7.2 LITERATURE

7.2.1 GREEN MARKETING

GM promotes goods that are thought to be safe for the environment. It encompasses a wide variety of actions, such as tweaks to products, production methods, packaging materials, and even marketing strategies. However, defining green marketing is not a straightforward undertaking due to the prevalence of multiple connotations related to this phrase, including social, environmental, and retail implications that often overlap and contradict one another. Environmental marketing and ecological marketing are two other synonyms for this concept.

Marketing practices that aim to minimize their impact on the natural world are called "green marketing," as defined by the American Marketing Association (2022). (i.e., designed to minimize negative effects on the physical environment or to improve its quality). Production, advertising, packaging, and recycling initiatives that take ecological considerations into account may also be described by this term. According to the Cambridge Dictionary (2022), "green marketing" is the process of promoting a company's goods or services to customers by highlighting their positive environmental impact. To put it simply, GM is the practice of advertising eco-friendly goods and services as well as green causes. To be more precise, "green marketing" encompasses a wide variety of approaches that are kinder to the planet. To create a sustained market for environmentally friendly goods, a business must engage in "green marketing" (Boada, 2021). GM, also known as ecological marketing, eco-marketing, and sustainable marketing (Katrandjiev, 2016), has introduced novel, environmentally friendly, and financially fruitful ways of conducting business. Among the many arguments in favor of GM are the need to reduce waste, increase awareness of eco-friendly practices among consumers, and propel the sustainability agenda in developing economies. There needs to be a GM attitude that affects organizational behavior and performance in emerging markets for GM techniques to be successfully conceived and implemented (Mukonza and Swarts, 2019). When a company takes a green marketing stance, it takes a more holistic approach to helping the environment (Papadas et al., 2017). Positive brand associations are the end goal of GM campaigns. By doing so, the brand's positive effect on the planet is reinforced. The goal of "green marketing" is to increase demand for goods and services by highlighting their positive effects on the natural world. Sustainable business practices, environmentally friendly product design and packaging, clear labeling of environmental benefits, etc. are all part of it. The benefits that can come from this type of advertising more than make up for the high prices that may be incurred (Boada, 2021). According to Marketingschools.org (2016), to be compliant with green practices, a company must take a comprehensive strategy for GM rather than focusing solely on the product. However, the company risks being branded a greenwashing if it fails to demonstrate genuine care and dedication for the environment across all of its operations, from procurement to employee involvement.

There have been three distinct phases of GM's development: ecological, environmental, and sustainable (Mishra and Sharma, 2014; Zampese et al., 2016; Lazar, 2017; Papadas et al., 2017). Toxic industries such as chemicals, mining, etc., and the damage they bring to habitats were the primary focus of researchers and practitioners in the first phase, known as the ecological phase (Papadas et al., 2017). The government's attention during this period is the key benefit. In the second stage, efforts were directed at developing pollution-free technologies that would result in new product innovations that would reduce waste and pollution (Lazar, 2017). In addition to businesses involved in the ecological phase, enterprises in the electronics, tourism, and apparel industries were a part of this era. In this stage, businesses struggled to sell their products to customers because of its "green" qualities and benefits. Nonetheless, it was in this era that packaging recycling first became widespread. During the 1990s, businesses showed a lot of enthusiasm for eco-friendly advertising, but that desire has since waned as many businesses saw GM as an unnecessary expense. A sustainable era began in 2000 when businesses began catering to customers' needs for consumption and production in a way that would not compromise future generations' quality of life (Peattie, 2001). This is the era in which businesses generally embrace GM. Sustainable advertising, looking ahead, and putting customers first all gained popularity among businesses across sectors (Katrandjiev, 2016). With an ever-increasing global awareness of environmental challenges, GM is continually developing.

7.2.2 GREEN MARKETING PRACTICES

The term "green marketing" refers to the practice of promoting environmentally friendly products, services, and lifestyle choices to individuals in a way that does not harm the natural world. This includes but is not limited to market research, product design, packaging, and advertising (Sarumathi, 2014),

7.2.3 CSR

A firm can take the initial steps toward sustainability by embracing CSR for its wrongdoings in the past and launching attempts to embrace more environmentally friendly practices. A corporation that has contributed to pollution or the depletion of natural resources can nonetheless rebrand itself to appeal to environmentally conscious consumers by adopting a more positive image.

7.2.4 ECO-DESIGN

When a company's products or services cannot legitimately be called "green," that company will resort to greenwashing. Creating eco-friendly products and services from the ground up is a key part of any successful GM campaign (Mitra and Masunda, 2019). You may make your products friendlier to the environment by using green strategies from the get-go in the design and development phases. To design in a sustainable manner means to make items that are easy on the environment, user friendly, adaptable, and durable (Foster and Partners, 2022). Typically used in the context of the building industry, "green designing" provides a potent alternative to the conventional building model by making greater improvements to occupant health and safety while simultaneously reducing the building model's use of scarce natural resources (Mitra and Masunda, 2019).

7.2.5 ECO-ALLIANCE

As managers become more aware of the importance of environmental management techniques, green efforts are becoming a more important factor in selecting business associates (Lee and Klassen, 2008). Organizations that want to do more green work could benefit from forming less formal partnerships or alliances with other businesses. Choosing the proper partner is critical to the success of both companies, according to research on partnerships, which is widespread in the field of cause-related marketing (Lichtenstein et al., 2004). Companies that can partner with causes that are a "high match" for them might lessen consumer skepticism because the partnership will be seen as both a smart business decision and a reflection of the company's core beliefs (Mitra and Masunda, 2019). A company's socially responsible actions (such as its support for an environmental cause) and its synergies in activities (i.e., what it is known for) are said to be a good fit if they both complement one another (Mitra and Masunda, 2019). Hence, businesses seeking collaborations with other organizations, for profit or not, should think about how those agreements might be perceived by various stakeholder groups.

7.2.6 GREEN PACKAGING (ECO-FRIENDLY PACKAGING)

"Green packaging" is another successful green marketing technique. Eco-friendly packaging is a powerful tool for businesses looking to attract environmentally conscious consumers. Goods that are packaged using environmentally friendly materials and processes have a smaller carbon footprint and less of an influence on the energy needed to produce them. The use of biodegradable packaging shows consumers that the business values environmental responsibility. Customers may be dissuaded from buying environmentally friendly goods if they come in unsustainable packaging. It has been stated that "green packing involves lowering the size, shape, and weight of packaging and using environmentally friendly materials" (Khan et al., 2016). A competitive business strategy that should be explored is green packaging (Tuwanku et al., 2018). Mohamed (2016) defines "green packaging" as employing "low environmental impact and energy consumption production methods and materials for packaging commodities." To achieve their economic, social, and environmental (triple bottom line) sustainability goals, firms can benefit from adopting green packaging practices (Maziriri, 2018). Packaging that is environmentally friendly (or "green") is meant to express a sense of corporate environmental concern and highlight the product's eco-friendly features (Ghodeswar and Kumar, 2014). Green packaging is the advocacy for and use of materials and practices that increase the usability of products (Kumar, Agarwal et al., 2017). When we talk about "green packaging," we are referring to containers that do not cause any harm to future generations, do not waste, instead, reduce the use of subsurface resources, pay fair salaries, and provide safe and healthy working conditions for their employees (Quoquab et al., 2017).

7.3 GREEN POSITIONING

To strengthen consumer recognition of a brand, green positioning communicates details about the product's eco-friendliness (Mitra and Masunda, 2019). Lack of clear communication of green branding qualities will limit the commercial viability of eco-friendly products. Green positioning, such as brand positioning, can have a practical or emotional effect on how consumers view a brand (Mitra and Masunda, 2019).

7.3.1 ECO-LABELS

An eco-label, or sustainable label, is a symbol shown on consumer-facing packaging to indicate that the product is safe and less detrimental to the environment than others of a similar nature (Mitra and Masunda, 2019). A product's environmental quality can be advertised with the help of an ecolabel, a tool utilized by businesses and governments. Indicators of a reliable eco-label include four main factors: Measured environmental/sustainable consumption outcomes, demonstrating conservation of natural capital; (4) uptake independence and acceptance; proof of label influence; (5) breadth of environmental issues covered, carrying capacity, range of label products covered (Horne, 2009; Majeed, 2022). Ecolabels are widely recognized as an effective method of informing modern consumers about the product's environmental friendliness. They enlighten customers in a way that encourages them to take action and buy environmentally friendly goods. Consumers will buy more and have a more positive impression of a product with an eco-label if they believe the label is legitimate (Majeed, 2022). Credible ecolabels not only guarantee the sustainable management of the manufacturing chain but also communicate the superiority of the product when compared to nonlabeled products (Riskos et al., 2021). Reputable eco-labels have a constructive effect on consumers' tastes and budgets. Consumers are more likely to choose, buy, and value eco-label-designated products when there is an ecolabel on them (Riskos et al., 2021).

7.3.2 GREEN ADVERTISING

When it comes to communicating the eco-friendliness of a company's goods and services to potential customers, "green advertising" is a crucial component, as stated by Kumar and Kumar (2017). The term "biophilia" describes the practice of including ecologically focused language to appeal to people who value protecting the planet (Kumar and Kumar, 2017). Awan and Wamiq (2016), who believe that customers are just buying things to meet their needs and wants, assert that the health and environmental components of advertisements are the most significant aspects of communication messages for customers. The environment is emphasized in ads by Chang et al. (2005) rather than social factors to boost communication efficiency. Customers place the greatest importance on health and environmental messages in advertising (Awan and Wamiq, 2016). Marketers employ green advertising as one tactic to portray their products as eco-friendly in the eyes of consumers (Rex and Baumann, 2007). This includes highlighting waste management and ecolabels on packaging, as well as recycling information (Eren-Erdogmus et al., 2016).

7.3.3 GREEN DISPOSAL (RECYCLING AND REUSE)

Green disposal considers the full life cycle of an item, from manufacturing through final disposal. Unsustainable disposal techniques pose risks to both the environment and human health, thus it is important to recycle outdated products and materials whenever possible. The push toward more environmentally friendly waste management has led to the development of food recycling programs and mechanical devices that process food scraps (Mitra and Masunda, 2019).

7.3.4 ORGANIZATIONAL GREENING (ECO-FRIENDLY PRACTICES IN ORGANIZATIONS)

Changing a company's culture to be more environmentally friendly is no easy feat, and there are many possible routes to take. To organize the important themes from our literature synthesis for this study, we divided them into three broad classes: green champions, green processes, and supply chain management (SCM). If a firm wants to realize its full green potential, it must adopt the motto of its green champions and incorporate green initiatives into every facet of the business. Unfortunately, this change rarely happens overnight. Instead, the initiative is driven by an individual or group of people. The term "green champion" describes these people. Policy entrepreneurs who care about the environment are more likely to take actions that support green strategies within their company. Among the many operations that go into making a product, "green" refers to those that take concrete steps to lessen their influence on the environment. In recent years, as the concept of sustainability has become increasingly central, there has been a surge of interest in "green" processes and products among businesses, governments, and academics. Last but not least, SCM. It is not enough for a company to simply green its internal operations; green solutions must be incorporated across the board throughout the supply chain. Companies with larger arcs (i.e., those having stronger linkages to trading partners in both upstream and downstream directions) do better, according to studies. It seems to reason that this also applies to efforts made to protect the environment.

7.3.5 GREEN INNOVATION (GI) (ENVIRONMENT-FRIENDLY TECHNOLOGICAL ADVANCEMENTS)

The traditional definition of green innovation (GI) by Dangelico and Pujari (2010) is a multifaceted process that highlights the environment's material, energy, and pollution needs at various points in a product's physical life cycle. There are generally two categories of GI works. The first defines GI as an organization's eco-friendly policies and procedures (Yakubu, 2017), while the second emphasizes the firm's competencies (Xie et al., 2019; Ho et al., 2009). Business practice GI is defined as "the hardware or software innovation related to green products or processes" (Song and Yu, 2018); it is proposed that GI consists of management practices and technological advancements that increase environmental and organizational performance (OP) and give firms an edge in the market (Eren-Erdogmus et al., 2016). Some academics define GI as "unique or modified systems, processes, products, and behaviors that offer an advantage to the environment and subside enterprises' sustainability" (Xie et al., 2019). The creation of novel or inventive environmentally friendly products is a common tactic used by GI. It is widely held that when an organization introduces novel green products or services, it demonstrates its commitment to sustainability and reassures its many stakeholders that it is serious about being green.

7.3.6 GREEN MARKETING MIX

A relatively recent idea, "green marketing" refers to the advertising of eco-friendly goods and services. Sustainable production entails minimizing environmental impact at every stage of the product life cycle (ideation, design, production, marketing, sales, usage, and disposal). Including new environmental concerns and other dimensions, the classic marketing mix (4Ps of Marketing) is re-imagined. Product, pricing, marketing, and distribution of eco-friendly goods are all discussed.

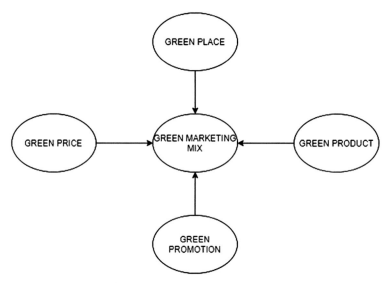

FIGURE 7.1 Green marketing mix.
Source: Authors

7.3.7 GREEN PRODUCT

What we call "green products" are those that have been made using environmentally friendly processes and have no negative effects on the natural world. The preservation of natural resources and long-term progress can only be achieved through the widespread adoption of green technologies and green consumer goods. When a product or service is advertised as "green," the idea is that it was created with environmental consciousness from the ground up, from the advertising to the product to the disposal of the product. With rising awareness of the effects of global warming, nonbiodegradable solid waste, and the harmful effect of contaminants, this is less detrimental to the environment. Ecology-based marketing is a method of advertising goods and services by taking advantage of their natural habitat. All potential environmental effects of making and using the product must be considered during its development. Similarly, management should evaluate the company's competitive advantage in the market (Mayakkannan, 2019). There has been a shift in consumer attitudes about products that have been linked to ecological disasters, such as palm oil, and consumers are rejecting those items as a result. Thus, there has been a rise in the number of fair trade campaigns. Recycled goods are gaining popularity with shoppers because of their eco-friendliness. This is yet another option for companies when it comes to branding, packaging, and product creation (Boada, 2021). Eco-friendly products, sometimes known as "green" products, cause no harm to the environment during any stage of their life cycle. Many environmental aspects were under evaluation as businesses and consumers alike sought to lessen their influence on the planet by, among other things, using less energy and producing less waste. The needs of consumers should guide the creation of the green product. Made from reclaimed resources, productions are possible (Mayakkannan, 2019). Products that conserve resources such as water, electricity, and money also have fewer negative effects on the natural world. The increasing focus on product enhancement is shown by green chemistry. A business can advertise the environmentally friendly items they make in their community using supplies from the area. There are two channels through which this approach might foster consumer loyalty. Mostly, the corporation will attract eco-conscious customers thanks to its investment in green initiatives. Second, purchasing regionally made goods can be good for the economy and the community. When it comes to human resources, operations, or marketing, developing environmentally friendly products necessitates creative problem-solving in the face of environmental and customer challenges. Strategies for GI are required if we are to meet the diverse, often contradictory, expectations of our many stakeholders (Hall and Vredenburg 2005). As part of their role in product management, marketers must relay market-driven characteristics and consumer demands for new features to the product designer. These were environmentally friendly, locally sourced, low-energy consuming, and chemically experienced (Mayakkannan, 2019). According to Kumar and Ghodeswar (2015), a product's entire lifecycle—from design to material procurement to production to storage to distribution to use to recycling—needs to be considered when attempting to make the product more environmentally friendly. These items need to be developed and commercialized with environmental sustainability in mind, not just profit. For instance, since packaging is a significant contributor to environmental pollution, a business should work to cut down on wasteful packaging by switching to recyclable materials.

7.3.8 GREEN PRICE

Currently, the cost of designing a product that is environmentally friendly is sometimes more than that of developing a traditional product. If customers know exactly what they are getting and why our product is worth more, they will gladly pay more for it. Green pricing takes into account society, the environment, and the economy. In addition to ensuring environmentally friendly output, it also ensures the health of businesses and their surrounding communities. Changing its form, expanding its capabilities, or making it uniquely yours are all ways to increase its worth (Mayakkannan, 2019). Modifications to the production process, such as packaging and disposal for environmental compliance, will incur additional costs for the company, which will be reflected in the final price. Green goods cost more than their conventional counterparts because of the extra money needed to cover environmental and social costs. As research has shown, this is the most significant factor preventing customers from buying eco-friendly goods (Weisstein et al., 2014). The term "green price" is used to describe a product's established cost that takes environmental factors into account (Yazdanifard and Mercy, 2011). The pricing takes into account the extra money needed to change the production method, the packaging, and the disposal procedure to minimize environmental and social costs. Such pricing has always led to green items costing more than their nongreen counterparts. It is possible that a price hike would not be a problem if buyers were willing to shell out the extra cash (Solaiman et al., 2015).

7.3.9 GREEN PLACE

The goal of Green Place's logistics planning is to reduce vehicle emissions. For this reason, we are promoting imported mango juice in India as a means of reducing our carbon footprint. Producing it locally under license is an option. By not having to ship the item from afar, the cost of delivery is reduced, and the product's significance is increased (Mayakkannan, 2019). As a result, the ship and any alternate form of transport will produce carbon dioxide. The campaign will succeed or fail based on how well the distribution and marketing teams collaborate. Improving fuel efficiency, shipment packing, and depot noise levels are just the tip of the iceberg when it comes to green distribution. Since the entire supply chain, from production to retail to final consumption, can affect a product's environmental friendliness, this system must ensure that all items on the market are environmentally friendly (Rivera-Camino, 2007; Li and Tang, 2010). Green distribution is all about getting the correct items into the hands of environmentally conscious buyers (Yazdanifard and Mercy, 2011). When we talk about the "internal" side of things, we're talking about how managers and workers within the organization need to be conscious of environmental challenges in the context of their work.

7.3.10 GREEN PROMOTION

Green advertising is a strategy used to raise awareness about eco-friendly products and influence consumer opinion (Yazdanifard and Mercy, 2011). Promoting our eco-friendly product effectively will help get the word out about its many benefits. The green product itself, sustainable lifestyle, or our company's environmental responsibilities are all possible avenues of discourse (Mayakkannan, 2019). The company may gain some loyal customers this way (Yazdanifard and Mercy, 2011), but it must be careful not to make any exaggerated claims lest it be seen as a "green-washer," which might cause people to disregard the ad, stop buying the product, or file a complaint with the authorities. GM and conventional marketing have identical goals and methods (Li and Tang, 2010), hence there are no essential distinctions between the two. The goals of green advertising are thus similar to those of traditional advertising: to teach consumers about the firm and the product, to encourage them to switch to a green brand and to remind them where and how to buy the items. Promoting the use of postconsumer recycled materials in product packaging or the use of less energy in the production process are examples of GM. Additionally, some businesses promote themselves as eco-friendly by contributing to environmental causes such as tree planting through a percentage of sales (Gupta and Ogden, 2018). Changing the settings on promotional machinery is an important part of green advertising. It included commercials, promotional materials, white papers, web pages, motion pictures, and talks. Papers and boards made by the Indian Tobacco Company (ITC Limited) are better for the planet. Entrepreneurs in the green economy can win over customers by highlighting the benefits their products provide in terms of efficiency, cost savings, health, and ease of use (Mayakkannan, 2019). For GM to be effective, it must inform customers of important environmental information that is directly related to a company's operations (Solaiman et al., 2015). If backed up by other corporate endeavors, green promotion may be a powerful strategic weapon. If not, customers may dismiss the ad as "greenwashing," leading to lost sales and maybe complaints to authorities. Customers are more likely to stick with a business that promotes its environmental responsibility through advertising, sales promotions, publicity, and CSR initiatives (Yazdanifard and Mercy,

2011) because they feel good about supporting a firm that cares about the environment. It is more difficult for businesses to use GM because it must be applied across the board (Marketing-schools.org, 2016). Marketing the eco-friendliness of a product or firm is pointless if the production and shipping processes are harmful to the environment. GM products have the following characteristics: they are naturally sourced; they are recyclable, reusable, and biodegradable; they contain nontoxic chemicals or chemicals that have been approved for use in consumer products; they do not harm or pollute the environment; they are not tested on animals; they come in environmentally friendly packaging (such as reusable containers and refillable containers). When businesses make significant efforts to reduce their carbon footprint, some customers are more likely to prefer those businesses' offerings over those of less environmentally responsible competitors. Such incentives include a company's use of recyclable materials, contribution to a good cause, or environmentally friendly packaging.

7.4   THE BENEFITS OF GM TO FIRMS

Several modern companies place a premium on environmental consciousness. To achieve the Sustainable Development Goals by 2030, firms will need to implement GM strategies (Chen and Yang, 2019). Since GM emphasizes environmental protection in all that it does, it can be thought of as a dependent variable on sustainable growth (Kinoti, 2011; Mukonza and Swarts, 2020). Nonetheless, many businesses have gone green due to the increased environmental consciousness of consumers, sometimes known as "green consumerism" (Chang et al., 2019). Reaching out to people who are keen on buying eco-friendly goods is the main objective of GM. Consumers are interested in supporting businesses who are making an effort to reduce their environmental impact (Indeed, 2022). Many buyers want information on the production process and the effects of product use on the natural world (Raman, 2023).

7.5   MAKE MORE MONEY WITH ECO-FRIENDLY ADVERTISING

The millennial generation places a premium on environmental responsibility. Individuals are prepared to pay a premium for goods and services that they believe to be environmentally friendly or socially beneficial. When consumers know that a product is safe for human and animal use and the environment because it is created from recyclable materials, they are more likely to purchase it. The goal of GM is to raise consumer knowledge so that they may make environmentally responsible purchasing decisions. Conscious consumers pay close attention to the goods they buy and use, so their increased involvement in promoting your product through word of mouth is a huge boon to your bottom line.

7.6 FOCUS ATTENTION ON PRESSING ENVIRONMENTAL OR SOCIETAL PROBLEMS

Partnerships with other industry leaders in environmental protection can be a key component of a company's GM strategy if it has any such ties. Any effort, be it an advertising campaign, an event, a training seminar, or something else, can benefit greatly from this.

7.6.1 ENHANCES CREDIBILITY

The organization's credibility will increase first and foremost among the benefits. A corporation needs a bright outlook if it is to generate sustainable profits. The green perspective is what makes this possible. Not only would customers flock to a company with a bright future, but so would partners in the industry who value its solid standing. GM is the most effective strategy for improving a company's image.

7.6.2 NEW MARKET ENTRY

One way a business might break into new markets is by emphasizing the beneficial environmental impact it has already had. Bringing attention to the benefits their product or service provides might help a company break into new markets. If the information is clear, succinct natured, and tailored to the needs of the residents, then maybe those people will start using solar panels when they have not considered it before. Highlighting sustainable manufacturing processes, using eco-friendly and organic items in the workplace, composting and recycling, and carpooling to and from work are all examples of GM's potential benefits. One could go on and on. Reducing or improving packaging, going paperless, reusing printer cartridges, reforesting, etc. all help lessen the environmental impact of a business or individual. Green marketing has many benefits, including the ability to expose businesses' efforts to new audiences and inform consumers about environmental issues.

7.6.3 EMOTIONAL CONNECTION

Using a GM approach can make a company more relatable to its target audience. It is a great way to get your business out there while also supporting a good cause. It will aid in making them more memorable to customers and will have a constructive effect on how customers view the company.

7.7 COMPETITIVE ADVANTAGE (A COMPETITIVE EDGE)

GM's competitive edge is one of its main benefits. Being the first to market eco-friendly goods and services can give a business a significant leg up on the competition. Additionally, it has the potential to entice shareholders interested in supporting environmentally and socially conscious businesses (Rahman, 2023). Those who choose "green marketing" are recognized as leaders in their field who are dedicated to doing the right thing. This is the case even for consumers who place less importance on ecological concerns. It also provides you with other selling factors to advertise and discuss with your customers, which you can use in addition to the tried-and-true methods of offering the best value, the longest lifespan, and the most En Vogue offerings. Instead of focusing exclusively on price and value, market the product's positive effects on the environment and society.

7.7.1 CUSTOMER GAINS

If consumers are serious about protecting the planet, they must support businesses that provide eco-friendly goods. In addition, a company's GM efforts will be more successful if they take the time to learn how customers value their products and services and how it may best position their offerings to meet their needs (Fernando et al., 2016). They gain a cleaner environment in which to live longer and healthier lives. The public wants eco-friendly goods that don't skimp on quality or functionality. Customers prefer to buy from companies that care about the environment (Lin et al., 2017). Businesses hoping to attract millennials as clients should adopt more ethical business practices.

7.7.2 ENVIRONMENTAL BENEFITS

The environment gains the most from GM. The majority of the greenhouse gases that contribute to global warming come from burning fossil fuels. Because more energy-efficient products are developed in response to GM initiatives, the amount of energy used by the general public is reduced. Air pollution is decreased when more hybrid cars are introduced to the market. Agricultural practices that forego the use of synthetic inputs such as pesticides, weed killers, and fertilizers prevent groundwater contamination by limiting the accumulation of excess nutrients.

7.7.3 PRODUCT BENEFITS

When people know that buying green items helps the planet, those products are more likely to sell well. The value and consumption of a product or service can be increased by including environmentally friendly features alongside those that boost price, quality, and performance. Any product that claims to be "green" must do more than just make the client happy; it must also help the planet. Eco-friendly packaging is something else that green marketers work on. Businesses are making strides to phase out plastics and other items made from Petrochemicals. Procter & Gamble (P&G) has reduced the amount of trash people throw away by eliminating the outer carton from its Sure and Secrets deodorants.

7.7.4 POSITIVE EFFECTS ON THE SUPPLY CHAIN

Waste can be reduced through the use of green strategies by analyzing truck loading and route planning in the shipping process. By planning a route, you may save money on fuel, increase vehicle utilization, and boost service quality for your customers. By fostering connections between the businesses that make up an organization's supply chain from mining to raw materials to finished products to the distribution network and finally to the consumers, GM enhances sustainability. Products are tracked by companies through their supply chains. Companies that use environmentally responsible methods of manufacturing and distribution can offer assurance that their goods will meet or exceed consumer expectations.

7.7.5 BENEFITS OF THE STRATEGY

Strategic advantages accrue to businesses that use eco-friendly marketing strategies. Businesses are realizing that promoting environmental sustainability is good for business and is increasingly reflected in their mission statements and communications with stakeholders such as customers, employees, shareholders, the government, investors, and the general public. Customers have a favorable impression of the company because of its environmental consciousness. It helps to bring in skilled workers and keeps them actively involved in the company's operations, which in turn boosts output. Investors are eager to back companies that work to solve the issues of rising fuel costs and decreasing greenhouse gas emissions.

7.7.6 PROGRESS IN THE ECONOMY

Reduced agricultural output, higher water use, higher sea levels, detrimental effects on ecosystems, and increased human illness are all direct results of climate change. They cause malnutrition and extreme poverty in emerging economies (Lin et al., 2017). GM strategies in production help mitigate global warming, which in turn lessens the severity of hunger and poverty. Migration issues from the countryside to the city plague economies still on the rise. As a result, GM strategies have an effect on the global environment and the consumption of resources in these regions. Businesses in these regions can get a leg up on the competition by using GM tools to promote eco-friendly products (Pink, 2022).

7.7.7 FIND FRESH AND SUSTAINABLE MATERIALS

Forcing businesses and industries to get inventive as we transition away from fossil fuels and other nonrenewable resources. Even though this shift could cause a temporary drop in production, it could ultimately spur innovation that leads to more efficient, environmentally friendly methods of production.

7.7.8 BOOST IN CUSTOMER SATISFACTION AND SALES

Businesses that offer products or provide services that strongly appeal to the Lifestyles of Health and Sustainability (LOHAS) market demography may see a rise in revenue and customer loyalty after adopting green practices and implementing a GM plan (Pink, 2022).

7.7.9 LOWERING SUPPORTING EXPENSES

Use of utilities such as water and electricity can be decreased by the implementation of renewable manufacturing techniques. One of the benefits of implementing a green production strategy is that it can help a business become more financially independent and reduce its reliance on external sources of energy (Pink, 2022).

7.7.10 CHALLENGES OF GM

Some businesses utilize GM for the wrong reasons or fail to forecast potential negative repercussions, even though it is meant to promote a more ethical approach to business and production. Some significant drawbacks of environmentally friendly advertising tactics include the following:

7.7.11 HIGH PRICES FOR ENVIRONMENTALLY FRIENDLY GOODS

Prices tend to go up when businesses try to be environmentally responsible. Particularly in India, buyers are price conscious and give preference to things that are reasonably priced. Although creating eco-friendly products and adopting renewable energy initiatives might have considerable environmental benefits, they may be out of reach for small enterprises. Likewise, regular people may not be able to afford these products and services since the high prices set by the manufacturers and suppliers are passed on to the customers (Pink, 2022). Green products cost more because extensive research and development and marketing are required to bring them to market. GM is the promotion of eco-friendly goods and services, including those that use renewable energy sources. Developing a new marketing strategy and implementing it may be a time-consuming and expensive process for businesses. Changing a company's brand to be more environmentally friendly can be costly, even though such initiatives and policies are meant to save money over time.

7.7.12 CONSUMPTION-BASED SKEPTICISM

Smart customers can spot fake attempts at GM, known as "greenwashing" or "eco-bleaching." For instance, a business may say it is working to lessen its environmental impact while only making cosmetic changes. Commercials and advertising efforts that employ greenwashing strategies frequently rely on market research or trends to deceive the public. Companies that make GM claims without having them backed up risk losing the trust of consumers who care about the environment but are skeptical of such assurances (Pink, 2022).

7.7.13 UNANTICIPATED REPERCUSSIONS FOR THE ENTIRE BUSINESS

While eco-friendly consumer trends may have good intentions at their inception, firms can wind up being short-sighted as a result of changes in supply and demand. A GM campaign might promote almond milk as an alternative to cow's milk, drastically lowering the demand for dairy products and the associated CO_2 emissions. However, almond producers would have to raise production to meet the rising demand, and this process uses a lot more water than dairy cow farming does. This hypothetical scenario depicts widespread drought and water constraints in almond-growing regions as a result of a shift in customer preferences (Pink, 2022).

7.7.14 RESILIENCE AND LONGSUFFERING

Marketers should consider the long-term benefits of this new green movement, and investors and corporations should see the environment as a big long-term investment opportunity. Expect to wait a long time for any progress to be made. There will be an adjustment period because it is novel (Lin et al., 2017).

7.7.15 STOPPING "GREEN MYOPIA"

One of the basic rules of GM is to always put the customer first and think about what they want. If done correctly, this can encourage customers to try new products or even pay more for one that is more environmentally friendly. Developing a product that is completely environmentally friendly in different ways but fails to meet the standards for customer happiness would not help. If this continues, people will get green myopia. The market appeal of eco-friendly goods will also decline if they are priced too expensive.

7.7.16 CONSUMERS' GENERAL LACK OF UNDERSTANDING

While there are many advantages to GM practices, the vast majority of consumers are still ignorant of them. There is a pressing need to inform and enlighten them on the subject. Eco-labels are a tool for encouraging people to buy environmentally friendly goods.

7.7.17 INSUFFICIENT UNIFORMITY

Currently, there are no universally accepted criteria for labeling a product as organic. There will be no way to verify the certifications unless official authorities are involved. For such labeling and licensing, a universal quality control board is required.

7.7.18 NOVEL IDEA (NEWNESS OF THE GREEN MARKETING CONCEPT)

The benefits of GM to consumers should include this element. More education about the benefits of eco-friendly goods among urban consumers is underway. However, the general public is still getting used to the idea. Consumers must be informed of the environmental risks they pose (Lin et al., 2017). It will take a long time and a lot of work for the new green movements to reach the public. Buyers understand the value of herbal and all-natural cosmetics. Yoga and organic food are only two of the many examples of healthy lifestyles that Indian consumers are exposed to. The consumer is already knowledgeable and predisposed to adopt green products in those regards.

7.7.19 AGGRESSIVE MARKETING

Companies should advertise the advantages of their green products more actively. Companies are producing and selling environmentally friendly goods, but they are not publicizing this shift in focus because it is still a novel idea.

7.7.20 TRUTHFUL CLAIMS

Corporations have an obligation to be forthright in their statements. Some companies' credibility is damaged and consumer trust is eroded due to their false advertising.

7.7.21 THE HIGH PRICE OF ENVIRONMENTAL CERTIFICATES

Getting environmental certifications for your products can be a time-consuming and expensive procedure, depending on your sector. Governments, trade organizations, expert organizations, and advocacy groups for consumers all issue certifications that guarantee a product is safe for the environment. Specifically, this is true for businesses involved in the recycling of garbage and the use of renewable energy sources. One of the major drawbacks of green marketing is the difficulty of adhering to these criteria. For the simple reason that businesses and consumers will have no reference point for evaluating the veracity of green "claims" without these governmental standards.

7.7.22 GREENWASHING

Because of the many benefits associated with GM, many large corporations have begun to adopt "greener" public personas. However, this is often just greenwashing on their part. This indicates that a business will focus on a little point to make something that is not sustainable appear environmentally friendly.

7.8 DISCUSSION

With pollutants, habitat destruction, climate change, woodland loss, etc. on the rise, a worldwide environmental disaster is looming (Emekci, 2019). Thus, there has been a rise in eco-consciousness among customers. Current consumers are more than happy to shell out more cash for environmentally friendly goods. Becoming green is not without its difficulties. Businesses engaging in "green marketing" should be transparent in all aspects of their operations and assertions. The assertions must be accurate. Socially responsible businesses should take into account the possibility that their current actions, while ecologically beneficial, may have unintended negative consequences in the future, and organizations should clearly state the environmental advantages, rationalize the comparison discrepancies, and consider the harmful consequences. Research into the difficulties of GM in India has been conducted by Verma (2015) and Nadaf and Nadaf (2014). They concluded that the government, consumers, and rival firms were all secondary factors in the development of GM in India. They examined the challenges and solutions facing GM in India. They cite factors such as false advertising, low levels of consumer knowledge, excessive prices, and a lack of trustworthiness as justifications for their position. To better manage GM, they advocated for tighter management oversight, updated technology, and a well-thought-out strategy. Singal, Garg, and Singla (2013) argue that for green products' claims to be credible, regulatory authority must certify and standardize them. They believe that the idea of "green marketing" and "green products" is novel and calls for further consumer education, so businesses should give it some thought. High investment in green technology, green power, etc., was cited by Welling and Chavan (2010) as an additional issue for the organization. According to Shafaat and Sultan (2012), companies that care about their consumers" satisfaction have started making eco-friendly products. Businesses must make wholesale changes to their supply chains if they are to respond to GM. By leading by example, brands may help consumers understand the negative effects their purchasing decisions have on the environment and motivate them to make better choices. As the strength of the green market grows, businesses will be able to implement GM strategies. Although they never intended for the green qualities of their products and business methods to be made public, they can now use the term "green" in promotional materials without having to change anything. Since there is no universally applicable GM plan, however, a generalized strategy is impossible, as stated by Ginsberg and Bloom (2004). So, businesses need to formulate their optimal strategy in light of their resources and the external environment. It is more likely that customers will use the information provided by eco-labels, which increases the likelihood that consumers will engage in sustainable behavior without compromising their freedom of choice (Majeed, 2022).

The term "green marketing" is used to describe the practice of selling goods and services with an emphasis on their positive impact on the natural world. Green items include things like eco-furniture and reusable paper or fabric shopping bags used in the creation of handicrafts. Because of the emphasis placed on environmental and social considerations, this method of advertising stands out from the crowd. Eco-friendly advertising has only been around since the 1980s. Now, more than ever, it is crucial that "green marketing" becomes the standard rather than the exception in the realm of advertising. Currently, it is most common among businesses that are dedicated to sustainable development and CSR, making those businesses' products more desirable. Those customers who are also concerned with social issues are more likely to remain loyal to the company as a result. The moral requirement of socially responsible behavior, legislative pressure to become more responsible, rivals' environmental actions, cost issues, etc. are just a few of the many motivating elements that push a firm to adopt green practices beyond only consumer loyalty (Moravcikova et al., 2017). Increased sales, lower operational and manufacturing costs, increased appeal to potential employees, a competitive edge, reduced risk of resource depletion in the long term, increased emphasis on CSR, improved environmental quality, etc. are all possible thanks to GM. Several obstacles, such as a lack of cooperation, a lack of customer awareness, a compromise between short-term and long-term cost-benefit analysis, a dearth of scientific knowledge, etc., exist because the industry is still in its infancy. As a result of the urgent situation on Earth, businesses of the future should work to overcome these obstacles and embrace GM (Nagarajan, 2016). According to market research, firms of all stripes can benefit greatly from consumers' growing interest in sustainability.

7.9 IMPLICATION

For their part, sustainable businesses must act responsibly in their dealings with all of their stakeholders. The pursuit of wealth is important, but so is the protection of the environment. The company culture should reflect a respect for the environment and a commitment to preserving it. Companies need to create and implement green technology to make their processes and goods more sustainable, cost-effective, and esthetically pleasing. There is an urgent need for businesses to invest in research development (R&D) facilities across a variety of industries, including the automobile sector (where they can reduce emissions and develop environmentally friendly vehicles), the tourism sector (where they can cultivate eco-tourism), the power sector (where they can cultivate green energy), and the housing industry (where they can cultivate green housing). It is possible that some businesses will invest more on marketing their eco-friendly goods than they did in developing those goods. Some customers may conclude that these businesses are using their environmental concerns for financial gain. It is necessary to invest heavily in R&D for some green projects because they include the usage of cutting-edge technology. Indeed, it could be challenging to pursue for tiny, cash-strapped businesses. Many clients may not be willing to pay a premium for green products and services because they are unaware of GM. Also, it is the marketer's duty to educate the buying public on the relevance and superiority of eco-friendly goods and services over their conventional counterparts. Customers are prepared to pay a premium for green products as part of GM initiatives. As a result, GM takes on even greater significance and relevance in Third World countries. Companies would do well to take note that customers are more likely to purchase from them if they offer items and services that ease their concerns about the environment. In this new environmental era, companies must look for ways to improve the environmental credentials of their products to boost their brand equity. Indeed, today's environmentally conscious consumers are putting pressure on firms to improve their environmental management. In addition, as demand for eco-friendly goods has increased, competition has heated up in the industry and marketplaces, with many companies producing green goods.

Hence, businesses should be aware that customers are more likely to prefer them if they offer products and services that satisfy customers' environmental concerns. In this new environmental era, companies must look for ways to improve the environmental credentials of their products to boost their brand equity. Indeed, today's environmentally conscious consumers are putting pressure on firms to improve their environmental management. Furthermore, the increasing demand for eco-friendly items has resulted in increased competition within the sector and its markets, with many different brands now creating eco-friendly products and businesses developing green brands to attract customers.

7.10 CONCLUSION

The rate of industrialization is accelerating, which will lead to greater environmental problems in the future. It's time for businesses around the world to embrace "green marketing." All countries need to do their part in enforcing rigorous duties, as green marketing is crucial to preventing global warming and its subsequent environmental consequences. From a business perspective, this makes sense because an astute marketer is one who not only wins over customers but actively recruits their participation in spreading the word about the product. GM must become the norm rather than the exception as the threat of global warming grows. Paper, metal, plastic, etc. recycling should be standardized and implemented globally in a way that protects the environment. Lighting and other electrical appliances that consume less energy must become the standard. Companies are becoming more eco-aware as a result of rising public awareness of environmental issues. The concept of "green marketing" has developed over the years and is rapidly entering the collective conscience of both consumers and businesses. To fully realize the potential of green marketing, it must be vigorously promoted through integrated marketing communication, with a primary emphasis on social media marketing, which has the potential for extensive audience penetration. At present, GM is more than just a strategy. With the intrinsic environmental and social dimension. Once weaker than conventional marketing, green advertising is now a formidable alternative. The concept of "green marketing" encompasses more than just advertising in general. Both parties are responsible for taking measures to preserve the natural world. As a result, the benefits of green advertising are readily apparent. Companies that see the green revolution as an opportunity can use this as a powerful marketing tool. However, businesses are cognizant of the fact that going green has certain unique problems. There are obstacles to GM, the most significant of which is the decline in interest and sales that has resulted from the inevitable price increases brought on by green practices. The literature surrounding the difficulties, reward, and potentials of GM has been reviewed. Green methods are good for everyone involved, not just the planet and society. Spreading this information far and wide is necessary to face and conquer its obstacles. Brands that support the green movement and see marketing it as a growth opportunity. It is common knowledge at this point that GM strategies are a must for any company that wants to survive and thrive in the long run.

Green packaging, green advertising, and GI are the three pillars of "green marketing." To attain sustainability objectives, green businesses must engage in activities, such as spreading the word about their environmentally friendly products and building their brand. Businesses can better convey and position themselves as a green brand with related consumer benefits by creating products that appeal to the consumers' social, functional, and emotional requirements.

KEYWORDS

- **green**
- **marketing**
- **price**
- **promotion**
- **place**
- **product**

REFERENCES

Ahmadzadeh, M.; Eidi, F.; Kagopour, M. Studying the Effects of Environmental Commitments on Green Marketing Strategies. *Int. J. Econ. Persp.* **2017,** *11* (1), 816–823.

AMA. Definitions of Marketing, 2022. https://www.ama.org/the-definition-of-marketing-what-is-marketing/ (accessed on 21 Jan 2022).

Awan, A. G.; Wamiq, S. Relationship Between Environmental Awareness and Green Marketing. *Sci. Int.* **2016,** *28* (3), 2959.

Boada, N. What Is Green Marketing? 5 Strategies, 9 Dec 2021. https://www.cyberclick.net/numericalblogen/what-is-green-marketing-5-strategies.

Cambridge Dictionary. Green Marketing, 2022. https://dictionary.cambridge.org/dictionary/english/green-marketing (accessed 21 Jan 2022).

Chang, R. Y.; Leung, T. K. P.; Wong, Y. H. The Effectiveness of Environmental Claims for Services Advertising. *J. Serv. Market.* **2005,** *20*, 233–250.

D'Souza, C.; Taghian, M.; Sullivan-Mort, G.; Gilmore, A. An Evaluation of the Role of Green Marketing and a Firm's Internal Practices for Environmental Sustainability. *J. Strategic Market.* **2015,** *23* (7), 600–615.

Dangelico, R. M.; Pujari, D. Main Streaming Green Product Innovation: Why and How Companies Integrate Environmental Sustainability. *J. Bus. Ethics* **2010,** *95* (3), 471–486.

Dangelico, R. M.; Vocalelli, D. "Green Marketing": An Analysis of Definitions, Strategy Steps, and Tools Through a Systematic Review of the Literature. *J. Clean. Prod.* **2017,** *165*, 1263–1279.

Emekci, S. Green Consumption Behaviours of Consumers within the Scope of TPB. *J. Consum. Market.* **2019,** *36* (3), 410–417. https:// doi.org/10.1108/JCM-05-2018-2694

Eren-Erdogmus, İ.; Lak, H. S.; Çiçek, M. Attractive or Credible Celebrities: Who Endorses Green Products Better? *Procedia Soc. Behav. Sci.* **2016,** *235*, 587–594.

Fernando, A. G.; Sivakumaran, B.; Suganthi, L. Message Involvement and Attitude Towards Green Advertisements. *Market. Intell. Plan.* **2016,** *34* (6), 863–882. https://doi.org/10.1108/MIP-11-2015-0216

Gupta, S.; Ogden, D. T. To Buy or Not to Buy? A Social Dilemma Perspective on Green Buying. *J. Consum. Market.* **2018,** *26* (6), 376–391.

GEO. UNEP Global Environment Outlook 6 (2019) Calls on Decision Makers to Address Pressing Environmental Problems Among Which Land Degradation as an Increasing Threat for Human Well-Being and Ecosystems. United Nations—Convention to Combat Desertification, 12th April 2019. https://knowledge.unccd.int/publications/unep-global-environment-outlook-6–2019-calls-decision-makers-address-pressing

Ho, Y.-H.; Lin, C.-Y.; and Chiang, S.-H. Organizational Determinants of Green Innovation Implementation in the Logistics Industry. *Int. J. Organ. Innov.* **2009,** *2*, 3.

Horne, R. E. Limits to Labels: The Role of Eco-labels in the Assessment of Product Sustainability and Routes to Sustainable Consumption. *Int. J. Consum. Stud.* **2009,** *33* (2). https://doi.org/10.1111/j.1470-6431.2009.00752.x

Indeed What Is Green Marketing? Benefits and Strategies, 2022. https://www.indeed.com/career-advice/career-development/green-marketing (accessed 20 Jan 2022).

Kasliwal, N.; Khan, I. Green Marketing: Trends, Challenges, Future Scope and Case Studies. In: *International Conference Make in India Initiatives, Roles, and Challenges for SMEs in the Global Perspective*, Feb 2016. file:///C:/Users/kabir/Desktop/poornimaconferencepaper-irum.doc.pdf

Katrandjiev, H. Ecological Marketing, Green Marketing, Sustainable Marketing: Synonyms or an Evolution of Ideas? *Econ. Altern.* **2016,** *1* (7), 71–82.

Khan, M.; Hussain, M.; Ajmal, M. M. *Green Supply Chain Management for Sustainable Business Practice: Advances in Logistics, Operations, and Management Science*; IGI Global: New York, 2016.

Kumar, P.; Kumar, P. Intents of Green Advertisements. *Asia Pac. J. Market. Logist.* **2017,** *29* (1), 70–79.

Lazar, C. I. Perspectives on Green Marketing and Green Businesses for Sustainable Development. *Bull. Transilvania Univ. Brasov* **2017,** *10* (59), 45–52.

Lin, J.; Lobo, A.; Leckie, C. Green Brand Benefits and Their Influence on Brand Loyalty. *Market. Intell. Plan.* **2017,** *35* (3), 425–440. https://doi.org/10.1108/MIP-09-2016-0174

Katrandjiev, H. Ecological Marketing, Green Marketing, Sustainable Marketing: Synonyms or an Evolution of Ideas. *Econ. Altern.* **2016,** *1* (7), 71–82.

Konar, S.; Cohen, M. A. Does the Market Value Environmental Performance? *Rev. Econ. Stat.* **2001,** *83* (2), 281–289.

Kumar, P.; Ghodeswar, B. M. Factors Affecting Consumers' Green Product Purchase Decisions. *Market. Intell. Plan.* **2015,** *33* (3), 330–347. DOI: 10.1108/MIP-03-2014-0068

Lee, S. Y.; Klassen, R. D. Drivers and Enablers That Foster Environmental Management Capabilities in Small and Medium Sized Suppliers and Supply Chains. *Prod. Operat. Manag.* **2008,** *17* (6), 573–586.

Lichtenstein, D. R.; Drumwright, M. E.; Braig, B. M. The Effects of Corporate Social Responsibility on Customer Donations to Corporate-Supported Nonprofits. *J. Market.* **2004,** *68*, 16–32.

Li, S.; Tang, Z. *Understanding Green Marketing with Marketing Mix—A Case Study on the Body Shop*; University of Gavle: Gavle, 2010.

Lin, C.-J.; Chen, H.-Y. User Expectancies for Green Products: A Case Study on the Internal Customers of a Social Enterprise. *Soc. Enterprise J.* **2016,** *13* (3), 281–301. https://doi.org/10.1108/SEJ-02-2016-0004

Marketing-schools.org. Green Marketing. Author, 10 Nov 2016. http://www.marketing-schools.org/types-of-marketing/green-marketing.html

Majeed, M. Green Marketing Communication and Consumer Response in Emerging Markets. In: Mogaji, E., Adeola, O., Adisa, I., Hinson, R. E., Mukonza, C., Kirgiz, A. C., Eds.; *Green Marketing in Emerging Economies: Palgrave Studies of Marketing in Emerging Economies*; Palgrave Macmillan: Cham. https://doi.org/10.1007/978-3-030-82572-0_3

Mitra I.; Masunda, K. S. Green Marketing. E2E, 2019. https://www.e2exchange.com/articles/5-effective-green-marketing-strategies/

Maziriri, E. T. The Impact of Green Marketing Practices on Competitive Advantage and Business Performance Among Manufacturing Small and Medium Enterprises (SMEs) in South Africa; Doctoral dissertation; University of the Witwatersrand, 2018.

Mayakkannan R. A Study on Green Marketing Practices in India. *Emperor Int. J. Finance Manag. Res.* **2019,** *5* (4).

Mishra, P.; Sharma, P. Green Marketing in India: Emerging Opportunities and Challenges. *J. Eng. Sci. Manag. Educ.* **2010,** *3* (1), 9–14.

Mukonza, C.; Swarts, I. Examining the Role of Green Transformational Leadership on Promoting Green Organizational Behavior. In: *Contemporary Multicultural Orientations and Practices for Global Leadership*; IGI Global, 2019; pp 200–224.

Mukonza, C.; Hinson, R. E.; Adeola, O.; Adisa, I.; Mogaji, E.; Kirgiz, A. C. Green Marketing: An Introduction. In: Mukonza, C., Hinson, R. E., Adeola, O., Adisa, I., Mogaji, E., Kirgiz, A. C., Eds.; *Green Marketing in Emerging Markets. Palgrave Studies of Marketing in Emerging Economies*; Palgrave Macmillan: Cham, 2021. https://doi.org/10.1007/978-3-030-74065-8_1

Moravcikova, D.; Krizanova, A.; Kliestikova, J.; Rypakova, M. Green Marketing as the Source of the Competitive Advantage of the Business. *Sustain.—Open Access J.* **2017,** *9,* 2218. DOI: 10.3390/su9122218.

Nagarajan, P. Strengths, Weakness, Opportunities and Threats of Green Marketing. *Int. J. Sci. Res. Manag.* **2016,** *4* (04), 4059–4061.

Mishra, P.; Sharma, M. P. Green Marketing in India: Future Opportunity for Business. *Elkjournals* **2011**. https://www.elkjournals.com/masteradmin/uploadfolder/4.%20green%20marketing%20in%20india%20future%20opportunity%20for%20business/4.%20green%20marketing%20in%20india%20future%20opportunity%20for%20b usincss.pdf

Mishra, P.; Sharma, P. Green Marketing: Challenges and Opportunities for Business. *BVIMR Manag. Edge* **2014,** *7* (1), 78–86.

Mohanty, V.; Nayak, S. Green Marketing—Its Application, Scope, and Future in India. *Indian J. Sci. Res.* **2017,** 111–116.

Nadaf, Y. B. R.; Nadaf, S. M. Green marketing: Challenges and Strategies for Indian Companies in 21st Century. *Int. J. Res. Bus. Manag.* **2014,** *2* (5), 91–104.

Papadas, K. K.; Avlonitis, G. J.; Carrigan, M. Green Marketing Orientation: Conceptualization, Scale Development and Validation. *J. Bus. Res.* **2017,** *80* (C), 236–246.

Peattie, K. Towards Sustainability: The Third Age of Green Marketing. *Market. Rev.* **2001,** *2* (2), 129–146.

Pink D. Green Marketing: Sustainable Marketing Pros and Cons, 2022. https://www.masterclass.com/articles/green-marketing

Rahman, M. Advantages and Disadvantages of Green Marketing, 2023. https://www.howandwhat.net/advantages-disadvantages-green-marketing/

Rahman, I.; Reynolds, D.; Svaren, S. How "Green" Are North American Hotels? An Exploration of Low-Cost Adoption Practices. *Int. J. Hosp. Manag.* **2012,** *31* (3), 720–727.

Riskos, K.; Dekoulou, P.; Mylonas, N.; Tsourvakas, G. Ecolabels and the Attitude–Behavior Relationship Towards Green Product Purchase: A Multiple Mediation Model. *Sustainability* **2021**, *13*, 6867. https://doi.org/10.3390/su13126867

Solaiman, M.; Osman, A.; Halim, M. S. Green Marketing: A Marketing Mix Point of View. *Int. J. Bus. Technopreneurship* **2015**, *5* (1), 87–98. http://dspace.unimap.edu.my/xmlui/bitstream/handle/123456789/40027/IJBT_Vol_5_Feb_2015_7_87–98. pdf?sequence=1

Sudhalakshmi, K.; Chinnadorai, K. Green Marketing Mix—A Social Responsibility of Manufacturing Companies. *Glob. J. Comm. Manag. Persp.* **2014**, *3* (4), 109–112.

Shafaat, A.; Sultan, A. Green Marketing. *Excel Int. J. Multidisc. Manag. Stud.* **2012**, *2* (5), 184–195.

Singal, R.; Garg, A.; Singla, S. Green Marketing: Challenges and Opportunities. *Int. J. Innov. Eng. Technol.* **2013**, *2* (1), 470–474.

Teo, Y. V.; Yazdanifard, R. Green Marketing Strategies, Sustainable Development, Benefits and Challenges/Constraints. *ResearchGate* **2014**, 1–10. https://www.academia.edu/8073438/Green_marketing_strategies_sustainable_development_benefits_and_challenges_and_constraints

Virgin. 10 Global Companies That Are Environmentally Friendly, 2021. https://www.virgin.com/virgin-unite/latest/10-global-companies-that-are-environmentally-friendly (accessed 20 Jan 2022).

Verma, A. Green Marketing: Importance and Problems Associated. *Int. J. Bus. Manag.* **2015**, *2* (1), 428–437.

Vilkaitė-Vaitonė, N.; Skačkauskienė, I. Green Marketing Orientation: Evolution, Conceptualization and Potential Benefits. *Open Econ.* **2019**, *2* (1), 53–62.

Welling, M. N.; Chavan, A. S. Analysing the Feasibility of Green Marketing in Small & Medium Scale Manufacturers. *Asia Pac. J. Res. Bus. Manag.* **2010**, *1* (2), 119–133.

Xie, X.; Huo, J.; Zou, H. Green Process Innovation, Green Product Innovation, and Corporate Financial Performance: A Content Analysis Method. *J. Bus. Res.* **2019**, *101*, 697–706. DOI: 10.1016/j.jbusres.2019.01.010

Xie, X.; Zhu, Q.; Wang, R. Turning Green Subsidies into Sustainability: How Green Process Innovation Improves Firms' Green Image. *Bus. Strategy Environ.* **2019**, *28*, 1416–1433. DOI: 10.1002/bse.2323

Yakubu, O. Addressing Environmental Health Problems in Ogoniland Through Implementation of United Nations Environment Program Recommendations: Environmental Management Strategies. *Environments* **2017**, *4*, 28. DOI: 10.3390/environments4020028

Yazdanifard, R.; Mercy, I. E. The Impact of Green Marketing on Customer Satisfaction and Environmental Safety. In: *2011 International Conference on Computer Communication and Management Proceedings of CSIT*; IACSIT Press: Singapore, Jan 2011. https://www.researchgate.net/publication/268502673_The_impact_of_Green_Marketing_on_Customer_satisfaction_and_Environmental_safety

Zampese, E. R. S.; Moori, R. G.; Caldeira, A. Green Marketing as a Mediator Between Supply Chain Management and Organizational Performance. *Revista de Administracao Mackenzie* **2016**, *17* (3), 183–211.

CHAPTER 8

Green Warehousing Practices for Firms

MOHAMMED MAJEED[1], AWINI GIDEON[2], and AHMED TIJANI[2]

[1]Marketing Department, Tamale Technical University, Tamale, Ghana

[2]Minerals Commission, Ghana

ABSTRACT

The chapter reviewed the literature to understand the effect of green warehousing (GW) on firms. Specifically: to identify the GW practices; and to understand the benefits of GW on firms. The review lists the following advantages: safer practices; decreased warehouse space requirements; customer satisfaction; new technology; enhanced processes; increased efficiency; improved company reputations; economy's functionality; performance standards for manufacturing procedures; decreased operating costs; and reduced waste. Creating environmentally friendly warehousing involves the following practices: harvesting rainwater; Location; superior efficiency lighting; sensors; energy management system; electric-powered stackers; renewable energy from the sun; climate change and sustainable solutions; building materials; paperless system; reliable stock-keeping; good storage systems; inventory control/optimization; training of employees; employee safety and health; introduction employees welfare schemes; building emergency rooms; controlling shift schedules by management; accuracy of stock; biodiversity; recyclable and reusable plastic pallets; system of man-made lights; retrieval and storage automation; landscaping and water usage; renewable energy sources; and eco-friendly packaging.

Green Supply Chain Management. Mohammed Majeed, Kirti Agarwal, and Ahmed Tijani (Eds.)
© 2025 Apple Academic Press, Inc. Co-published with CRC Press (Taylor & Francis)

8.1 INTRODUCTION

In the current corporate world, global warming and pollution of the environment are two of the biggest news items. As a result of the undeniable fact that companies are living entities, sustainability and being environmentally friendly have become important tenets for many corporations. Integration, equilibrium, and control of economic, ecological, and human outcomes and inputs of activities in green buildings are often thought of nowadays when the term "sustainable green warehouse" is mentioned (Akandere, 2016). A sustainable and green warehouse is a collection of technological and organizational solutions that maximize warehouse productivity while also protecting the environment and upholding the highest ethical standards. Also, there is a rising pattern of countries enacting legislation that take nature conservation into account. Thus, scientists and environmentalists have proposed go-green concepts to lessen the impact on the environment and cut down on emissions of greenhouse gases (Khan et al., 2018). Businesses' supply chain activities—including the release of greenhouse gases, poor waste management, the manufacture of nonbiodegradable products, the storage of hazardous and explosive substances, and the overexploitation of natural resources—have contributed to environmental pollution, global warming, climate change, and the loss of human life (Khan, 2019). Green supply chain management (GSCM), is gaining traction in several sectors, including the automotive industry, chemicals, textiles, oil and gas exploration, pharmaceuticals, metal production, fast-moving consumer products, electronics, construction, plastics, and tourism. This section provides a brief overview of the research on GSCM (Khan et al., 2018). Companies rely heavily on product storage as a vital part of their supply chain management. Expenses will be reduced over time as the warehouse's capacity is utilized and the merchandise is safely stored. The chapter reviewed the literature to understand the effect of green warehousing (GW) on firms. Specifically: (1) to identify the GW practices, and (2) to understand the benefits of GW on firms.

8.2 LITERATURE

8.2.1 GREEN WAREHOUSING

The goal of the management approach known as "green warehousing" is to lessen the facility's carbon footprint, electricity expenses, and greenhouse gas emissions by incorporating and enforcing environmentally friendly measures. GW involves not only the adoption of environmentally responsible management methods, but also the incorporation of various systems, techniques, and equipment. For GW to succeed in India, technological development is essential since relying too much on management methods puts too much strain on scarce human resources (Khan et al., 2018). Clean logistics, which includes green warehouses, is described as contract logistics locations that employ green machinery, software, and procedures to lessen their environmental footprint. Many people, organizations, and places practice the three R's of waste management: reduction, reuse, and recycling. This idea serves as a cornerstone for the energy-saving and productivity-boosting practices of many "green" warehouses.

8.2.2 GREEN WAREHOUSE PRACTICES

Firms and people now prioritize environmental issues. By streamlining all supply chain processes, businesses may create environmentally friendly warehouses. Businesses can provide quality service while having a smaller impact on the environment if they adopt more efficient procedures. In this post, we will look at how sustainable warehousing may reduce energy use across the board, from the warehouse's lighting and climate control to its inventory management and traffic flow.

8.2.2.1 HARVESTING RAINWATER

The warehouse industry can benefit greatly from rainwater collection technologies. The environment would benefit greatly from the recycling of rainwater and sewage water for uses such as gardening and toilet flushing (Slyer, 2022). Several cold storage facilities, such as those used for frozen and chilled food storage, collect rainwater for reuse, reducing their water use and, in turn, their utility bills. These storage facilities are becoming more eco-friendly and productive thanks to water-saving measures.

8.2.2.2 LOCATION PROXIMITY

A warehouse's location is crucial to its long-term viability. Inventory that is strategically placed has been shown to increase efficiency and production by reducing the amount of manual labor required to access the stock in question. As a result, workers will have more time on their hands, allowing them to more efficiently complete assignments. Consequentially, this philosophy will lead to a dramatic increase in financial success (Inbound Logistics, 2018). Energy usage can be quite high when products are being moved from a storage facility to retail and residential areas. Logistics facilities that are close to both distribution hubs and end users save money and time by minimizing wasteful travel and waiting times. Water and power supplies, for example, are less likely to need to be expanded to accommodate a warehouse that is conveniently positioned near major roads, ports, and airports (Slyer, 2022).

8.2.2.3   SUPERIOR EFFICIENCY LIGHTING

Using light-emitting diode (LED) lighting in warehouses instead of incandescent lights can cut down on carbon dioxide emissions (Slyer, 2022). Using LED lights is a wise financial and environmental decision because of the significant savings in both energy and maintenance costs. LED lights may cost more upfront, but they last longer, are more energy efficient, and respond quickly. They make the environment less hot, which solves several issues (Aaj Enterprises, 2021). Sensors and natural tube lighting are two further methods used to reduce energy use. Energy is conserved by the use of sensors that monitor room usage while no one is there, and through the use of natural tube lighting throughout the day, which reduces energy usage while also improving visibility (Kaplan, 2019). Businesses can reduce their carbon footprint by using energy-efficient lighting and letting in more natural light. Skylights, solar panels, and sensors are some of the most often used resources. To maximize the usefulness of electrical resources, energy management systems can also be put into place. Whenever they are not in use, machines, for instance, can be turned off. Companies may lessen their reliance on fossil fuels and their carbon footprint with the help of these alternatives. Keeping the warehouse at an adequate light level to save energy and money is simple. The management of a warehouse may need to contact with electricians to determine how many lights should be installed in various sections. Energy efficiency can also be improved by the use of well-chosen lighting fixtures (Baker and Marchant 2015).

8.2.2.4   SENSORS

They can be utilized for the management of gas and water supplies in addition to lighting and room occupancy. Submeters can keep tabs on the energy use of appliances including refrigerators, machines, and more (Kaplan, 2019).

8.2.2.5 ENERGY MANAGEMENT SYSTEM

Consumption can be reduced through careful management. With little no-human intervention, energy management systems keep track of a building's whole energy consumption (Inbound Logistics, 2018). Energy management systems determine the most effective ways to utilize available resources, such as power, gas, heat, and water, while minimizing wastage, through the coordination of various timers, thermostats, and gauges. This is crucial to environmentally friendly systems as it allows businesses to save money and reduce their consumption of renewable resources.

8.2.2.6 ELECTRIC-POWERED STACKERS

All-electric forklifts can do away with their need for petroleum products. In addition to being better for the planet, this also reduces risks to workers. Workers are now spared the peril of coming into contact with battery acid, antifreeze, or transaxle fluid (Inbound Logistics, 2018). This has the potential to increase profits by reducing the number of accidents that occur when handling dangerous materials. It is as easy as plugging in an electric forklift before and after use to get it up and running.

8.2.2.7 RENEWABLE ENERGY FROM THE SUN

Solar power has many advantages over other renewable energy sources, including its low environmental impact, low cost, and ability to control electricity use. Energy-efficient solar panels, commonly known as photovoltaic panels, are gaining in popularity. Large, flat roofs are common in warehouses, making them ideal locations for solar panel installations (Aaj Enterprises, 2021). Also, because of its central location in the tropics and the sheer volume of sunlight it receives, Africa is a prime area for solar panel installations. Warehouse rooftops are typically wide and flat, making them ideal locations for solar panels and other forms of solar power producing equipment. Warehouses in India can benefit from solar energy systems because of the country's high levels of sunshine. The warehouse's design should maximize access to natural light. Many factors are involved including the building's height and orientation, aisle width, available daylight, etc. Windows, doors, and roof openings are the typical sources of natural light. Careful consideration of the local climate and topography is required when determining their total quantity and specific placement. Light-colored ceilings and walls also aid in the diffusion of natural light. Combining natural and artificial sources of light is also crucial. It is important to adjust the brightness of the warehouse's artificial lighting to match the natural light coming in through the windows, which may be at varying levels in different areas (CarbonTrust, 2007). Make good use of daylight or energy-efficient artificial lighting. To save costs and waste in the warehouse, it is essential to have an efficient lighting system installed. Skylights are among the most affordable and simple options for letting natural light into a space (neoco, 2020). Some fascinating possibilities to save money, manage energy use, and become less reliant on traditional energy sources include solar panels (which produce clean energy) and LED sensors (which are activated by movement and can be installed, for instance, in low-consumption lamps) (neoco, 2020).

8.2.2.8 CLIMATE CHANGE AND SUSTAINABLE SOLUTIONS

The use of air conditioning, particularly in cold and freezer rooms, results in significant energy usage. The goal is to minimize energy use while maintaining optimal storage conditions for these items. The building's layout poses a challenge to effective climate management. Warehouses are often big industrial structures with high ceilings and several openings to the street, allowing the cold air to flow in. How can firms lessen its impact? A common solution is to construct warehouses out of insulating materials like sandwich panels, which limit heat loss. Put in doors with insulation to prevent heat or cold from escaping. These doors will keep the warehouse's interior at a constant temperature by sealing off any drafts. In this manner, firms can keep the house at a comfortable temperature while cutting down on our monthly energy costs (neoco, 2020).

8.2.2.9 BUILDING MATERIALS

Worker comfort and energy savings both benefit from insulation's use. Building air quality can be enhanced and less chemicals used in their manufacturing by switching to low-emitting materials such certain types of paints, adhesives, wood products, sealants, and carpeting (Kaplan, 2019).

8.2.2.10 PAPERLESS SYSTEM

Reducing the consumption of paper towels, toilet paper, and other single-use items in warehouses is another environmentally friendly method that contributes to a more sustainable supply chain. Paper consumption in warehouses may be drastically cut down with the use of paperless dock management and handheld technology, which also serve to increase productivity (Aaj Enterprises, 2021). To lessen the use of waste paper, Indian warehouses should adopt computerized order picking, barcoding, and radio frequency identification (RFID) systems. To a large extent, the usage of disposable papers can be reduced if technological advances are put to good use.

8.2.2.11 SPACE-SAVING DATA STORAGE

A sustainable warehouse may be made possible with the use of high-density storage technologies. These creative storage options make full advantage of vertical space to accommodate more items. Low energy usage per pallet is achieved through the use of compact solutions in temperature-controlled storage areas. The term "high-density system" refers to a collection of storage solutions, each with its own set of advantages and drawbacks. Space constraints and the need to accommodate several flows will inform the decision between possible solutions.

8.2.2.12 ROOFING

Roofing solar panels can be installed on roofs. Use anything white or very light in color, such as a reflecting substance, to accomplish this. This deflects light rather than soaking up the rays of the sun. Also, it aids local efforts to mitigate the urban heat island effect, in which one area of a region is abnormally hotter than others as a result of human development (Kaplan, 2019).

8.2.2.13 RELIABLE STOCK-KEEPING

With the use of a warehouse management system (WMS), shipping, transportation, and retail operations may all be digitally coordinated. By utilizing a WMS for inventory control, green warehouses can operate with the minimum amount of stock necessary, thereby reducing unnecessary stock and making better use of available storage space (Aaj Enterprises, 2021).

8.2.2.14 STORAGE SYSTEM

To retain (or store) goods or materials of varying types, forms, and sizes, a storage system is an essential component of the internal layout of a warehouse. There are structural characteristics that deal with the system's physical layout, and there are performance characteristics that pertain to things like data storage capacity, accessibility, efficient resource allocation, and storage regulations. Block stacking, selective racks (single-deep racks), drive-in/drive-through racks, double-deep racks, mobile racks, flow-through/push-back racks, and flow-through/push-back racks are only some of the many storage options available. Choosing a storage system is a strategic decision made at the design stage (Aaj Enterprises, 2021). In Kaplan (2019), the SLAP is explored in depth. When it comes to the monetary aspect of sustainability, the command cycle of storage systems is another crucial feature. The highest possible levels of efficiency in a given warehouse could be attained using either a single or dual command.

8.2.2.15 INVENTORY CONTROL/OPTIMIZATION

If firms want to reach sustainability goals, optimizing their inventory is a must. When inventory levels are too low, businesses risk losing sales and running out of essential items too soon, while when they are too high, they risk having too much of a limited supply on hand. Inventory optimization is difficult since it depends on several factors, including but not limited to replenishment lead times, forecasting, visibility, future inventory prices, available warehouse space, customer returns, obsolete inventory, carrying costs, quality of supply, etc. (neoco, 2020). To obtain optimum inventory levels, it is necessary to strike a balance between these opposing elements. Warehouse management software, better supply chain communication, the removal of old stock, more accuracy in demand forecasting, standardized parts/components/ingredients, vendor-managed inventory (VMI) or just-in-time (JIT) inventory management systems, etc. are all good places to start.

8.2.2.16 INBOUND PROCESSES

Tasks like unloading, receiving, reworking, and putting away are all part of the inbound procedures. At the inbound dock, also known as the receiving dock, counterbalanced forklifts unload shipments to a staging area (a partition in the receiving department) (Aaj Enterprises, 2021). The goal is to update the WMS after a thorough quality check has been performed on the goods, making them ready for storage.

8.2.2.17 OUTBOUND PROCESSES

The term "outbound" refers to operations that are not internal, and typically include the transfer of inventory to fulfill customer orders. The goods are moved from the pick (or forward) location to the outgoing staging area, where they are loaded and then sent on their way to the clients. Customizing pallets or repackaging products into a different format (or standard) are two examples of outbound operations that can be performed to meet the needs of a wide variety of customers and industries.

8.2.2.18 TRAINING OF EMPLOYEES

Warehouse workers need regular safety training to guarantee a secure and productive workplace. Staff training is a topic that is heavily discussed in the many books and articles written about warehouses and supply chains. Hence, this component has been highlighted in greater detail within the "warehouse personnel" framework. Analysis of the surrounding environment uncovered numerous types of training, including those for the safe and efficient use of MHEs, manual handling, neutralizing hazardous substances, personal hygiene, stress and fatigue management, emergency egress, warehouse operations, storage equipment audits, maintenance, stock counts, dealing with spills and breaks, using fire-fighting equipment, etc.

8.2.2.19 EMPLOYEE SAFETY AND HEALTH

There has been a lot of study done in this area, likely due to the legal obligations that businesses face. Occupational health and safety (OHS) refers to the prevention of illness and injury in the workplace. This includes both paid and unpaid labor in any setting. There is some evidence in the literature to suggest that effective OHS management raises output.

8.2.2.20 WELFARE MATTERS

Water fountains, lockers, showers, bathrooms (both men's and women's), a kitchen, a dining hall, and a storage area are all provided free of charge. The laws of most developed countries, both federal and state, set these standards as a bare minimum. In the event of a warehouse, it is also necessary to provide unique amenities for overnight drivers and night shift workers. There may be a fitness center, locker rooms, a TV lounge, and a sports room stocked with table tennis, foosball, chess, arcade games, and the like. Constant reminders to practice good personal hygiene, including the importance of keeping bathrooms and changing areas clean, as well as the dining hall neat and free of pests, should be posted. All workers need access to parking facilities.

8.2.2.21 EMERGENCY ROOMS

A warehouse needs to have access to first aid supplies at all times. Having a daytime medical center manned by a physician and nurse is ideal. Some of the guards should have first-aid and cardiopulmonary resuscitation (CPR) training, and the facility as a whole should have the appropriate signs and instructions posted. A minimum of two beds, a few cabinets for keeping dressings, linen, and medications, an appropriate disposal system, a stretcher, a workbench or dressing cart, a wash basin with hot and cold water, etc., should all fit comfortably in the emergency room.

8.2.2.22 CONTROLLING SHIFT SCHEDULES

Recent studies have revealed that shift work, and particularly night employment, is one of the leading causes of weariness, which in turn causes cognitive and physical impairment (Dzanuska, 2022). Also, people are wired to sleep at night and be active during the day, thus their level of alertness shifts during the day. The term "shift work" refers to "any job pattern that produces a disturbance in typical sleep habits" (New Zealand Department of Labour, 2007). Sleep deprivation and a "sleep debt" are the unfortunate consequences of shift employment, which often occurs in the wee hours of the morning or late at night.

8.2.2.23 ACCURACY OF STOCK

Being a company's asset, inventory counts and records must be reliable. It is important to conduct periodic counts of inventory—money in the form of commodities or materials—to ensure valuation accuracy, ensure enough supply, and prevent loss. Insurance firms need accurate stock counts in the event of a natural disaster, seasonal product availability must be guaranteed, and high-value or frequently used commodities must be strategically placed in the warehouse. When examined through the lens of sustainability, the importance of counting inventory, already one of the most important operations, increases dramatically. The occurrence of natural disasters such as floods, earthquakes, and tsunamis has become routine throughout a year. Businesses must know the worth of their stock to protect themselves from potential disasters.

8.2.2.24 BIODIVERSITY

Natural flora, woods, animals, microbes, streams, and ecosystems are all examples of the biological diversity that may be found in any given area. It would be impossible to keep life on Earth without biological variety. People, cities, and corporations alike all benefit from a healthy biodiversity. Property values near parks and other green areas are found to be, on average, 8% higher than those located further away (Commission for Architecture and the Built Environment, 2005). Companies that take steps to improve their environmental impact tend to attract and retain a healthier, more productive workforce.

8.2.2.25 RECYCLABLE AND REUSABLE PLASTIC PALLETS

Plastic pallets that may be used and recycled multiple times, Pallets manufactured from recycled plastic that can be recycled once they have served their purpose in the warehouse will help us greatly lessen our waste and impact on the environment. As these pallets are lightweight and homogeneous in weight and dimension, they are ideal for automated systems that handle the handling, calibration, and distribution of products (neoco, 2020).

8.2.2.26 SYSTEM OF MAN-MADE LIGHTS

Although its effects on sustainability are rarely mentioned, content analysis reveals that it is one of the most crucial factors. Recent studies have shown that it has a significant effect on employee productivity in addition to lowering costs and carbon emissions. About 80% of sensory information comes through the eyes, so a poor lighting scheme can severely hinder visibility, which in turn reduces productivity. It has also been shown that workers' moods and levels of alertness improve under high-quality lighting, which, in turn, can greatly cut down on accidents in a warehouse. Supports healthy levels of cortisol, serotonin, and endorphins, the hormonal balance responsible for waking people up, making people sleep less, and making people happy (Dzanuska, 2022).

8.2.2.27   RETRIEVAL AND STORAGE AUTOMATION

Automated tools in warehouses boost productivity, cut down on product returns, and decrease the likelihood of mistakes being made by employees. In addition, it minimizes carbon emissions, optimizes space more efficiently, and reduces energy use. These are just some of the measures that can be carried out if firms want to have a green and sustainable storage facility. It is an investment with great potential that improves the environmental impact, economic profitability, and reputation of any company.

8.2.2.28   LANDSCAPING AND WATER USAGE

Even though not all warehouses will win beauty and design awards, they can still be attractively maintained, using water-efficient landscaping. Other water features can include rainwater harvesting, plumbing fixtures to reduce water use indoors, and sensors to monitor water usage (Kaplan, 2019).

8.2.2.29   RENEWABLE ENERGY SOURCES

This factor necessitates that the warehouse as a whole be designed to make effective use of energy. Warehouses with ambient temperatures have energy costs that are 5–10% of operating costs, while those with temperature control have energy costs that are 15–20%. It has an immediate effect on both the environment and the running costs, and it is one of the key inputs alongside materials and water (Nathan, 2005).

8.2.2.30   ECO-FRIENDLY PACKAGING

A sustainable warehouse, while helpful, is only a piece of the puzzle. Besides from reducing the demand for additional energy, sustainable packaging also helps to promote a more circular system through recycling (Dzanuska, 2022). For instance, the Spanish company Logifruit is a logistics service provider with a focus on the cleaning, administration, and rental of recyclable packaging. The company has reduced its carbon footprint by 20% thanks to its innovative steps toward a circular economy.

8.2.3 BENEFITS OF GREEN WAREHOUSING

8.2.3.1 SAFER PRACTICES

Any warehouse will have chemicals and other things that are harmful to people and the environment. Using less toxic chemicals, such as solvents and degreasers, is a primary goal of "green warehousing," which also seeks out more eco-friendly substitutes. This has two major advantages: first, it reduces the risk to the firm's employees, so the firm's warehouse is less likely to incur the costs of washing and cleaning or the company delays that can result from hazardous spillages, and second, it reduces the costs associated with handling and disposing of toxic chemicals.

8.2.3.2 REDUCE THE SPACE OCCUPIED BY THE WAREHOUSE

Inefficient warehouse layout and architecture can increase operating costs, land consumption, and labor expenditures (Dzanuska, 2022). The total cost of operation for a warehouse can be drastically reduced by investing in materials handling technology and a warehouse layout that are both environmentally friendly and make efficient use of the building's internal storage space. Some techniques to make the most of a warehouse's horizontal and vertical storage capacity include making aisles smaller and installing taller pallet racking (Hinz, 2022). By making the most of available warehouse space, expanding businesses can put off the inevitable move or construction of a new, larger building until necessary.

8.2.3.3 CUSTOMER SATISFACTION

Customers' expectations of businesses to act as good corporate citizens, which is taking into account environmental and social concerns such as global warming, are growing (Hinz, 2022). Sustainable warehousing practices are more than just a nice thing for businesses to do; they may also influence customers' purchasing decisions as a reflection of a company's commitment to corporate social responsibility. Customers that are concerned about the environment are more likely to do business with a firm that shares their values and is actively pursuing sustainability measures (Dzanuska, 2022). Businesses that actively promote environmental responsibility are more likely to keep their current clientele and win over new ones.

8.2.3.4 NEW TECHNOLOGY

Even if a firm's warehouse rental does not provide very sophisticated technology, such as robotics and automation, there are far simpler but equally cost-effective solutions any warehouse can explore. While the initial investment in LED lighting may be costlier, the long-term savings from the lights' durability and reduced energy use more than make up for the difference. Companies may begin to quickly green their storage as each nonelectric machine reaches the end of its useful life, and the UK forklift market is quite evenly divided between diesel or LPG powered machines and battery-driven electric ones. When it comes to cooling a warehouse, high-volume, low-speed fans may replace forklifts. Large fans like this can reduce indoor temperatures by up to four degrees without significantly increasing firm's electricity bill, saving organization's money in the long run.

8.2.3.5 IMPROVED PROCEDURES

Cross docking is one method through which warehouses are implementing the JIT principle by bypassing the warehouse entirely and going straight from receiving goods from suppliers to delivering them to customers. While this can only be a small part of overall warehouse logistics, any time this kind of process can be created, it results in significant savings in time, money, and resources. Improved inventory practices aren't typically thought of as environmentally friendly, but doing things like reducing risk, minimizing spoilage, and speeding up the pick-and-pack process can lead to reduced insurance premiums and injury rates, better stock utilization, and more orders completed per day.

8.2.3.6 BOOST EFFICIENCY

Incorporating eco-friendly and sustainable practices into the workplace has the potential to boost output by giving workers a more positive and enjoyable place to work. When employees' personal values and those of their employers coincide, all parties benefit. This makes for a more committed and effective workforce (Dzanuska, 2022). Providing employees with the opportunity to share their thoughts and suggestions on how their organization can become more environmentally friendly is a great way to foster a sense of community and pride in their work, both of which contribute to increased engagement and productivity.

8.2.3.7   *REPUTATION OF COMPANIES*

Any company with a warehouse operation can benefit from spreading environmental awareness within their consumer base, just as bad food and poor logistics quickly go viral. From encouraging reuse of packaging (discussed further below) to promoting the installation of green roofs, these are the kinds of environmental messages that will resonate with customers and help to distinguish firm's business from the wasteful, widely publicized, and largely empty boxes sent out by competing businesses and subsequently criticized on social media.

8.2.3.8   *FUNCTIONALITY OF THE ECONOMY*

Numerous businesses engage in environmentally friendly practices to boost company profits and lessen their negative effects on the planet (Baah and Jin, 2019). GW entails making the most efficient use of available space and energy so as to maximize profits and minimize expenses (Feng et al., 2018). In addition, businesses may be able to avoid paying environmental fines by switching to GW practices such as using renewable energy sources. In addition, high-energy performance certificate warehouses have a lower energy footprint, which is great for the environment and the bottom line (Indrawati et al., 2018).

8.2.3.9   *PERFORMANCE STANDARDS FOR MANUFACTURING PROCEDURES*

One strategy for improving output and product quality is to implement "Lean Manufacturing." Waste, which can take the shape of human effort, superfluous resources, or any action that wastes space or time, can be reduced by eliminating non value added procedures, recognizing problems along with processes, fixing them, and preventing them in the future (Dzanuska, 2022). In order to create ecologically sustainable practices, it is crucial to get rid of any processes that get in the way of optimizing quality. Doing so helps anticipate and prevent potential negative effects on the environment (Hinz, 2022). Maintaining the highest standards requires routine inspections and reviews. This not only helps a company save money by getting rid of unnecessary materials, but it also helps the company look more professional and care about the environment.

8.2.3.10 CUT DOWN ON RUNNING EXPENSES

While the upfront cost of creating a greener warehouse may appear hefty, the long-term savings on operating costs more than make up for it (Dzanuska, 2022). Whether a firm uses a fully automated pick and pack system or a simple pallet storage outlet, operating expenditures are a significant portion of the firm's warehouse's budget. Even while fossil fuels have, up until recently, seemed to be the most cost-effective option, recent studies have shown that they increase costs in the long run due to their inefficiency and the waste they generate. Although the initial investment in renewable energy may be more, the resulting shift in mentality can lead to significant savings in the long run through order consolidation, route optimization, and other creative approaches to energy consumption. Hinz (2022) provided several examples of both large and small changes that can be made to a warehouse to make it more sustainable and reduce overall operational costs, such as: (1) installing solar panels on the warehouse roof to generate electricity, which will save money on utility bills in the long run; (2) harvesting rainwater from roofs and grey water from bathrooms, which can lower water costs by reducing the amount of freshwater required in the long run; and (3) printing on both sides of the paper, which can reduce.

8.2.3.11 LESS WASTE

While it may seem like an extra expense at first, using recyclable (or recycled) packaging can save money in the long run because the materials can be reused. Compostable cellulose packaging, as opposed to noncompostable plastic, can lessen the carbon footprint of a warehouse, improve a company's reputation for sustainability, and make employees happier in their jobs. The daily operations of a warehouse inevitably result in the accumulation of waste. In a sustainable warehouse, waste management is a crucial responsibility. Companies can cut expenses by recycling recyclable materials, complying with local environmental standards, and providing a more pleasant working environment by employing an effective waste management strategy and putting it into practice (Redox, 2005). Although while it may seem that logistics and fulfillment are the only areas where waste can be reduced, there is another component of the storage process that might benefit from a green approach. Warehouses generate unnecessary paper waste when they print packing slips, order confirmations, shipment alerts, and return papers without considering the frequency with which these documents are needed. There are several expenditures connected with excessive paper use, including but not limited to printing, storing, and copying. However, the percentage of necessary records is often significantly smaller than the amount of data created. The disposal of paper records is an additional expense because it often necessitates the use of dedicated equipment such as shredders and professional clean-up crews. Similarly, many distribution centers can extend the life of pallets and storage materials through reuse, which, in turn, prevents waste from going to landfills and cuts costs associated with disposing of it.

8.3　IMPLICATIONS

Management can benefit from the study's findings. The findings provide a rationale for integrating green storage, logistical optimization, and social values and ethics into supply chain sustainability initiatives. In addition, managers can use this research as a guide and an argument for why it's important to incorporate socially responsible and ethical procedures into the supply chain. To further enhance the sustainability of the supply chain, the report recommends that managers implement logistics optimizations, green warehouses, and societal ethical and moral values. The researchers are confident that their findings will have far-reaching benefits for all of society. Companies' logistics operations are a major source of hazardous greenhouse gases and particle pollution. According to the results of this research, GW, and logistics optimization help cut down on waste, pollution, and hazardous gas emissions. In turn, this benefits people's overall health in the community. In addition, businesses can better address the demands of their final consumers and other stakeholders while also helping to preserve natural resources for future generations and improve Earth's environment by switching to renewable energy sources and cutting down on waste and energy usage. Furthermore, this study reveals practices that seek the well-being and safety of employees and community members, suggesting that social values and ethics have a positive influence on supply chain sustainability. Solar thermal, solar photovoltaic, wind, biofuels, biomass (wood chips or other waste), geothermal resources, and energy recovered from process waste should all be used whenever possible (such as heat from air compressors, etc.).

8.4 CONCLUSION

This chapter's focus is on how GW might benefit businesses. The goals of this study are twofold: to catalog the various GW techniques; and to comprehend the positive effects of GW on businesses. Unlike previous generations, today's millennial shoppers are keenly aware of the ecological consequences of their purchases and are eager to find eco-friendlier alternatives. Sustainable supply chain procedures, in addition to environmentally friendly products, are usually a selling point for this demographic. On the other hand, logisticians gain a great deal from GW practices because they cut down on energy waste, wasted resources, and dead inventory. Greener methods are thus required for storage facilities in India. The operators and the country, as a whole, would gain greatly from the increased business that better green applications would bring in. Reliable stock keeping, good storage systems, inventory control/optimization, training of employees, employee safety and health, and the introduction of employee welfare are all essential components of an environmentally friendly warehouse. Other factors to consider include the location of the warehouse, the efficiency of its lighting, the presence of sensors, the effectiveness of its energy management system, the use of electric-powered stackers, the effects of climate change, and the use of renewable energy from the sun. The demand from the public sector rises as more people, both domestic and international, make use of the finished items to satisfy their needs thanks to the warehouse's green uses. Authorities also need to know the results of this desktop data since they may be used to create and implement new warehouse policies that will help to ensure that the public sector maintains its high quality. The review identifies the following benefits: safer practices; reduce the space occupied by the warehouse; customer satisfaction; new technology; improved procedures;

boosted efficiency; reputation of companies; functionality of the economy; performance standards for manufacturing procedures; cut down on running expenses and less wastages.

KEYWORDS

- **environment**
- **green**
- **warehousing**
- **waste**
- **firms**
- **ecological**

REFERENCES

Aaj Enterprises. Importance of Green Warehousing in India; How Do We Go Green? 14 Dec 2021. https://www.aajenterprises.com/importance-of-green-warehousing-in-india-how-do-we-go-green-2/

Akandere, G. The Effect of Logistic Businesses? Green Warehouse Management Practices on Business Performance. Proceedings of International Academic Conferences 4106594, International Institute of Social and Economic Sciences, 2016.

Baah, C.; Jin, Z. Sustainable Supply Chain Management and Organizational Performance: The Intermediary Role of Competitive Advantage. *J. Manage. Sustain.* **2019**, *9*, 119.

Baker, P.; Marchant, C. Reducing the Environmental Impact of Warehousing. In: *Green Logistics: Improving the Environmental Sustainability of Logistics*; McKinnon, A.; Browne, M.; Piecyk, M.; Whiteing, A.; Eds.; 3rd edn.; Kogan Page Limited: London, 2015; pp 194–226.

Dzanuska, H. Why Become a Sustainable Warehouse? 2022Combilift. (accessed 8 Feb 2022).

Indrawati, D.; Lindu, M.; Denita, P. Potential of Solid Waste Utilization as Source of Refuse Derived Fuel (RDF) Energy (Case Study at Temporary Solid Waste Disposal Site in West Jakarta). In: *IOP Conference Series: Earth and Environmental Science*, Vol. 106; IOP Publishing, 2018; p 012103.

Feng, M.; Yu, W.; Wang, X.; Wong, C.Y.; Xu, M.; Xiao, Z. Green Supply Chain Management and Financial Performance: The Mediating Roles of Operational and Environmental Performance. *Bus. Strategy Environ.* **2018**, *27* (7), 811–824.

Hinz, P. 5 Reasons to Become a Sustainable Warehouse, Feb 2022. https://www.adaptalift.com.au/blog/5-reasons-to-become-a-sustainable-warehouse.

Inbound Logistics. 5 Ways Warehousing Is Going Green, 2018. https://www.inboundlogistics.com/articles/5-ways-warehousing-is-going-green/

Khan, S.A.; Kusi-Sarpong, S.; Arhin, F. K.; Kusi-Sarpong, H. Supplier Sustainability Performance Evaluation and Selection: A Framework and Methodology. *J. Clean. Prod.* **2018**, *205*, 964–979.

Khan, I. Power Generation Expansion Plan and Sustainability in a Developing Country: A Multicriteria Decision Analysis. *J. Clean. Prod.* **2019**, *220*, 707–720.

Kaplan, D. A. 7 Elements of the Sustainable Warehouse—And Why Shippers are Moving in, 5 Mar 2019. https://www.supplychaindive.com/news/building-sustainable-warehouse-shippers-cost-benefits/549625/

neoco. Green Warehouses: Why Bet on This Logistics Trend and How to Apply It, 27 July 2020. https://naeco.com/en/news/green-warehouses-why-bet-on-this-logistics-trend-and-how-to-apply-it/

Redox. Operational Environmental Management Plan. Waste Management Plan, 2005; pp 1–13. http://www.redox.com/content/pdf/mintowastemanagementplan.pdf. (accessed 2 April 2016).

Slyer, K. 5 Best Practices for Green and Sustainable Warehousing. *The Times of India* 3 Nov 2022. https://timesofindia.indiatimes.com/blogs/voices/5-best-practices-for-green-and-sustainable-warehousing/

CHAPTER 9

Green Manufacturing

AHMED TIJANI

Minerals Commission, Accra, Ghana

ABSTRACT

More and more businesses today understand the importance of creating environmentally friendly goods, services, and procedures. With the goal of preserving natural resources for future generations and recycling materials, green manufacturing (GM) prioritizes the development of better production methods over the regulation of technology. For economic development, it has been shown to reduce resource depletion, trash production, and pollution of all kinds, according to a number of studies. This chapter analyzes the positives, negatives, and green manufacturing methods. Waste and pollution levels can both be lowered thanks to genetic modification. If done right, it can help firms in terms of both finances and general perception. Firms face difficulties in implementing GM due to their scarcity of information and resources. The story went on to explain how GM helps save money and boost product quality, which is good for business and the planet. Environmental concerns and legislation; green image, global marketing and competitiveness; social and environmental responsibility; organizational capabilities and awareness; government rules and legislation; scarcity of resources, increased waste generation, and a waste disposal problem; customer awareness, pressure, and support; demand for environmentally friendly products; e. Incompatibility with different management and manufacturing systems; lack of research and empirical studies; lack of customers; increase in overall cost or financial burden; lack of awareness in companies; inadequate coordination between different departments; need of development of new analytical tools and models; lack of management commitment; lack of necessary tools;

lack of necessary skills and knowledge; loose government legislation; and inability to adopt are all factors that impede the successful implementation of GM.

9.1 INTRODUCTION

Industry around the world must adopt eco-friendly production methods because of rapid environmental loss and rising CO2 emissions. Green manufacturing (GM) practices, from this vantage point, were conceived of and implemented by large businesses in advanced economies. Natural resources are being depleted rapidly as a result of rapid development and urbanization. Therefore, the international society is at a pivotal point in which it must deal with an extreme scarcity of resources (Kothawade, 2017). There have been instances where environmental concerns have triggered or at least disrupted regional cooperation and even conflict (Tol, 2018). Green production (GM) techniques have become standard across all member countries of the cooperation to foster regional cooperation and protect natural resources. Many manufacturing companies have implemented GM strategies like the six "R"s (reduce, reclaim, recover, redesign, remanufacture, and recycle), zero waste production, and lean manufacturing (Cimatti et al., 2017). Companies benefit monetarily from these types of GM practices because they guarantee efficient use of resources and generate revenue from discards (Tumpa et al., 2019). Environmental and occupational safety costs are reduced (due to the recycling of waste rather than the purchase of virgin materials), company image is boosted, and production costs are cut thanks to green manufacturing (i.e. decrease in negative environmental impact by the public). Last, but not the least, this research adds new information by looking into the connections between the various obstacles to implementing GM practices.

9.2 LITERATURE

9.2.1 GM

The term "green manufacturing" (GM) is used to describe production processes that not only minimize environmental damage and resource consumption, but also prevent any scrap from ever ending up in a dump (Tumpa et al., 2019). When a company commits to "green manufacturing," it makes an effort to reduce its impact on the ecosystem by decreasing its consumption of raw materials and other natural resources. In addition, green buildings make every effort to minimize their environmental effect by reducing waste and carbon emissions. It is becoming increasingly common for companies to cut expenses and increase output thanks to "green" initiatives (Hjemdahl, 2020). In addition, there are more resources than ever before to help you become viable. In most cases, GM is a green procedure that reduces its negative effects on the environment. The Intergovernmental Panel on Climate Change (IPCC) recently released a report indicating that the average global temperature has risen by 0.850 C over the past century (Porter et al., 2018). Recycling, conserving resources, managing trash, protecting the environment, adhering to regulations, reducing pollution, and other similar concerns are all addressed in the GM production process. The term "green manufacturing" (GM) refers to production methods that minimize their impact on the natural ecosystem. No matter what you call it, the objective is the same: to create and distribute goods whose manufacturing, consumption, and disposal have as little impact on the ecosystem as possible.

9.2.2 BENEFITS OF GM

Businesses are increasingly "going green" as environmental consciousness grows. The transition to more sustainable manufacturing practices can be daunting, but it can have a beneficial effect on a company's bottom line if the manufacturer is committed to it. Sales can be boosted, operational expenses reduced, and more with these advantages.

9.2.3 BUDGET CUTS

Turning green can help businesses save money and get started quickly and easily. To cut down on your long-term electrical expenses, you could, for instance, put in energy-efficient lighting. You can save a lot of money over time by decreasing your water consumption and your waste removal requirements. If the green transitions are implemented with careful planning, a manufacturer may see a reduction in its overall running costs. Utility costs can be slashed significantly by utilizing renewable energy sources like solar and wind, as well as by installing energy-efficient machines and appliances. Supply expenses can be reduced by increasing recycling efforts and shifting to paperless billing and record-keeping.

9.2.4 CREATING A RECOGNIZABLE IMAGE

Customers are more likely to support businesses that care about them and their values, as well as the things they care about. Taking initiatives to reduce environmental impact and improve energy efficiency demonstrates to clients that you value the well-being of the earth and its inhabitants. Consumers now care about sustainability, so if you can make an impact in this area, it will be excellent for your brand's image. It is possible to expand your customer base and generate more revenue with a company rebrand. After all, everyone on Earth, not just the company, stands to gain from greater environmental protection. These initiatives are well received by customers and help win over the general confidence. Long-term, this kind of confidence in your business can lead to devoted patronage (Hjemdahl, 2020).

9.2.5 GAIN A COMPETITIVE ADVANTAGE THROUGH GOVERNMENT PARTNERSHIPS

Securing a government contract is a wonderful achievement for a manufacturer, but the market is notoriously cutthroat. The company has a better chance of landing a lucrative deal if it adopts environmentally friendly practices. Many contracts are set aside for environmentally conscious companies, opening up even more space for expansion and ownership.

9.2.6 SUSTAINABLE ENERGY PRACTICES

Energy use in manufacturing is typically very high. There will be less of an effect on the energy supply and the ecosystem if businesses switch to renewable energy (The Manufacturer, 2023).

9.2.7 SPEND LESS

There is no doubt that switching to more sustainable production practices will reduce costs. As we have seen above, switching to LED lights from incandescent ones is a great way to save money on utility bills. To further aid in the efficiency of building operations, outdated equipment can be swapped out for EnergyStar models. Taking steps to reduce energy usage benefits both the environment and the bottom line.

9.2.8 RAISE REVENUES

Seventy-eight percent of respondents to a 2021 GreenPrint survey said they were more inclined to buy a product if it bore an environmental label (Business Wire, 2021). Increasing sales in today's cutthroat market can be as simple as implementing "green policies" to satisfy consumers' wants. Seventy-six percent of people polled said they would switch to a company that offsets carbon emissions from their activities, demonstrating the financial potential of going green. Because transporting goods from abroad adds to environmental pollution and raises greenhouse gas emissions, factories can benefit from relying on local alternatives by decreasing their use of nonrenewable energy sources. A company can save money on supplies and speed up delivery time by working with a provider in the same region. Green production allows for the use of only environmentally friendly methods and products throughout an entire facility (Tarantino, 2021).

9.2.9 MAKE EMPLOYMENT AVAILABLE

The green workforce is constantly adapting to meet the changing needs of the green production industry. "[C]lean and green manufacturing generated 35,382 jobs between 2003 and 2010 while the rest of the industry shed in numbers," claimed Goodwin University (2016). The creation of economic and social value is pushed forward by the search for new ideas and intermediary positions. Workers in the clean economy "earn 13% higher salaries than other employees of the U.S. economy" because of the unique skills they bring to the table.

9.2.10 RAISE EMPLOYEE SPIRITS

Workers prefer to be employed by a company in which they feel secure and can take pleasure; such a business will naturally be environmentally conscious. Poor worker health and even long-term illness can be the outcome of indoor air pollution caused by inefficient manufacturing processes. The increased output seen in green offices can be directly attributed to the fact that employees are more invested in their work for a business that shows concern for the environment and the local community (Golden Arrow, 2023).

9.2.11 IMPROVEMENTS IN COMMUNITY SUPPORT

The greatest advantage is the gift of life itself. The corporate world has a significant effect on global and local societal well-being. Businesses can reduce their environmental impact by working toward a cleaner future one sustainable project at a time. As a whole, green production aims to reduce harmful emissions and make the world a better place to live for all inhabitants (Golden Arrow, 2023).

9.2.12 ASSIST WITH CUSTOMER NEEDS

More and more shoppers are learning about the hazards that production can pose to the planet. As a result of their newfound knowledge, consumers are demanding that businesses use renewable resources and less harmful processes when producing their products. Manufacturers can gain a competitive edge by going green to satisfy these demands (Hjemdahl, 2020).

9.2.13 BUILD A MORE SECURE OFFICE

When given opportunity, a green workplace improves conditions for everyone involved. A positive work environment is good for morale, productivity, and business pride. The company's dedication to environmental preservation will be further demonstrated by its adoption of eco-friendly practices such as paperless correspondence and electronic paychecks in addition to green technology, recycling programs, and green cleaning supplies (Hjemdahl, 2020).

9.2.14 LESSEN DISCARDED MATERIAL

A waste assessment is another tool available to businesses for preventing the unnecessary disposal of resources. It is possible that some primary resources could be downcycled or repurposed for use in alternative endeavors. Waste minimization has long-term financial and productivity benefits for any organization (Hjemdahl, 2020).

9.2.15 USING ONLY SAFE COMPONENTS

Many businesses today are going the extra mile by using environmentally favorable materials rather than the conventional alternatives. These companies are switching to natural and organic products instead of synthetic ones.

For instance, petroleum-based oil is used in the production of the foam used by conventional cushion manufacturers. However, eco-friendly mattresses swap out some of the petroleum for plant-based oils to lessen their impact on the earth. There will be less environmental damage and the product will be secure for consumers if this is done (Hjemdahl, 2020).

9.2.16 IMPROVED SOCIAL STANDING

Consumers' growing demands for openness have been a major factor in the rise of the sustainable manufacturing sector. More and more consumers are drawn to brands whose products and methods of manufacturing are more eco-friendly. Thousands of sustainable companies can be found all over the world, each promising complete openness and eco-friendly production methods. A clean nameplate does more for a company's reputation than any other single factor. Further, it aids eco-friendly producers in competing effectively with their non-green counterparts (Tarantino, 2021).

9.2.17 SAVINGS ON EXPENSES

Implementing a more environmentally friendly production method can help reduce overhead costs, which is one of the many indicators of a flourishing company. It is always profitable for businesses to begin recycling waste products in order to manufacture new and usable products using renewable energy sources. Adopting eco-friendly production practices negates the need to import costly materials from elsewhere (Tarantino, 2021).

9.3 RESULTING MINIMAL CARBON IMPACT

People all over the globe have noticed a drastic shift in the climate as the new decade begins. All these natural disasters are linked to the degrading state of our world, which has been hastened by a crisis in nonrenewable energy sources. However, with a minimal impact on the environment, things can change for the better (Tarantino, 2021). Green manufacturing is essential for lowering the carbon footprint of numerous sectors, which have contributed significantly to the current environmental imbalance. As a result of adopting green manufacturing practices, businesses and organizations have been able to significantly reduce their carbon impact.

9.4 GREATER ELECTRICITY CONSERVATION

Companies can alter both their energy consumption and the efficiency with which their goods are produced (The Manufacturer, 2023).

9.5 LESSENING OF CONTAMINATION

A company's efforts to reduce its environmental effect by cutting down on pollution can have significant results. To achieve this, we can recycle more and create cleaner technologies (The Manufacturer, 2023).

9.6 REDUCE FIRM'S IMPACT ON THE ENVIRONMENT BY PRESERVING NATURAL SUPPLIES

Large factories usually have negative effects on the surrounding ecosystem, so one way for factories to make amends is by pledging to preserve natural habitats (The Manufacturer, 2023).

9.7 EXEMPTIONS FROM TAXES

Governments at all levels are increasingly willing to reward businesses that adopt environmentally friendly production practices. Although there may be substantial preliminary expenses, there are many incentives to help businesses get started with green initiatives. Governments do not want major offenders based in their countries, so it is in everyone's best interest to push for environmentally friendly production methods. Taking advantage of this will make the shift a little bit smoother for the company (The Manufacturer, 2023). Choosing environmentally responsible production methods can simplify your financial obligations. Depending on where you live, you may be able to avoid paying certain fees if you invest in green manufacturing facilities. In the United States, for instance, businesses can receive a refund on a certain share of their sustainable energy expenditures. The manager of the factory should consult an accountant before making any of the above transactions to make sure they qualify for these tax breaks. One of the main reasons a sustainable future seems within our grasp is federal incentives for greener company (Tarantino, 2021).

9.8 BARRIERS OF GM

An organization faces challenges, or barriers, when trying to adopt GSCM (Dube and Gawande, 2016). Identifying and removing these obstacles is crucial for the GM practices adoption shift (Tumpa et al., 2019).

9.9 INSUFFICIENT MONITORING AND EVALUATION TOOLS

Sustainable manufacturing at scale is difficult to achieve without widespread collaboration, and this difficulty is compounded by a dearth of readily available and relevant data. Companies on all scales (local, national, international) that lack accurate methods of measuring data and tracking success typically develop unrealistic sustainability goals (Mareana, 2022). In order to combat this, businesses must improve their monitoring and assessment systems, which should extend to all aspects of business operations, such as environmentally friendly production methods and long-term strategic initiatives and projects. Efficacy and productivity can always be better, so it is important to implement a method of continuous improvement. Businesses and governments alike should look beyond the bottom line when assessing the value of an initiative. There is some thought that smart manufacturing powered by AI could help with this. The article claims that

9.10 LACK OF SUPPLIER/VENDORS COMMITMENT

One of the first exterior obstacles pinpointed is a lack of commitment from supply chain partners, which affects every step of the supply chain (Tumpa et al., 2019). The dedication of suppliers to a green supply chain is critical to the success of an end-to-end green supply chain and must be prioritized. Companies' efforts to adopt green practices may be hampered by a dearth of environmentally conscious vendors (Tseng et al., 2018). Additionally, suppliers may be hesitant to supply green products due to concerns about the complexity of GSCM practice implementation and a lack of familiarity with GSCM theory and practice (Dhull and Narwal, 2016). The failure to educate suppliers on the advantages of mutual commitment and incentive programs to motivate the adoption of green practices is another possible cause of the slow uptake of these measures.

9.11 A FAILURE TO SELL OR GENERATE INTEREST

Not having support from other influential people and the population at large could also be an issue (Sangwan, 2011). Low consumer spending, a lack of knowledge about the benefits of green products, and the desire of customers to purchase cheaper non-green products could all contribute to a lack of demand for green products (Tumpa et al., 2019).

9.12 LAWS, REGULATIONS, AND GOVERNMENT POLICY

Implementing GSCM can be hampered by governmental policies and regulations, as well as a lack of assistance from the government (Dube and Gawande, 2016). There is a risk that businesses in countries with strict policies and regulations will struggle due to factors like a dearth of necessary infrastructure or the high cost of maintaining a compliant environment (Dhull and Narwal, 2016).

9.13 INSUFFICIENT INTERNAL KNOWLEDGE

One prevalent challenge to implementing sustainable manufacturing initiatives is a lack of talent within manufacturing companies, specifically data scientists and sustainability experts (Mareana, 2022). Companies can get past this challenge by enlisting the help of experts or outside vendors who specialize in the necessary tools, knowledge, and expertise.

9.14 FINANCIAL AND ECONOMIC CONSTRAINTS

Inadequate funding and the lengthy period of time required to see a return on investment (ROI) are two of the biggest challenges to GSCM's widespread adoption (Dube and Gawande, 2016). Initial investment costs, such as those associated with purchasing new equipment and processes or hiring and training new workers, can be prohibitive for many businesses. There will likely be some downtime in production as a result of these preliminary expenditures, which will have a negative effect on the company's bottom line and market dominance in the near term (Niemann et al., 2016). In general, corporations put wealth and expansion ahead of human rights and environmental protection (Mareana, 2022). The perception that sustainability is too costly is a factor. Consequently, a paradigm shift is required to achieve sustainable manufacturing, from viewing the environment as a component of the economy to viewing the economy as an integral element of the environment. So, businesses need to adjust the economy so as to ensure the preservation of the ecosystem. Even though green manufacturing has the potential to greatly lessen our global carbon impact, it is not always easy for businesses to implement. Threatening competition from foreign firms that do not maintain the same standards could be their greatest obstacle. Some of these businesses' low operating expenses can be attributed to their disregard for environmental concerns.

9.15 INABILITY TO THINK CREATIVELY/LACK OF INNOVATION

There needs to be more cooperation between academic institutions and the business world to make up for the dearth of innovation-focused study in the academy. Students graduating from colleges and universities may not be equipped to deal with environmental and ecological issues in the real world (Mareana, 2022). The best hope for solving this kind of issue is a tight partnership between academic researchers and economists.

9.15.1 DRIVERS OF GM

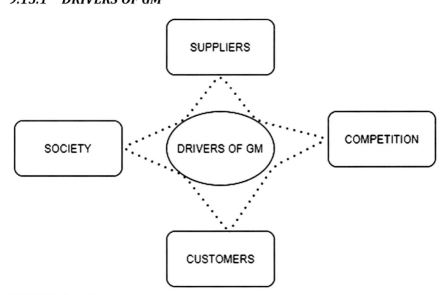

FIGURE 9.1 Drivers of GM.
Source: Authors.

9.15.2 COMPETITION

As has been noted by numerous academics, rivalry is indeed a motivator of GSCM. Firm success can be enhanced through the adoption of GSCM practices due to competition with key rivals.

9.15.3 SOCIETY

The adoption of environment consciousness practices is hindered by the public's lack of knowledge about environmentally friendly products and services. Min and Galle (2001) claim that consumers' continued ignorance of the environmental advantages of going green is due to a general lack of information about the topic (An et al., 2008).

9.15.4 SUPPLIERS

GSCM is a crucial factor in choosing a sustainable provider. It has been noted that vendors can offer valuable suggestions that aid in the implementation of customers' environmental initiatives and services.

9.15.5 CUSTOMERS

There are many interesting questions to consider when thinking about customers as a driver of green supply chain management practices, given the central position they play in GSCM. As a result of consumer demand for eco-friendly goods and rising environmental consciousness, more and more businesses are adopting GSCM strategies (Abdallah et al., 2015).

9.16 IMPLICATION

Implications for managers tasked with putting GM principles into action are substantial based on the findings of our study. This study will aid business owners and managers in pinpointing the biggest obstacles to implementing GM strategies. Because of how crucial it is for manufacturing companies to embrace GM practices, managers need to investigate what might stand in the way of doing so. They should devise effective solutions to the issue by weighing the significance of the various groups and obstructions. Waste and pollution levels can both be lowered thanks to genetic modification. If done right, it can help SMEs in terms of both finances and general perception. Due to their lack of personnel and funding, GM can be difficult to implement in SMEs. It was also covered in this piece how GM helps save money and improves product quality, which is good for the economy and the planet. Impacts on the environment and legislative action; ecofriendly image, brand building, and competitive edge; responsibility for the environment and society; capabilities of the organization and consciousness; legal regulations and legislative action; resource shortages; increased waste generation and disposal problem; customer awareness, pressure, and support; demand for environmentally friendly products; e. Incompatibility with different management and manufacturing systems; lack of research and empirical studies; lack of customers; increase in overall cost or financial burden; lack of awareness in companies; inadequate coordination between different departments; the need for development of new analytical tools and models; a lack of management commitment; a lack of necessary tools; a lack of management skills and knowledge; lenient government legislation; and an inability to adopt are all barriers to GM.

9.17 CONCLUSION

The emission of greenhouse gases has been steadily rising, and the industrial sector is a major contributor. Green manufacturing has garnered popularity over the years as a means to reduce pollution and support sustainable practices. Positives, drawbacks, and environmentally friendly production techniques are broken down in this chapter. Because of genetic engineering, we can reduce garbage and air pollution. When executed properly, it can boost a company's bottom line and public image. To put it simply, businesses struggle to adopt GM because they lack the necessary data and tools. As the narrative progressed, I learned how GM benefits businesses and the environment by reducing costs and improving quality. Government regulations and mandates; resource scarcity; increased waste generation and a waste disposal problem; customer awareness, pressure, and support; demand for environmentally friendly products; e. Incompatibility with different management and manufacturing systems; lack of research and emphasis on environmental issues.

9.18 RECOMMENDATIONS

Awareness and education efforts should be required to work for government-funded non-governmental organizations. The goal is to raise awareness about the need for eco-friendly goods and services in the community at large, which should lead to an increase in the market for such goods and services.

It is imperative that producers do everything in their power to reduce the environmental damage they have caused. Eco-friendly factories are able to pinpoint their emission generators and take remedial action. They must work with environmental authorities to devise practical methods of cleaning in order to reduce the risks associated with their activities.

Modernizing resource flows in sequential industrial facilities is central to conventional approaches to increasing productivity. Manufacturing companies are tasked with redesigning and optimizing their goods and services all the way through to the point of sale as part of the modernization process. As an illustration, raw material utilization, process regularity, and peak operational performance are just some of the goals of the controls implemented in the production process. The standard of the products is well-established, and there are few surprises. Gains in environmental effect are realized through waste minimization, pollution eradication, and research and development that lessens the use of hazardous and polluting substances, shrinks the size of component parts, and lightens products. Emerging ideas, like eco-efficiency, help advance environmental progress.

The government should increase its spending on R&D in order to encourage the creation of domestic green innovations in tandem with the country's specialized academic institutions. In addition, the government should help businesses acquire and use tested technologies.

The use of renewable energy sources is not the only method that factories can become environmentally friendly. They can also attempt cutting back on their energy consumption. Energy efficiency has become a major design goal for many modern machines.

Furthermore, in order to compel businesses to invest in green technologies, the government should enact necessary environmental laws on par with that of technologically developed countries.

The government should construct and improve the facilities required to successfully enforce environmental laws. To prevent polluting factories from moving to areas of the country with less stringent regulations, the federal government should guarantee that environmental laws are uniform across the country.

KEYWORDS

- green
- manufacturing
- sustainable
- energy
- practice
- system

REFERENCES

Abdullah, M.; Zailani, S.; Iranmanesh, M.; Jayaraman, K. Barriers to Green Innovation Initiatives Among Manufacturers: The Malaysian Case. *Rev. Managerial Sci.* **2015**, 1–27.

An, H. K.; Amano, T.; Utsumi, H.; Matsui, S. *A framework for Green Supply Chain Management Complying with RoHS Directive*; Queen's University Belfast, 2008.

Business Wire. GreenPrint Survey Finds Consumers Want to Buy Eco-Friendly Products, But Don't Know How to Identify Them, 22 May 2021. https://www.businesswire.com/news/home/20210322005061/en/GreenPrint-Survey-Finds-Consumers-Want-to-Buy-Eco-Friendly-Products-but-Don't-Know-How-to-Identify-Them

Cimatti, B.; Campana, G.; Carluccio, L. Eco Design and Sustainable Manufacturing in Fashion: A Case Study in the Luxury Personal Accessories Industry. *Procedia Manuf.* **2017**, *8*, 393–400.

Dhull, S.; Narwal, M. S. Drivers and Barriers in Green Supply Chain Management Adaptation: A State-of-Art Review. *Uncertain Supply Chain Manag.* **2016**, *4*, 61–76. https://doi:10.5267/j.uscm.2015.7.003

Dube, A. S.; Gawande, R. R. Analysis of Green Supply Chain Barriers Using Integrated ISM-Fuzzy MICMAC Approach. *Benchmark.: Int. J.* **2016**, *23* (6), 1558–1578. https://doi.org/10.1108/BIJ-06-2015-0057

Goodwin University. What Is Green Manufacturing and Why Is It Important? 2016. https://www.goodwin.edu/enews/what-is-green manufacturing/#:~:text=Green%20manufacturing%20is%20the%20renewal,operations%20within%20the%20manufacturing%20field.&text=Green%20manufacturers%20research%2C%20develop%2C%20or,their%20impact%20on%20the%20environment

Hjemdahl, P. W. Green Manufacturing: The Business Benefits of Sustainability. rePurpose, 2020. https://repurpose.global/blog/post/green-manufacturing-the-business-benefits-of-sustainability

Kothawade, N. S. Green Manufacturing: Solution for Indian Climate Change Commitment and Make in India Aspirations. *Int. J. Sci. Res.* **2017**, *6*.

Mareana. Top Barriers to Achieving Sustainable Manufacturing—And How to Overcome Them, 2022. https://mareana.com/top-barriers-to-achieving-sustainable-manufacturing-and-how-to-overcome-them/

Tarantino, J. The Benefits of Green Manufacturing, 8 Oct 2021. https://www.theenvironmentalblog.org/2021/10/the-benefits-of-green-manufacturing/

The Manufacturer. What Is Green Manufacturing and How Can It Benefit Your Business, 2023. https://www.themanufacturer.com/press-releases/green-manufacturing-can-benefit-business/

Tol, R. S. The Economic Impacts of Climate Change. *Rev. Environ. Econ. Policy* **2018**, *12* (1), 4–25.

Tseng, M.; Islam, M.S.; Karia, N.; Fauzi, F.A.; Afrin, S. A Literature Review on Green Supply Chain Management: Trends and Future Challenges. *Resour. Conserv. Recycl.* **2018**, *141*, 145–162. https://doi.org/10.1016/j.resconrec.2018.10.009

Tumpa, T. J.; Ali, S. M.; Rahman, M. H.; Paul, S. K.; Chowdhury, P.; Rehman Khan, S. A. Barriers to Green Supply Chain Management: An Emerging Economy Context. *J. Clean. Prod.* **2019**, *236*.

CHAPTER 10

Green SCM in the Fashion Sector

JOANA AKWELEY ZANU[1], SHERIFATU ABAS[2], and REBECCA LARTEKAI LARTEY[2]

[1]Department of Fashion and Design, Tamale Technical University, Northern Region, Ghana

[2]Department of Textiles Technology, Tamale Technical University Northern Region, Ghana

ABSTRACT

Mankind now confronts a rather real problem in the form of industrial contamination. Customers are becoming increasingly environmentally conscious as a result of global pollution and increased consciousness. In this age of broad environmental consciousness, "green" practices and policies were quickly adopted as essential for businesses. External barriers, such as legislation, poor supplier loyalty, and manufacturing barriers, were also found in the chapter, in addition to internal ones like price and credibility. This review also suggests that organizations are affected by both external and internal factors. Both corporate and exterior factors can facilitate or impede an organization's efforts to implement effective environmental supply chain management.

10.1 INTRODUCTION

The green movement, which sprouted in the late 1960s, has had a profound impact on the spread of eco-awareness around the world. The competitive landscape in many sectors has shifted as a result of rising public knowledge about environmental problems and the subsequent tendency toward adhering

---

Green Supply Chain Management. Mohammed Majeed, Kirti Agarwal, and Ahmed Tijani (Eds.)
© 2025 Apple Academic Press, Inc. Co-published with CRC Press (Taylor & Francis)

to global precautionary principle (Baig et al., 2020). Consumers are searching for and anticipating goods that help safeguard the natural ecology, and businesses, especially in the fashion industry, are rushing to promote their environmental practices by creating sustainable products to attract them. With green fabrics, shoppers have more options that are easier on the planet. Here, "environmental words" refer to statutes, commodities, principles, and policies that cause the least possible harm to the planet (Walsh, 2013). Increasing numbers of clothing companies are committing to eco-friendly operations, and the fashion industry is no exception. The garment industry is one of the world's most important in terms of its contribution to the economies and workforces of both consumer and supplier nations. Also, keeping sustainability parameters in line with the United Nations (UN) development goals is especially difficult for the textile and apparel business (Baig et al., 2020). Because of the widespread outsourcing that occurs in developing nations, the textile industry worldwide is in disarray. There is a dearth of visibility into the supply chain because suppliers are spread out across the globe (Köksal et al., 2017). Because of the textile industry's significance, immediate action is required to mitigate the negative effects of its production on the natural ecosystem and human culture (Desore and Narula, 2018).

Reduced emissions of gases, chemicals, and solid refuse throughout the supply chain—from sourcing raw materials to designing and producing products to delivering finished goods—is one of the primary goals of green supply chain management (GSCM). Cleaner production in the textile and apparel sectors has also made efficient use of energy a priority. Investment in energy-efficient technology, say Saberi et al., not only reduces the negative effects of production and delivery on the environment, but also lowers the costs associated with both (Saberi et al., 2018). Researchers have spent the last decade trying to adapt supply chain management (SCM) to the needs of sustainable development, thus expanding the field into sustainable supply chain management (SSCM) (Pagell and Wu, 2009; Tseng et al., 2015). By fusing the goals of GSCM/ESCM and CSR, SSCM provides assistance to businesses in improving their performance across the economic, social, and environmental spheres (Esfahbodi et al., 2016). Since there has not been a lot of time invested in studying GSCM in developing nations, those nations' practices are relatively nascent (Galal and Moneim, 2016). For this reason, supply networks in emerging and developing economies are less likely to implement sustainability measures than their more developed counterparts (Silvestre, 2015). It is essential for businesses to learn strategies for incorporating sustainability into the textile supply chain by reducing risks associated with the adoption of environmentally friendly procedures and societal practices (Esfahbodi et al., 2016; Köksal et al., 2017). (Freise and Seuring, 2015).

When compared to other major polluters, such as the oil business, the fashion industry ranks in at a close second (Market Watch, 2019). Water consumption is a major issue in the fashion industry because the production of textiles uses about 93 billion cubic meters of water annually; moreover, a lot of wastewater containing bleaches, acids, dyes, and softeners is released, polluting water supplies around the world (Market Watch, 2019). Spinning, weaving, knitting, printing, washing, bleaching, dying, and finishing are just some of the many steps involved in making a single fashion item, and as a result, the fashion industry employs a large number of people. For scientists, GSCM remains a prime area for investigation. There are, however, few studies that look into the challenges that developing nations face when trying to adopt GSCM (Aslinda et al., 2012). Limitations to green practice implementation in companies are rarely studied. Benefits to society and the environment have been highlighted in many of the available studies on business environmental management (Zhu et al., 2007). Since GSCM implementation is so important in the Ethiopian leather manufacturing industry, this study's primary objective is to better understand the obstacles these businesses encounter. The present benefits and barriers of GSCM in decreasing textile waste must be identified, and a review of current fashion business practices is essential. More research into the existing GSCM practices from an industry standpoint is needed to improve textile and apparel circularity. This chapter therefore aims to bridge the divide in the literature by reviewing desk research on the benefits and challenges faced by businesses in the fashion/textile industry supply chain when implementing green practices.

10.2 LITERATURE

10.2.1 FASHION INDUSTRY

It includes the textile, clothing, and fabric industries. More attention is being paid to sustainability impact in the clothing sectors in order to boost productivity, revenue, and public perception of the brands (Nema et al., 2013). When it comes to environmental impact, the fashion business ranks second only to the oil industry (McNeill et al., 2020). Because of its excessive consumption of water, power, and substances, the fashion business is widely recognized as the sector with the highest "resource intensity" (Riba, 2020). There has been a general uptick in the production and disposal of textiles due to the rising world's population and the prevalent buy-and-throwaway society. Landfills received 11.2 million tons of fabrics in 2017. (EPA, 2019). High quantities of recyclable materials, including dyeing compounds and poisonous fumes, and excessive packing are hallmarks of conventional supply chain processes. Many clothing manufacturers are adopting eco-friendly procedures to lessen their impact on the natural world. The views of major American clothing stores like Patagonia on the importance of sustainable practices have been presented (Michel et al., 2019).

10.2.2 GREEN SCM

Using renewable resources as input variables and undergoing transformation by agents whose byproducts are easily recyclable constitutes a green supply chain process. The components of a green supply chain are ones that can be repurposed and recycled after they have served their original purpose. A sustainable supply network is born from this action. The formulation of a green supply chain and the adoption of practices to support it is an overarching idea. There are many points along the supply line at which special attention must be paid. Natural fibers can be used in the production process. Nonhazardous processes can be used to clean fabrics. The durability of the textile and the fairness of the manufacturing process can inform your color and pattern options. The final goods can be packaged using ecologically responsible and suitable components. By incorporating environmental concerns, "Green Supply Chain Management" (GSCM) works to reduce pollution caused by manufacturing operations. GSCM has gained widespread support in the scholarly community and among professionals. Organizations in the textile manufacturing are increasingly focused on increasing the visibility, effectiveness, and cost-effectiveness of their supply chains as a result of the widespread interest in the concept of a "green supply chain" (Charter and Tischner, 2017). Organizational capabilities, environment pollution, and associated rules and laws all played a role in propelling early GSCM practice. Thus, GSCM is applied with the goal of protecting and bettering environmental advantages in mind. The execution of complete environment protection within the business, via ISO14001 quality systems licensing, green production, clean pollution, and other operations, can support GSCM even more, as noted by Carter (2018) and other scholars. Put in a good effort to help the planet. Reviewer Julia Wolf (2014) thinks businesses can improve their environmental performance through GSCM adoption.

Descriptions of GSCM have only evolved since the 1980s, but according to Kaur et al. (2018), it has become an important and effective tool which integrates about the issues related to society and the environment with the viewpoint of supply chain management in order to enhance the quality solutions (Hahn et al., 2018). Researchers advocated for more holistic environmental policies in supply chain management until the 1990s (Kirchoff et al., 2016). However, green buying is said to have been the first step in GSCM's introduction in 1994 (Charter and Tischner, 2017). In later years, as social and environmental worries grew, GSCM's role in SCM grew as well. Green supply chain management (GSCM) practices are described as those that take into account environmental concepts in the management of an organization's internal environment, including green purchasing, eco-friendly design, and the successful recoupment of investment costs (Soda et al., 2018). Meanwhile, Hahn et al. (2018) stated that green initiation, green design, green building, green operation and maintenance, and reverse logistics are all essential parts of GSCM practice in the construction industry. Researchers (Kaur et al., 2018; Moktadir et al., 2018), among others, argue that the basic GSCM practices of "green building design, green purchasing, green transportation, green construction, and end of life management" constitute an accurate description of GSCM. It appears that GSCM practice implicates distinct elements due to the conditions of different industries in different countries.

10.3 GSCM PRACTICES

10.3.1 LOGISTICS

The supply network would not function without transportation. It is a major environmental risk because it produces so many harmful gases and particles. Transport-related issues, such as picking the best method of transportation or determining the best vehicle or fuel, have received surprisingly little research attention. Integration of environmental effect improvement with expense, effort, and revenue improvement can be achieved through the use of statistical equations. Storage facilities and harbors are examples of structures that can affect sustainable development (Bastas and Liyanage, 2018). This area of transportation research has barely begun. Transportation handling, layout choices, and other issues can all be handled more efficiently with the help of tools from the field of systems analyzation.

10.3.2 GREEN PROCUREMENT (ECOLOGIC BUYING PRACTICES)

First implemented in GSCM practice is the concept of green purchasing (Sajjad et al., 2020). With this definition in mind, it is clear that green buying involves careful evaluation of the environment before, during, and after the transaction. The term "green procurement" refers to the practice of buying eco-friendly goods and working together with suppliers to better the ecosystem. Purchasing companies need collaborative activities like training, joint study, and information sharing to help their suppliers achieve their environmental goals (Kirchoff et al., 2016). To account for environmental concerns, the selection process includes the provision of an eco-design specification to suppliers that details the necessary conditions for the products to be purchased (Sajjad et al., 2020).

10.3.3 GREEN DESIGN

When new products or production methods are designed with environmental impact reduction in mind, we call this "greening the product" (Kirchoff et al., 2016). A more sustainable, fruitful, and improved life cycle is what we mean when we talk about eco-design (Sajjad et al., 2020). Waste processing and recycling expenses can typically be reduced through eco-design. The sustainability of an organization is a key consideration in all design choices. Fashion entrepreneurs should take note of a new business trend: catering to customers' desire for eco-friendly goods (Fortuna and Diyamandoglu, 2017). Low resource and energy use, biodegradable product design, reusable, recyclable, recoverable materials and component parts design, zero waste mechanisms, natural dyeing techniques, slow fashion methods, and customer collaboration as part of eco-design are all examples of green design implementation criteria (Scur and Barbosa, 2017). Similarly, the only method to think of environmentally friendly new products to cut down on textile and clothing waste is through life cycle design (LCD). Ultimately, the goal of the life cycle design (LCD) approach is to reduce any and all negative impacts throughout the product's entire lifecycle, from before manufacturing to after consumption. Bastas and Liyanage (2018) revealed that roughly 80% of product impacts on the environment originate from the design stage, demonstrating the importance of green design. As a result, businesses actively pursue strategies that incorporate recovered materials. The most up-to-date strategy involves coordinating with businesses along supply chains to accomplish sustainable development. Ultimately, it is up to consumers as the final link in the value chain to make the switch to eco-friendly goods. As a consequence, businesses will be pushed to make green supply chain investments so they can gain a competitive edge (Kang, 2019).

10.3.4 GREEN PRODUCTION

Green production focuses on reducing resource use and waste generation through the application of cleaner technologies, more efficient processes, and higher-quality raw materials (Sajjad et al., 2020). The term "green production" refers to a production cycle that makes use of inputs that have minimal negative impacts on the environment and high efficiency. Also, businesses can boost output and ecologic effectiveness through green products (Bastas and Liyanage, 2018). Integrated environmental machinery is used to handle and discard pollutants and wastes generated by green production, and carbon output and wastes are reduced, repurposed, and eliminated through cleaner technologies like recycling, reuse, and process innovation (Kirchoff et al., 2016). Trying to simplify the production process and streamlining the design are two ways in which the green production process can save energy, reduce pollution, and cut down on usage, thereby reaping substantial economic and environmental benefits. Many aspects of the green supply chain depend on the manufacturing phase, such as the availability of sustainable resources, the integration of recycled or repurposed parts, the ease with which components can be disassembled, and so on (Kang, 2019).

10.3.5 REVERSE LOGISTICS

Reverse logistics and closed-loop supply chains are topics that have been explored at length before, but their significance as a means of enforcement still stands out. Since sustainable green supply chain methods have not received much attention so far, this area offers room for investigation. The terms "reverse logistics" and "circular economy" are intertwined, with both referring to the reduction, reprocessing, and reusing of materials in the manufacturing process (Geng et al., 2017). When compared to the conventional (linear) business model, the actions in a circular business model include remanufacturing, repairing, refurbishing, recycling, sharing, and taking back (Stal and Corvellec, 2018). Furthermore, there is an abundance of qualitative and quantitative research on the subjects of sustainable/green logistics and reverse supply chain management (Ma et al., 2018). When it comes to Reverse Logistics, network design is a crucial area of study. Because of this, not only has environmental safety suffered, but so has the bottom lines of many companies (Sajjad et al., 2020). It is feasible to investigate and connect storage and transportation issues with location decisions linked to reverse supply chain processes. This means that recycled materials can be further processed to increase their worthwhile also reducing their environmental impact. Also, better waste handling is an important step toward implementing eco-friendly policies. Detailed research into waste management and recycling options is possible. Plan for environmentally-friendly operations. The components of the green logistics design are organized in a specific order, which is represented by the array symbol.

10.4 DRIVERS OF FASHION FIRMS IMPLEMENTING GSCM

10.4.1 MARKET

The green supply chain can trace its origins back to the consumers themselves. This is so because consumers want drives production. As the idea of "green consumption" is championed by the government and sociologists, consumers are beginning to prioritize environmental concerns. A portion of buyers may also be willing to back initiatives to create environmentally friendly supply chain businesses (Kang, 2019). Consistent green and environmental preservation advocacy raises public support for eco-friendly goods and services, which in turn helps businesses gain loyal clientele. Products with a high environmental value also tend to be better for end users and offer other advantages. However, in order to win over more environmentally conscious customers, the business is actively developing sustainability practices and supporting sustainable strategy implementation (Kang, 2019).

10.4.2 TOP MANAGEMENT SUPPORT

The dedication and backing of top management is also essential to the success of any SSCM initiative (Bastas and Liyanage, 2018). Senior leadership's "desire to do the right thing" can be seen in actions beyond mere legal compliance and financial gain, as proven by the findings of Lieb and Lieb (2010). Despite this, some research suggests that a lack of management backing could hinder SSCM's widespread adoption (Correia et al., 2013).

Negative views on sustainability are likely to blame for the absence of leadership backing (e.g., sustainability practices increase business costs or lack of perceived benefits from engaging in SSCM implementation; Sajjad et al., 2015).

10.4.3 GOVERNMENT

It can be prohibitively expensive for some small- and medium-sized enterprises (SMEs) to adopt a green supply chain at this time in technology's development. Sometimes, they just do not have the drive to improve. Government incentives play a significant part here. It is a motivation for the government to intervene in the business world by drafting rules or providing financial support (Kang, 2019).

10.4.4 THE SIZE OF THE FIRM

The scale of a company is a crucial consideration in the sustainability implementation process (Lee, 2019). Large clothing firms are widely believed to be adopting environmentally and socially responsible practices as a means of taking responsibility and of tackling global sustainability issues. In addition, bigger clothing firms are able to invest more heavily in R&D, financing, marketing, and the social compact, and they use these advantages to strive for sustainable performance (Sancha et al., 2015). Due to limited resources and competitive pressures, small- and medium-sized businesses (SMEs) pay less attention to environmental concerns than their larger counterparts (Li and Huang, 2017). However, small- and medium-sized clothing firms are crucial to the growth of many developing countries. Small- and medium-sized clothing firms account for the vast majority of the textile industry. An additional moderating factor between GSCM practices and success is the size of the firm (Wang et al., 2018).

10.4.5 COST

The maximization of profits is regarded as the pinnacle of success in conventional supply chain management. Some businesses will deliberately pollute the environment in an effort to save money (Kang, 2019). Core businesses will not proactively address environmental breaches in the supply chain because doing so would compromise their ability to maximize profits. It does not matter if they find out or not; they won't mandate that affected businesses make changes. By incorporating ecological environmental protection measures into supply chain management, the green supply chain improves the supply chain's meaning and repositions it as a whole. A small business should not make such an expenditure if it cannot expect to recoup its costs in a reasonable amount of time. As a result, most businesses are unable to adopt green supply chain management due to the associated costs (Kang, 2019).

10.5 CHALLENGES OF GSCM IN THE FASHION INDUSTRY

10.5.1 STAKEHOLDER PRESSURE

Companies implement SSCM projects in response to external pressure, most notably from government agencies, nongovernmental organizations, and other stakeholders (Sajjad et al., 2020). Reduced governmental oversight is a major hindrance to sustainability efforts (Oelze, 2017). After consumers and states, stakeholders are the most powerful group when it comes to sustainability. Allies in the supply chain and other players in developing nations are often uninformed about ecology and their role in achieving it (Moktadir et al., 2018; Soda et al., 2015). The fashion business is one that has been under scrutiny for its lack of progress toward sustainability in recent years. Increased production and wastage have been seen in the fashion business due to the rapid shifts in style. According to Remy (2016), annual production of fashion garments has surpassed 100 billion since 2014, doubling from 2000 levels. One garbage truck's worth of textiles is thrown away every second due to this high rate of output, leading to an estimated 92 million tons of textile waste per year. Consumers and sustainable industry players have required long-term shifts in response to rising awareness of these problems.

10.5.2 FAST CHANGE

Because of the extremely short product cycles and constantly shifting market demands in the fashion industry, new suppliers, products, and materials are sometimes required to be brought on rapidly in order to keep up with demand (Zimmerman, 2022). Brands concerned with minimizing their environmental effect should look at potential suppliers through the lens of sustainability, in addition to the quality and cost. Consistently high standards for environmental performance across supply chains can be challenging for brands to achieve due to time and expense constraints during the procurement process (Zimmerman, 2022).

10.5.3 ISSUES OF ACCOUNTABILITY

It is challenging to establish universal standards for environmental performance when you have so many suppliers in your supply chain, and it is even more challenging to ensure they are upheld consistently (Zimmerman, 2022). A supply chain analysis may show that, rather than requiring vendors to make changes to meet new standards, switching suppliers is the quickest way for brands working on the sustainability of their products to reduce environmental impact; however, this is not without its own difficulties (Brix-Asala et al., 2018).

10.5.4 DATA EXTRACTION

A clear starting point for enhancing the environmental performance of the supply chain can be established through life cycle assessment (LCA), which can reveal where your goods have the greatest effect. However, LCAs necessitate precise and reliable data from each step of a product's supply chain, which can be difficult to obtain for a number of reasons (Zimmerman, 2022). Some suppliers may not have or be able to easily provide the data you need, and even if managers do obtain the correct data, it can be challenging to keep track of such large and complicated quantities of data without the proper sustainability data management system in place (Oelze, 2017).

10.5.5 GSCM'S DIFFICULTY

Even though it may not seem so at first glance, the fashion industry's supply chain is among the most intricate of any business (Xiao et al., 2019). The multi-tiered nature of the fashion industry's supply networks is a major contributor to their complexity (Zimmerman, 2022).

10.6 BENEFITS OF GSCM IN THE FASHION INDUSTRY

10.6.1 FINANCIAL GAINS

While going green may not always be the most cost-effective option, many businesses will see an increase in profits after making the transition to more eco-friendly suppliers and materials. Life cycle assessments and supply chain analyses, when done thoroughly, also disclose ways to improve efficiency and reduce costs that might not have been obvious without such investigation (Zimmerman, 2022).

10.6.2 COMPANY REPUTATION

Establishing high expectations for the sustainability practices of your merchandise is one means of standing out effectively in a competitive market as more companies come under scrutiny for their negative effect on the environment. Brands that take a stand on social and environmental impact (and convey it well) could become famous in the era of conscientious consumerism, where the word "green" is becoming increasingly common as a marketing descriptor (Xiao et al., 2019). Better sales performance, greater investor interest, and more enthusiastic employees are just some of the byproducts of a company's efforts to improve its brand image (Zimmerman, 2022).

10.6.3 STRONG INDUSTRY DOMINANCE

Many shoppers now base their purchasing decisions on how environmentally friendly an enterprise is, as consumers are more committed than ever to minimizing their individual environmental impacts. Sixty-seven percent of buyers took into account the use of sustainable materials when making a purchase decision, and 57% have made major changes to their lifestyles to reduce their environmental effect (Zimmerman, 2022). Fashion companies will increase their market share if they can enhance the environmental performance of their products and effectively convey their influence.

10.6.4 MARKET LEADERSHIP

Successful supply chain sustainability storytelling places brands in a prime position to dominate their industries (Hajmohammad and Vachon, 2016). Pioneering brands can raise the bar for their entire industry by raising customer expectations, influencing competitor performance, and setting stricter standards for their suppliers. This has an effect that extends far beyond the scope of the company's own operations (Zimmerman, 2022).

10.7 IMPLICATIONS

There has been a recent uptick in the amount of scholarly attention paid to concern for the environment and the adoption of green approaches throughout the supply chain. Countries and businesses all over the world are starting to take environmental and climate warming, as well as the negative consequences of careless handling, more seriously. This chapter comes at a good moment, as managers will benefit from having a better grasp on the forces that encourage or discourage businesses from adopting GSCM. The transition to more environmentally friendly supply chain methods is a long-term investment for any company. It is important for the business to prepare for a healthier distribution network in light of both its immediate and long-term objectives as well as its financial situation. For reference, the firm's goal of reducing overhead costs would be at odds with its desire to use eco-friendly packaging for its merchandise. Thus, the business must deliberate and make the right choices regarding the policies and available options in order to achieve a balance between the two. Worldwide, well-known companies are adopting eco-friendly policies. They have developed novel logistics strategies that will increase their profits and lessen their impact on the earth. Accordingly, this chapter emphasized the importance of managers addressing and controlling GSCM issues in order to effectively execute SSCM. In particular, building trusting, collaborative relationships with suppliers and providing them with daily communication and responses can help resolve supplier-related problems and lessen the need for their close monitoring. A number of factors, including successful laws and political backing, can be viewed as motivators for GSCM. It is imperative that policymakers take the initiative to introduce and enact laws that create a competitive environment for businesses to adopt GSCM. It would be challenging for businesses to expand GSCM in the absence of efficient legal and regulatory initiatives. Also, the government can help with demand-side problems by raising customer and consumer knowledge of ecology.

10.8 CONCLUSION

The manufacturing sector has, in the last few decades, come to recognize the importance of environmental management, and has begun implementing environmental management initiatives in order to remain competitive in the global market. As a result, green supply chain management (GSCM) has become a crucial company strategy in the present day. The global clothing business is massive and must not be undervalued. This study makes an effort to measure the effect that green SCM factors like green design, green procurement, green manufacturing, and reverse logistics have on the environment and on businesses in the apparel sector. We also analyzed the opportunities and threats that Green SCM poses to the fashion business. As a result, the challenge and complexity of the subject of how to lessen the environmental impact of the textile industry has grown. Recent studies and published works on green supply networks have mostly concentrated on providing an overarching theoretical introduction. The goal of GSCM, as an innovative environmental activity, is to reduce or eliminate waste at every step of the supply chain, from initial product conception to final product delivery and disposal. Global supply chain management is, as its name suggests, a subset of SCM. Companies were compelled by fierce rivalry to engage in environmentally responsible practices with social and ethical dimensions. Explicit outcomes, like firm and environmental success, are the best barometers of GSCM's value.

KEYWORDS

- green
- SCM
- fashion
- environmental
- pollution

REFERENCES

Akter, S.; Ji, X.; Sarker, M.; Cai, L.; Shao, Y.; Hasan, M.; Abir, S.; Quan, V. Clean Manufacturing and Green Practices in the Apparel Supply Chain. *Open J. Bus. Manag.* **2020**, *8*, 104–113. DOI: 10.4236/ojbm.2020.81007.

Baig, S. A.; Abrar, M.; Batool, A.; Hashim, M.; Shabbir, R. Barriers to the Adoption of Sustainable Supply Chain Management Practices: Moderating Role of Firm Size. *Cogent Bus. Manag.* **2020**, *7* (1), 1841525. DOI: 10.1080/23311975.2020.1841525

Bastas, A.; Liyanage, K. Sustainable Supply Chain Quality Management: A Systematic Review. *J. Clean. Prod.* **2018**, *181*, 726–744. https://doi.org/10.1016/j.jclepro.2018.01.110

Brix-Asala, C.; Geisbüsch, A. K.; Sauer, P.; Schöpflin, P.; Zehendner, A. Sustainability Tensions in Supply Chains: A Case Study of Paradoxes and Their Management. *Sustainability* **2018**, *10* (2), 424. https://doi. org/10.3390/su10020424

Carter, C. R.; Rogers, D. S. A Framework of Sustainable Supply Chain Management: Moving toward New Theory. *Int. J. Phys. Distrib. Logist. Manag.* **2018**, *38*, 360–387. https://doi. org/10.1108/09600030810882816

Correia, F.; Howard, M.; Hawkins, B.; Pye, A.; Lamming, R. Low Carbon Procurement: An Emerging Agenda. *J. Purchas. Supply Manag.* **2013**, *19* (1), 58–64.

Charter, M.; Tischner, U. *Sustainable Solutions: Developing Products and Services for the Future*; Routledge: London, 2017.

Desore, A.; Narula, S. A. An Overview on Corporate Response Towards Sustainability Issues in Textile Industry. *Environ. Dev. Sustain.* **2018**, *20* (4), 1439–1459. https://doi.org/10.1007/s10668–017–9949–1

EPA. Textiles: Material-Specific Data, 2019. https://www.epa.gov/facts-and-figures-about-materials-waste-and-recycling/textilesmaterial-specific-data (accessed 13 July 2020).

Fortuna, L. M.; Diyamandoglu, V. Optimization of Greenhouse Gas Emissions in Second-Hand Consumer Product Recovery through Reuse Platforms. *Waste Manag.* **2017**, *66*, 178–189. https://doi.org/10.1016/j.wasman.2017.04.032

Geng, R.; Mansouri, S. A.; Aktas, E. The Relationship between Green Supply Chain Management and Performance: A Meta-Analysis of Empirical Evidences in Asian Emerging Economies. *Int. J. Prod. Econ.* **2017**, *183*, 245–258. https://doi.org/10.1016/j.ijpe.2016.10.008

Hahn, T.; Figge, F.; Pinkse, J.; Preuss, L. A Paradox Perspective on Corporate Sustainability: Descriptive, Instrumental, and Normative Aspects. *J. Bus. Ethics* **2018**, *148* (2), 235–248. https://doi.org/ 10.1007/s10551-017-3587-2

Hajmohammad, S.; Vachon, S. Mitigation, Avoidance, or Acceptance? Managing Supplier Sustalnability Risk. *J. Supply Chain Manag.* **2016**, *52* (2), 48 65.

Hasan, M. M.; Nekmahmud, M.; Yajuan, L.; Patwary, M. A. Green Business Value Chain: A Systematic Review. *Sustain. Prod. Consumption* **2019**, *20* (2019) 326–339. https://doi.org/10.1016/j.spc.2019.08.003

Kang, S. Research on Green Supply Chain in Textile and Apparel Industry. World Maritime University Dissertations. The Maritime Commons: Digital Repository of the World Maritime University, 2019; 1476. https://commons.wmu.se/all_dissertations/1476

Köksal, D.; Strähle, J.; Müller, M.; Freise, M. Social Sustainable Supply Chain Management in the Textile and Apparel Industry—A Literature Review. *Sustainability* **2017**, *9* (1), 100. https://doi.org/10.3390/ su9010100

Kaur, J.; Sidhu, R.; Awasthi, A.; Chauhan, S.; Goyal, S. A DEMATEL Based Approach for Investigating Barriers in Green Supply Chain Management in Canadian Manufacturing Firms. *Int. J. Prod. Res.* **2018**, *56* (1–2), 312–332. https://doi.org/10.1080/ 00207543.2017.1395522

Kirchoff, J. F. Tate, W. L.; Mollenkopf, D. A. The Impact of Strategic Organizational Orientations on Green Supply Chain Management and Firm Performance. *Int. J. Phys. Distrib. Logist. Manag.* **2016**.

Lee, D. Implementation of Collaborative Activities for Sustainable Supply Chain Innovation: An Analysis of the Firm Size Effect. *Sustainability* **2019**, *11* (11), 3026. https://doi.org/10.3390/su11113026

Lieb, K. J.; Lieb, R. C. Environmental Sustainability in the Third- Party Logistics (3PL) Industry. *Int. J. Phys. Distrib. Logist. Manag.* **2010,** *40* (7), 524–533. https://doi.org/10.1108/09600031011071984

Li, Y. H.; Huang, J. W. The Moderating Role of Relational Bonding in Green Supply Chain Practices and Performance. *J. Purchas. Supply Manag.* **2017,** *23* (4), 290–299. https://doi.org/10. 1016/j.pursup.2017.06.001

Meixell, M. J.; Luoma, P. Stakeholder Pressure in Sustainable Supply Chain Management: A Systematic Review. *Int. J. Phys. Distrib. Logist. Manag.* **2015,** *45* (1), 69–89. https:// doi.org/10.1108/IJPDLM-05-2013-0155

McNeill, L. S.; Hamlin, R. P.; McQueen, R. H.; Degenstein, L.; Wakes, S.; Garrett, T. C.; Dunn, L. Waste Not Want Not: Behavioural Intentions Toward Garment Life Extension Practices, the Role of Damage, Brand and Cost on Textile Disposal. *J. Clean. Prod.* **2020,** 121026.

Michel, G. M.; Feori, M.; Damhorst, M. L.; Lee, Y. A.; Niehm, L. S. Stories we wear: Promoting Sustainability Practices with the Case of Patagonia. *Fam. Consum. Sci. Res. J.* **2019,** *48* (2), 165–180.

Moktadir, M. A.; Ali, S. M.; Rajesh, R.; Paul, S. K. Modeling the Interrelationships Among Barriers to Sustainable Supply Chain Management in Leather Industry. *J. Clean. Prod.* **2018,** *181*, 631–651. https://doi.org/10.1016/j.jclepro.2018.01.245

Market Watch. Fashion Industry Moving to Improve Sustainability Footprint, 2019. https://www.marketwatch.com/press-release/fashion-industry-moving-to-improve-sustainabilityfootprint-2019–02–14 (accessed on 15 Feb 2019).

Ma, X.; Ho, W.; Ji, P.; Talluri, S. Contract Design with Information Asymmetry in a Supply Chain under an Emissions Trading Mechanism. *Dec. Sci.* **2018,** *49*, 121–153. https://doi.org/10.1111/deci.12265

Nema, N.; Soni, S. R.; Talankar, A.; Nougriaya, S. Green Supply Chain Management Practices in Textile and Apparel Industries: Literature Review. *Int. J. Eng. Technol. Manag. Res.* **2013,** *1*, 330–336.

Oelze, N. Sustainable Supply Chain Management Implementation-Enablers and Barriers in the Textile Industry. *Sustainability* **2017,** *9* (8), 1435. https://doi.org/10.3390/su9081435

Riba, J.-R.; Cantero R.; Canals T.; Puig R. Circular Economy of Post-Consumer Textile Waste: Classification Through Infrared Spectroscopy. *J. Clean. Prod.* **2020,** *272*, 1–29.

Saberi, S.; Cruz, J. M.; Sarkis, J.; Nagurney, A. A Competitive Multiperiod Supply Chain Network Model with Freight Carriers and Green Technology Investment Option. *Eur. J. Operat. Res.* **2018,** *266*, 934–949. https://doi.org/10.1016/j.ejor.2017.10.043

Sandin, G.; Peters, G. M. Environmental Impact of Textile Reuse and Recycling—A Review. *J. Clean. Prod.* **2018,** *184*, 353–365. https://doi.org/10.1016/j.jclepro.2018.02.266

Soda, S. Sachdeva, A.; Garg, R. Green Supply Chain Management Drivers Analysis Using TISM. In: *Flexibility in Resource Management*; Springer, 2018; pp 113–135.

Stal, H. I.; Corvellec, H. A Decoupling Perspective on Circular Business Model Implementation: Illustrations from Swedish Apparel. *J. Clean. Prod.* **2018,** *171*, 630–643. https://doi.org/10.1016/j.jclepro.2017.09.249

Scur, G.; Barbosa, M. E. Green Supply Chain Management Practices: Multiple Case Studies in the Brazilian Home Appliance Industry. *J. Clean. Prod.* **2017,** *141*, 1293–1302. https://doi.org/10.1016/j.jclepro.2016.09.158

Remy N. Stylish, Affordable Clothing Has Been a Hit with Shoppers. Now Companies Are Trying to Reduce Its Social and Environmental Costs 20 Oct 2016. https://www.mckinsey.com/capabilities/sustainability/our-insights/style-thats-sustainable-a-new-fast-fashion-formula

Sajjad, A.; Eweje, G.; Tappin, D. Managerial Perspectives on Drivers for and Barriers to Sustainable Supply Chain Management Implementation: Evidence from New Zealand. *Bus. Strategy Environ.* **2020,** *29* (2), 592–604. https://doi.org/10.1002/bse.2389

Sancha, C.; Longoni, A.; Giménez, C. Sustainable Supplier Development Practices: Drivers and Enablers in a Global Context. *J. Purchas. Supply Manag.* **2015,** *21* (2), 95–102. https://doi.org/10.1016/ j.pursup.2014.12.004

Soda, S.; Sachdeva, A.; Garg, R. K. GSCM: Practices, Trends and Prospects in Indian Context. *J. Manuf. Technol. Manag.* **2015,** *26* (6), 889–910. https://doi.org/10.1108/JMTM-03-2014–0027

Walsh, M. The Green Supply Chain Choosing and Setting up an Eco-Friendly Workflow. *LOGOS J. World Book Community* **2013,** *24*, 16–23.

Wang, J.; Zhang, Y.; Goh, M. Moderating the Role of Firm Size in Sustainable Performance Improvement Through Sustainable Supply Chain Management. *Sustainability* 2018, *10* (5). https://doi.org/10. 3390/su10051654

Wolf, J. The Relationship Between Sustainable Supply Chain Management, Stakeholder Pressure and Corporate Sustainability Performance. *J. Bus. Ethics* **2014,** *119*, 317–328. https://doi.org/10.1007/s10551–012–1603–0

Xiao, C.; Wilhelm, M.; van der Vaart, T.; van Donk, D. P. Inside the Buying Firm: Exploring Responses to Paradoxical Tensions in Sustainable Supply Chain Management. *J. Supply Chain Manag.* **2019,** *55* (1), 3–20.

Zimmerman, A. Greenstory, 3 Jun 2022. https://blog.greenstory.io/the-opportunities-and-challenges-of-supply-chain-sustainability-for-fashion-brands

CHAPTER 11

Impact of Green Structural Capital on Green Supply Chain Agility

RASEEM ABDUL KHADER[1] and P. NISSAR[2]

[1]Department of Commerce, Ansar Arabic College Valavannur, Kerala, India

[2]Department of Commerce & Management Studies, PSMO College Tirurangadi, Kerala, India

ABSTRACT

Green structural capital refers to the environmental resources, processes, and systems that support sustainable development and reduce the negative impact of business operations on the environment. Green supply chain agility refers to the ability of a company's supply chain to respond quickly and effectively to changes in environmental requirements, regulations, and consumer preferences while minimizing the negative impact on the environment. It involves the integration of environmental considerations into supply chain operations, including the use of sustainable materials, reduction of waste and emissions, and the adoption of innovative green practices. The present study examines the impact of green structural capital on green supply chain agility. The present study is based on a sample of 136 small and medium manufacturing firms in Kerala. The study found a strong positive impact of intellectual capital on green supply chain agility.

11.1 INTRODUCTION

Green supply chain agility refers to the ability of companies to quickly respond to changes in customer demands, regulations, and environmental concerns while simultaneously reducing their environmental impact. The aim of this paper is to discuss green supply chain agility and its impact on the environment and society. This paper also examines how companies can incorporate green supply chain agility into their business practices, and the benefits that can be achieved through such initiatives.

Green supply chain agility involves the integration of environmentally conscious principles into the supply chain management process. The goal of green supply chain agility is to create a sustainable supply chain that minimizes the negative impact on the environment and society, while at the same time remaining competitive and responsive to changing market conditions.

Green supply chain agility encompasses a wide range of activities, such as reducing waste and emissions, sourcing materials and energy from renewable sources, and designing products that can be easily recycled. By adopting a green supply chain approach, companies can enhance their corporate social responsibility (CSR) image, improve operational efficiency, and reduce costs.

To incorporate green supply chain agility, companies can adopt a variety of strategies. Some of these strategies include using renewable energy sources—Companies can use renewable energy sources such as wind and solar power to reduce their carbon footprint and decrease their dependence on fossil fuels, reducing packaging waste; Companies can reduce packaging waste by using eco-friendly materials and reducing the size of packaging, recycling, and reusing materials; Companies can recycle and reuse materials to minimize waste and reduce their environmental impact, implementing green logistics; Companies can use green logistics practices such as route optimization, fuel-efficient vehicles, and reverse logistics to reduce their carbon footprint, collaborating with suppliers; Companies can work with suppliers to ensure that they are also adopting green practices, such as using eco-friendly materials and reducing their energy consumption.

Incorporating green supply chain agility can have several benefits for companies including improved

1. Corporate social responsibility (CSR)—By adopting green practices, companies can enhance their CSR image, which can lead to improved brand reputation and increased customer loyalty.
2. Reduced costs—Green supply chain practices can lead to reduced costs by minimizing waste, increasing efficiency, and reducing energy consumption.
3. Competitive advantage—Companies that adopt green supply chain practices can gain a competitive advantage by differentiating

themselves from their competitors and appealing to customers who are environmentally conscious.
4. Regulatory compliance—Green supply chain practices can help companies comply with environmental regulations and avoid costly penalties.

Green supply chain agility is an important concept that can help companies reduce their environmental impact while remaining competitive and responsive to changing market conditions. By adopting green supply chain practices, companies can improve their CSR image, reduce costs, and gain a competitive advantage. There are several strategies that companies can use to incorporate green supply chain agility, such as using renewable energy sources, reducing packaging waste, and collaborating with suppliers. Overall, incorporating green supply chain agility is a win–win for both companies and the environment.

Green Structural Capital is a critical component of Green Intellectual Capital, which represents the intangible assets that enable organizations to develop and implement environmentally sustainable practices. This article will explore the concept of Green Structural Capital as part of Green Intellectual Capital, and its importance for sustainable business practices.

Green Structural Capital is a type of intangible asset that represents the knowledge, skills, and expertise of an organization's employees, customers, and partners related to environmental sustainability. It is built on the foundation of an organization's human capital and is characterized by the values, culture, and leadership that support environmental sustainability practices.

Green Structural Capital is made up of two components: environmental knowledge and environmental capabilities. Environmental knowledge refers to the awareness, understanding, and application of environmental sustainability concepts, such as waste reduction, energy conservation, and pollution prevention. Environmental capabilities refer to the ability to implement these concepts in practice, through the use of technology, process redesign, and stakeholder engagement.

Green Structural Capital is an essential element of Green Intellectual Capital as it provides organizations with the capability to integrate environmental sustainability into their operations, products, and services. Organizations that possess high levels of Green Structural Capital are better equipped to identify, develop, and implement environmentally friendly practices, products, and services. This leads to improved environmental performance, increased customer satisfaction, and reduced costs.

Research has shown that organizations with high levels of Green Structural Capital are more likely to engage in environmentally sustainable practices (Bansal, 2005). These practices include the adoption of green technologies, the reduction of waste and emissions, and the promotion of sustainable products and services. This not only benefits the environment but also enhances the organization's reputation, leading to increased customer loyalty and brand recognition.

Green Structural Capital also enables organizations to adapt to changing environmental conditions and regulations. Organizations that possess high levels of Green Structural Capital are better equipped to respond to environmental challenges such as climate change, water scarcity, and natural resource depletion. This allows organizations to maintain their competitive advantage and avoid potential legal and financial risks associated with noncompliance.

Green Intellectual Capital is a broader concept that includes not only Green Structural Capital but also other types of intangible assets related to environmental sustainability. These include: Green Human Capital which involves knowledge, skills, and expertise of an organization's employees related to environmental sustainability, green relational capital which means relationships that an organization has with its stakeholders, such as suppliers, customers, and regulators, related to environmental sustainability.

Together, these components of Green Intellectual Capital provide organizations with the capacity to develop and implement environmentally sustainable practices, products, and services.

Green Structural Capital is a critical component of Green Intellectual Capital and represents the knowledge, skills, and expertise of an organization's employees, customers, and partners related to environmental sustainability. It is essential for organizations to develop and enhance their Green Structural Capital to integrate environmental sustainability into their operations, products, and services. By building Green Structural Capital, organizations can not only improve their environmental performance but also benefit from increased customer loyalty, brand recognition, and reduced costs. Organizations with high levels of Green Structural Capital are better equipped to adapt to changing environmental conditions and regulations, maintain their competitive advantage, and avoid potential legal and financial risks associated with noncompliance.

Building Green Structural Capital requires a strategic and long-term approach that includes leadership and culture, employee training and development, partner engagement, and technology and innovation. By implementing these strategies, organizations can develop and enhance their Green Structural Capital and contribute to a more sustainable future.

11.2 HYPOTHESIS DEVELOPMENT

Environmental sustainability has become an increasingly important focus for businesses in recent years. Organizations are seeking to enhance their environmental performance and reduce their environmental impact through the adoption of sustainable practices and the development of sustainable supply chains. One way that organizations can achieve this is by investing in Green Intellectual Capital, which includes Green Structural Capital and Green Supply Chain Agility.

Green Structural Capital refers to the knowledge, skills, and expertise related to environmental sustainability that an organization possesses. Green Supply Chain Agility, on the other hand, refers to an organization's ability to quickly and effectively respond to environmental changes and challenges within its supply chain. This research aims to explore the relationship between Green Structural Capital and Green Supply Chain Agility and how it can contribute to environmental sustainability.

Green Structural Capital is an essential element for organizations seeking to enhance their environmental sustainability. It involves the development and enhancement of an organization's knowledge, skills, and expertise related to environmental sustainability. Bansal (2005) suggests that companies that develop and invest in their Green Structural Capital can build a strong foundation for sustainable development. Epstein and Roy (2001) further argue that Green Structural Capital is critical for achieving sustainable performance and that companies that invest in it can gain a competitive advantage in the market.

Green Supply Chain Agility is another essential element for organizations seeking to enhance their environmental sustainability. It refers to an organization's ability to quickly and effectively respond to environmental changes and challenges within its supply chain. Organizations that possess high levels of Green Supply Chain Agility can adjust their operations and supply chains to respond to environmental changes quickly. Gibson (2006) suggests that Green Supply Chain Agility is essential for organizations seeking to enhance their environmental sustainability and that it can contribute to significant improvements in environmental performance.

Relationship between Green Structural Capital and Green Supply Chain Agility:

Based on the literature, it can be hypothesized that there is a positive relationship between Green Structural Capital and Green Supply Chain Agility. By investing in the development of their Green Structural Capital, organizations can enhance their knowledge and expertise related to environmental sustainability, which in turn can enable them to better respond to environmental changes and challenges within their supply chain. Additionally, organizations with high levels of Green Structural Capital may be better positioned to identify and implement sustainable practices and innovations throughout their supply chain, further enhancing their Green Supply Chain Agility.

H1: There is a positive relationship between Green Structural Capital and Green Supply Chain Agility.

11.3 RESEARCH METHODOLOGY

The relevant data for the study were collected from 145 manufacturing units in Kerala using random sampling method. After removing invalid questionnaire 136 questionnaires were considered as final sample. Questionnaire includes measurement scales that were derived from well-established scales in the existing literature.

TABLE 11.1 Descriptive Statistics.

Variable	Mean	SD	Min	Max	Cronbach's alpha
Green Structural Capital (GSC)	4.2	0.75	2.5	5.0	0.88
Green Supply Chain Agility (GSCA)	3.8	0.80	1.5	5.0	0.91

Source: Field work (2023).

Based on the descriptive statistics, the mean score for Green Structural Capital (GSC) was 4.2 out of 5, with a standard deviation of 0.75. This indicates that, on average, the sample perceived a relatively high level of GSC in their organization. The minimum value of 2.5 suggests that there were some respondents who perceived a lower level of GSC in their organization, while the maximum value of 5.0 suggests that some respondents perceived a very high level of GSC.

Similarly, the mean score for Green Supply Chain Agility (GSCA) was 3.8 out of 5, with a slightly higher standard deviation of 0.80. This indicates that, on average, the sample perceived a slightly lower level of GSCA in their organization compared to GSC. The minimum value of 1.5 suggests that there were some respondents who perceived a very low level of GSCA in their organization, while the maximum value of 5.0 suggests that some respondents perceived a very high level of GSCA.

TABLE 11.2 Results.

Analysis	Result
Correlation	Correlation coefficient: 0.68
	P-value: <0.001
SEM analysis	Direct effect of GSC on GSCA: 0.78
	Standard error: 0.05
	Coefficient value: 0.76
	Chi-square test: 10.12
	CFI: 0.94
	RMSEA: 0.08

Source: Field work (2023).

Based on the results of the SEM analysis, the study found that there is a significant positive relationship between green structural capital (GSC) and green supply chain agility (GSCA). Specifically, the direct effect of GSC on GSCA was found to be statistically significant with a coefficient value of 0.76, indicating that for every one-unit increase in GSC score, GSCA score is predicted to increase by 0.76 units.

This finding is consistent with prior research that has shown that investing in green structural capital can help organizations achieve greater agility in their green supply chain. For example, building sustainable partnerships with suppliers, implementing eco-friendly manufacturing practices, and investing in green technology can help organizations become more flexible and responsive to changes in the market.

11.4 CONCLUSION

This research has demonstrated that there is a positive relationship between Green Structural Capital and Green Supply Chain Agility. Organizations that invest in the development of their Green Structural Capital can enhance their knowledge and expertise related to environmental sustainability, which in turn can enable them to better respond to environmental changes and challenges within their supply chain. Additionally, organizations with high levels of Green Structural Capital may be better positioned to identify and implement sustainable practices and innovations throughout their supply chain, further enhancing their Green Supply Chain.

The study has important implications for managers and policymakers who are looking to improve the sustainability and agility of their supply chains. By investing in green structural capital, organizations can not only reduce their environmental impact but also enhance their ability to respond to changing market conditions and stakeholder demands. This, in turn, can help them maintain a competitive advantage and achieve long-term success.

In conclusion, the study provides empirical evidence for the positive relationship between green structural capital and green supply chain agility. Further research could investigate the role of other factors, such as green human capital and green relational capital, in achieving greater sustainability and agility in the supply chain.

KEYWORDS

- **intellectual capital**
- **green structural capital**
- **green supply chain agility**
- **manufacturing**
- **small**
- **medium firms**

REFERENCES

Bansal, P. Evolving Sustainably: A Longitudinal Study of Corporate Sustainable Development. *Strategic Manag. J.* **2005,** *26* (3), 197–218. https://doi.org/10.1002/smj.441

Chang, Y. H.; Lin, C. H. Exploring the Relationship Between Green Supply Chain Management and Supply Chain Agility: An Empirical Study. *J. Clean. Production* **2019,** *211*, 120–129.

Epstein, M. J.; Roy, M. J. Sustainability in Action: Identifying and Measuring the Key Performance Drivers. Long Range Planning **2001,** *34* (5), 585–604. https://doi.org/10.1016/S0024-6301(01)00068-6

Gibson, R. Sustainability Assessment: Basic Components of a Practical Approach. *Impact Assess. Project Appraisal* **2006,** *24* (3), 170–182. https://doi.org/10.3152/147154606781765336

Gibson, B. J. A Green Supply Chain Is a Requirement for Profitability. *Int. J. Operat. Prod. Manag.* **2006,** *26* (7), 721–740.

Gopalakrishnan, M.; Yusuf, Y. Y. A Review on Supply Chain Agility: Concept, Taxonomy, Antecedents, and Outcomes. *Int. J. Prod. Econ.* **2018,** *206*, 107–124.

Jabbour, C. J.; De Sousa Jabbour, A. B.; Govindan, K.; Teixeira, A. A.; Souza Freitas, W. R. Environmental Management and Operational Performance in Automotive Companies in Brazil: The Role of Human Resource Management and Lean Manufacturing. *J. Clean. Prod.* **2013,** *47*, 129–140.

Kumar, M.; Chutia, S. K. Exploring the Impact of Green Supply Chain Management Practices on Supply Chain Agility: An Interpretive Structural Modeling Approach. *Resour. Conserv. Recycl.* **2018,** *141*, 244–258.

Lee, C. K. M.; Chen, Y. C.; Chen, C. H.; Chen, L. Y. Green Supply Chain Agility in Circular Economy: The Mediating Effect of Environmental Management. *Sustainability* **2020,** *12* (1), 327.

Mishra, A.; Gunasekaran, A.; Papadopoulos, T.; Childe, S. J.; Dubey, R. Green supply chain agility: A Review and Proposed Conceptual Framework. *J. Clean. Prod.* **2019,** *207*, 520–533.

Sarkis, J.; Zhu, Q.; Lai, K. H. An Organizational Theoretic Review of Green Supply Chain Management Literature. *Int. J. Prod. Econ.* **2011,** *130* (1), 1–15.

Sarkis, J.; Zhu, Q.; Lai, K. H. Green Supply Chain Management Innovation Diffusion and Its Relationship to Organizational Improvement: An Ecological Modernization Perspective. *J. Eng. Technol. Manag.* **2011,** *30* (1), 21–44.

CHAPTER 12

The Role of Industry 4.0 Software Tools in Creating Sustainable Supply Chain Management in Emerging Markets

KETAN RATHOR

Senior Project Manager, GyanSys Inc., Bengaluru, India

ABSTRACT

In the context of Industry 4.0, sustainable supply chain management may be one of the technology applications that drives the industry's development; however, it is also one of the most significant barriers to the sector's performance in terms of its competitiveness, environmental impact, and social impact. A future picture of the production system as it should be, "Industry 4.0," also known as the "Fourth Industrial Revolution," With the intention of raising the overall degree of automation found within the manufacturing sector, the German government initially suggested and then embraced the concept of Industry 4.0 in the year 2011. In order to make the world a more sustainable place, the objective of the fourth industrial revolution, also known as Industry 4.0, is to fully automate and link all of the systems that are a part of the manufacturing process. The Internet of Things is only one example of a technology that may be disruptive (IoT). This means that all components of the supply chain are now online and are able to share data in real time. The Internet of Things is comprised of a combination of a wide range of computer hardware and software, including a variety of sensors, networks, algorithmic frameworks, and application programmes (IoT). With the assistance of the Internet of Things, businesses may be able to improve their levels of production and simplify their supply chains.

The innovations of today are having a profound impact, not just on the day-to-day lives of individuals but also on the very fabric of our civilization as a whole. Changes in the climate, loss of resources as a result of increasing output, and waste generated by industry are only some of the environmental challenges that have been brought on by Industry 4.0. The current research aims to show how Industry 4.0 might affect the functioning of a sustainable supply chain and what advantages that could bring about. Individuals, non-governmental organisations (NGOs), and governments have banded together to demand that businesses modify how they run their supply chains in order to better adhere to the sustainability principle of "filling today's requirements without sacrificing the capacity of future generations to meet their own needs." At first, a high-level summary of the three major industrial revolutions and an explanation of the fourth iteration of Industry were provided.

The present age, which was brought about by advancements in dynamic data processing and cyber-physical systems that link the actual world to the web, has resulted in value chains being connected from the very beginning to the very end. Formerly human-managed functions in "smart factories" are being taken over by robots instead, including production scheduling and inventory management, for example. The fundamental objective of this line of study is to get an understanding of the relevance of industry 4.0 software tools in the development of sustainable supply chain management in developing countries such as India. The findings of this study emphasise many critical components of sustainable development, including the preservation of the environment, increased collaboration and integration of supply chain systems, and decision making that is driven by data.

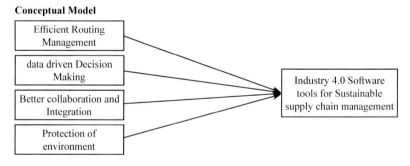

12.1 INTRODUCTION

The most significant advantages that have resulted from the digitalization of processes in recent years have been for private, professional, and creative endeavours. The manufacturing sector is one of the most essential sectors that must be successful for Industry 4.0 to be implemented. The usage of this information is very beneficial to the choices about investment, production, costs, marketing, and distribution. In addition to this, it improves both the performance of processes and the efficiency of activities throughout supply chains, which ultimately leads to improved resource utilisation optimization. (Legenvre, 2020). This helps to outline a new paradigm for the industrial revolution. Implementing practises of circular economies and operating under moral principles that direct the chain's participants in what and how to maintain value and reciprocity relationships in order to gain a competitive edge in the global market are central to the sustainable supply chain management's optimization of resource consumption.

Industry 4.0 is an initiative that combines infrastructure design and technical improvements to allow the interconnection and integration of processes. At its core, sustainable regional supply chain performance is at the centre of this initiative. Those industries that have not yet adopted these innovations will face increasing disadvantages in the global competitive landscape, while industrial ecosystems that are committed to the initiatives of Industry 4.0 will thrive. As more industries adopt these innovations, those that have not yet done so will face increasing disadvantages in the global competitive landscape. Because of the burden that this places on both industrial organisations and the countries in which they operate, it is important to determine what is preventing the full adoption of these technological advancements in order to boost logistics and commercial performance. This will allow for greater efficiency in both areas. Because of the constantly changing nature of the system, it is common knowledge that not all manufacturing organisations are now in a position to apply technology 4.0 at the same time (Yavas, 2020). From the commencement of the industrial revolution, companies have placed an emphasis on maximising their profits as their primary objective. In the early days of industrialization, increasing production alone was all that was necessary to increase profits since there was such a huge demand for goods and there was so little competition. Yet in the years that have passed since then, quite a bit has changed (Bag, 2018). Several companies are searching for cost-cutting strategies in order to raise their profitability in the face of increasing competition and a corresponding increase in the number of suppliers available to satisfy customer demand. This is because there are now more suppliers available to fulfil customer demand. When undercutting the competition only via lower pricing was not enough, more flexible production processes were developed, and new management practises were used in order to further reduce costs while simultaneously increasing production flexibility and quality. Since then, companies that are part of the supply chain often collaborate, making use of technology and making purposeful attempts to increase both their productivity and their profits (Chalmeta, 2020).

The influence that modern society has had on the natural environment has a number of repercussions, one of which is climate change. The increased use of natural resources has led to a growth in the amount of trash produced by industries, which has prompted reactions from people, non-governmental organisations, governments, and enterprises alike (Gupta, 2020). As a result of the development of systems that can satisfy an endless amount of demand, it is no longer practical to manage activities in the supply chain with simply financial objectives in mind. As the world struggles to keep up with its present demands(Palladino, 2020). These issues have recently gained prominence as the world struggles to keep up with its present demands. As a result, companies have begun placing a higher priority on the environmentally friendly aspects of sustainability.

In order to accomplish monetary, ecological, and social goals, sustainable supply chain management must cater to the requirements of all parties involved in the chain's production and distribution, beginning with the producers and ending with the customers (Osterrieder, 2020). The term "supply chain" refers to the whole process, beginning with the conception of an idea and continuing through the procurement of raw materials, the production of completed items, distribution, consumption, and finally disposal. New regulations are being passed that are in line with concerns about carbon emissions, ecological footprints, and other issues of a similar kind in order to prevent pollution that is the result of inappropriate waste management and recycling programmes (Yadav, 2020). The concept of Industry 4.0 centres on the integration of digital infrastructure with more conventional methods of production. This approach for industrial integration involves a great deal more than just the internal automation of value chains as an element of its scope. This system is both intelligent and adaptable since all of the actions that take place along the value chain are interacting with one another and adapting to one another in real time. It will be possible to integrate environmentally friendly management procedures all the way through the supply chain if the concept of Industry 4.0 is updated to include the most cutting-edge technological advancements (Manavalan, 2019).

Smart factories are able to maintain a continuous flow of product because the interdependence of their automated equipment and the storage of crucial data by sensors makes it possible for them to do so. Companies have been sluggish to accept this notion because they have struggled to locate the proper integrated solution that would give them with a larger return (Wang, 2020). This has caused the adoption rate to be slower than it otherwise would have been. Unmanned aerial delivery, sometimes known as "drone" delivery, is a concept that has applications in the last mile of supply chain delivery. This idea comes under the purview of Industry 4.0 and is sometimes referred to as "drone" delivery. The problem of city logistics, which entails the movement of goods inside a metropolis, may be helped by the development of this new piece of technology, which may be of assistance to companies (Bai, 2020). The traditional means of automobile distribution are being phased out in favour of delivery through unmanned aircraft. Deliveries that are not only effective but also kind to the environment have emerged as a top focus for a variety of businesses. Customers who purchase products from Amazon with a total weight that does not exceed 5 kilogrammes are eligible for the new 30-minute delivery option. Companies like as Google and DHL are exerting a lot of effort to deliver this technology to the market as soon as possible. The German manufacturing industry has been an early user of these technologies, and numerous companies, notably Volkswagen, BMW, and Daimler, have started to effectively implement and utilise them in their products (Raj, 2020).

The governments of several nations, such as India, have started programmes such as "Made in India" in an effort to increase output via sectoral digitalization. In today's economy, which is more linked on a worldwide scale, businesses are coming under growing pressure to prioritise sustainable development from the perspectives of economics, ecology, and society. As a strategic and competitive advantage, organisations actively endeavour to strengthen the long-term viability of their business operations (Palmaccio, 2021). It is for this reason that it is of the utmost importance that digital manufacturing systems enable firms to innovate and be environmentally responsible. These are two aspects that are generally accepted as being the driving forces behind the rise of the global economy. As a result, manufacturers of all sizes are working to develop solutions that will make the environmental impact of their manufacturing processes much lower. Nevertheless, the level of knowledge and skills that are now accessible is not adequate to properly integrate sustainability into the process of supply chain management. The production of greenhouse gases has a pattern of increasing in line with the advancement of technology (Weking, 2020). A direct result of this is a quickening of the warming of the planet. Yet, broad use of these cutting-edge technologies helps solve the difficulties associated to sustainability by reducing the amount of time needed for lead times and maximising the use of all resources that are accessible (Meneghello, 2019).

Over the course of the last ten years, some of the most innovative companies in the world have been exploring the potential benefits of digitally transforming conventional manufacturing companies. Research into the advances was also required because of the potentially enormous influence they may have on the market. The implementation of these technologies into the distribution network poses a substantial obstacle for companies operating in the manufacturing industry. Yet, a number of studies have previously broken out what "Industry 4.0" is, what its fundamental principles are, and how those ideas connect to pre-existing industrial organisations.

12.2 LITERATURE REVIEW

The goal of the "Industry 4.0" initiative is to integrate digital technology into manufacturing processes that are already well-established. This kind of industrial integration goes far beyond the simple automation of enterprises since it is both intelligent and has the capacity to improve itself over time. As a direct result of this, it ensures that connections at all points throughout the value chain are kept active and current at all times. The eventual result of implementing Industry 4.0 will be to have completely automated factories that are continually interacting with one another and coordinating the activities of their many machinery, integrated computer systems, and sensors (Feng, 2020). If robots and computers could simultaneously share data and make choices, manufacturing would use less time, energy, raw materials, and labour to produce bigger quantities of better quality things, while at the same time creating higher quality goods at a higher volume. It is possible to discover where an item came from by using either its one-of-a-kind serial number or any other identifying information. The internet always provides access to the tools as well as the final goods that are used in the manufacturing process of these items. They will be equipped with sensors that allow them to react properly to their surroundings, and they will be able to communicate in real time with other Internet-connected devices situated anywhere on the planet (Bezai, 2021). When it is fully implemented, the fourth industrial revolution will have an effect not only on individuals and society as a whole, but also on factories, industries, and all other kinds of enterprises. Because Industry 4.0 was responsible for making these advancements possible, we owe it a tremendous lot of gratitude.

Because of the Internet of Things, machines and other cyber-physical systems now have access to distributed databases that include information about suppliers, manufacturers, and distributors (Mani, 2019). As a result of this, it is now feasible to link all of the stages of the supply chain. By way of illustration, owing to the Internet of Things, depleted raw material stockpiles for a product may be automatically refilled from sources located in other countries. This ensures that a quantity of raw materials that is estimated, used in an appropriate manner, and utilised effectively throughout the production process. There is yet another illustration of this in the realm of business. It discusses how the internet and other services are being included into the manufacturing process as well as the distribution of finished products (Govindan, 2020).

Processing techniques are required for the analysis of large data collections The term "big data" refers to data sets that are either too extensive or too complicated to be adequately analysed using the methods that are more traditionally used. The day-to-day operations of an organisation are susceptible to being impacted by a variety of outside factors. There are several examples, some of which include production logs, financial accounts, and studies based on market research (Sony, 2020). Non-traditional sources such as the Internet, search engines, social media, and the sensors integrated into smart things (in part because of the Internet of Things) are some examples of where we may now get the information that is necessary for us to make choices (e.g., Google, Facebook, Twitter). Big data is a word that is used to describe the massive quantities of data that have been lately collected and stored from a variety of kinds of digital media. This data is referred to as "big" data. As a consequence of developments in information technology and declining prices associated with data storage, an increasing number of individuals are ingesting and analysing enormous amounts of data. While doing strategic planning and evaluation, having the ability to anticipate fluctuations in consumer demand via the analysis of enormous data sets may be valuable.

12.2.1 ROBOTICS

Robots are adaptable robots that can move or remain still under the supervision of pre-stored computer programmes in their onboard processors. These programmes are run by the robots' onboard processors. It's possible that the software created by humans and already installed on robots holds the key to solving their difficulties. Intelligent robots, on the other hand, may alter their programming in response to the lessons that they have gained from the mistakes that they have made. In addition, students often provide fresh points of view and methods for approaching problems that need to be solved (Mangla, 2018).

Make Sure That Both the Horizontal and the Vertical Axis of Integration Are Considered: For the vertical integration concept of Industry 4.0 to be put into practise, all machines, workstations, computers, and other pieces of production equipment, in addition to all of the company's internal business operations, need to be connected to one another and able to communicate in both directions (including product design, procurement, production, marketing, and distribution, among other things). Companies in the value chain should engage in horizontal integration, which entails digitally coordinating their production and planning processes with those of other companies in the value chain, in order to ensure that all unnecessary steps are removed and flow is optimised. This can be accomplished by coordinating their production and planning procedures with those of other companies in the value chain. The successful operation of the value chain will be ensured as a result of this (Culot, 2020). The procedure of developing a product that functions as a whole entity is referred to as "whole engineering." Connecting the digital engineering systems used in the factory with those used by other stakeholders, including the end users, requires the usage of interfaces and systems that are analogous to those used by those stakeholders. Integration on both the vertical and the horizontal planes might be incorporated in an alternative formulation.

12.2.2 CLOUD COMPUTING

Due of computing in the "cloud," a company's information may be kept privately and safely on a distant server and accessible from any location in the world with an Internet connection. Hackers have the ability to target gadgets that are linked to the internet. Each and every financial transaction is secured using encryption, and only authorised computers are permitted to access to the network. There is a level of cyber security risk associated with both horizontal and vertical integration techniques, especially with respect to the theft or manipulation of personal or commercial data and information. Cyber-interventions in manufacturing processes and equipment also pose a threat since they might result in a halt in output or perhaps the cessation of all manufacturing altogether.

It is essential for supply chains that are committed to sustainability to pay particular attention to the design of their goods in order to guarantee that the manufacturing process does not include the use of any chemicals that are hazardous to either human or environmental health. Since the product has a lengthy lifetime, less of the resources that go into making it will be wasted after they have accomplished their function. It is very necessary for these raw materials and their suppliers to adhere to the 6R principles. This is especially the case in terms of reuse and remanufacturing. Reducing the total quantity of material used in manufacturing and packaging is just as important as making use of environmentally friendly items. Redesign projects reduce the negative effects of production on the environment by reusing resources that are already in use.

It will be possible to monitor the state of a product at every step of its manufacturing and distribution with the help of Internet of Things, a technology that is part of the Industry 4.0 initiative. This will make it much simpler to adopt 6 Sigma and other practises that are analogous to it. Creating intelligent objects that are able to connect with one another across the Internet of Things calls for further thought. By the use of simulation, one is able to evaluate the compatibility of materials with the practises as well as their impact on human health and the environment. Because of the horizontal and vertical integration, information about the design of products that comply with the standard may be supplied to internal processes. Sharing one's knowledge about one's own design processes with other partners in the supply chain helps to ensure the effectiveness of sustainability components that can be performed with closed-cycle product life cycles, such as reduction and reuse. Integration on both the horizontal and the vertical planes necessitates the use of precursor technologies such as cloud computing, big data, and analytics in order to guarantee the confidentiality of all data that is exchanged.

12.2.3   GATHERING DATA AND INFORMATION FROM DECISION MAKING

Acquiring, shopping, and gathering information: Throughout the stages of sourcing and procurement, it is essential for a sustainable supply chain to choose suppliers that engage in environmentally friendly production practises and make use of environmentally friendly products. When it comes to procuring raw materials and components, it is best to utilise techniques that are favourable to the environment, and the same can be said for the manufacturing process itself. The highest priority should be placed on machines and systems that reduce waste, electricity consumption, and emissions of carbon dioxide. It is crucial to put the 6 Sigma and concepts at the centre of your decision-making when it comes to making purchases. For example, if raw materials and supplies are recovered, recycled, or reused, this may prolong the product's lifetime while simultaneously reducing the total resource consumption and waste production of the supply chain as a whole. In order to advance the cause of social sustainability, businesses should be selected based on their ability to meet the sustainability standards for working conditions, and the terms of the contracts for purchasing goods and services should make specific reference to the working conditions of the workforce.

Integration of technology from the fourth industrial revolution in both horizontal and vertical directions has a significant impact on the performance of sustainability measures throughout the procurement process. If suppliers are subjected to frequent monitoring of both the safety of the raw materials used and the things produced, as well as the safety of the working circumstances of the workers who make those items, then the suppliers may be compelled to improve their own working conditions in order to satisfy the requirements of the monitoring. It is possible that the use of technology for additive manufacturing might assist economically developing nations by enabling commerce with suppliers who were previously inaccessible. Businesses will be able to assess a broad range of possible suppliers and resources thanks to the use of big data and analytics. This will enable the firms to make choices that are more economically sound and will result in cost savings. Vertically integrated manufacturers will be able to inform their horizontally integrated suppliers of the time and amount of the needed material by keeping track of raw material and supply utilisation in real time through the Internet of Things. This will allow horizontally integrated suppliers to operate with less stock and speed up delivery times. Vertically integrated manufacturers will be able to inform their suppliers of the time and amount of the needed material.

Researchers intend to maximise the environmental element of supply chain sustainability by thinking up and implementing techniques and technologies that minimise waste output, energy use, and raw material utilisation. This will allow us to maximise the sustainability of the supply chain. The decreased use of resources like energy, raw materials, and supplies will bring about cost reductions, which will be beneficial to the enterprise as a whole. The management of production in the vast majority of supply chains is primarily focused with either boosting productivity or cutting expenditures, with little consideration for the health and safety of the people who are actually carrying out the work. As part of the social pillar of sustainability, efforts are made to increase access for employees to things like fair pay, safe working conditions, and health safeguards. In order to ensure the continued viability of society over the long term, it is imperative that all members of society have access to equal work opportunities, regardless of criteria such as gender, age, or any other personal traits. While developing their industrial workforces, companies should keep in mind the requirement to offer diverse social groups with equal job opportunities, fair pay, and other social rights. This obligation should be a priority for businesses. For the nation as a whole to have sustainable development economically, the distribution of income and chances for employment must be equitable.

Now that we have intelligent robots and automated production lines, potentially dangerous industrial processes that would have previously put people in risk may be carried out without the need for human involvement. Because of this, reducing the amount of wasted resources is one of the most significant things that can be done to safeguard the environment. Businesses are able to adapt production and are ready for expected fluctuations in demand with the help of real-time data from smart industrial applications. This enables firms to substantially reduce the amount of stock they have on hand. Because of advancements in additive manufacturing technology, it is becoming more unnecessary to complete all stages of production in a single site. This might result in some manufacturing being relocated to less developed regions or countries.

12.2.4 BETTER DISTRIBUTION

The distribution function of the supply chain is responsible for the shipment of products and services from the various suppliers to the various production facilities and then from the manufacturing facilities to the various distributors, retailers, consumers, and end users. One of the most useful functions is making sure that products are distributed through supply chains that are beneficial to the environment. Traditional supply chains prioritise cost reduction by selecting the method of distribution that results in the least amount of environmental damage. In contrast, sustainable supply networks place a higher priority on finding solutions that will have the opposite effect. Driving in a way that is less harmful to the environment should be a top concern since there is a clear link between the kind of gas used in automobiles and the amount of damage they do to the environment. Since the number of distribution trips has a direct influence on the amount of gasoline that is used, many participants in the supply chain utilise mathematical models for precise planning in order to reduce the total number of distribution trips.

The Internet of Things enables the whole distribution network to maintain visibility over all of the resources and components that will be put to use. Because of horizontal integration and cloud computing, all of the partners in a distribution chain now have access to the data, which enables businesses to make use of distribution channels. Since these technologies allow the simultaneous interchange of data on demand and production at all stages of the supply chain, it is now possible to both anticipate and factor future needs into distribution planning. This was previously impossible. There is a possibility that cyber-physical systems, such as the navigational software that is put in delivery trucks, may be able to cut down on the amount of time that is spent travelling.

The client was successful in transitioning the supply chain from one based on conventional practises to one that is sustainable by requiring sustainable business practises throughout all stages of the product's life cycle. Customers have the ability to play an important role in the policing of unsustainable business practises in the supply chain by choosing to purchase only products that are made with non-hazardous materials, remaining loyal to brands that are committed to social sustainability practises such as providing decent working conditions, and avoiding companies that use processes that are in question.

12.3 DISCUSSION

This section involved in presenting the critical analysis based on the data sourced from the respondents, the focus of the study is to understand the importance of using Industry 4.0 tools in creating sustainable supply chain management in Emerging markets. The data are mainly sourced from the respondents who are working in supply chain industry. The analysis involves in presenting the demographic variables through frequency analysis, and further analysis is performed using tools like correlation, regression and chi square test.

12.3.1 FREQUENCY ANALYSIS

TABLE 12.1 Frequency Analysis.

Gender	Frequency	Percent
Male	95	56.9
Female	72	43.1
Age	**Frequency**	**Percent**
Less than 30 years	52	31.1
31–40 years	54	32.3
41–50 years	22	13.2
Above 50 years	39	23.4

The Role of Industry 4.0 Software Tools in Creating Sustainable Supply Chain 209

TABLE 12.1 (Continued)

Current Position	Frequency	Percent
Lower level management	76	45.5
Middle level management	60	35.9
Top level management	31	18.6
Type of Family	**Frequency**	**Percent**
Nuclear Family	98	58.7
Joint Family	69	41.3
Education	**Frequency**	**Percent**
Completed UG	77	46.1
Completed PG	39	23.4
Completed Professional course	29	17.4
Others	22	13.2
Work experience	**Frequency**	**Percent**
Less than 5 years of experience	45	26.9
5–10 years	45	26.9
10–15 years	30	18
15–20 years	33	19.8
Above 20 years	14	8.4
Total	**167**	**100**

Based on analysis from Table 12.1, it is noted that nearly 56.9% were male respondents and 43.1% were female respondents, 31.1% were in the age group of Less than 30 years, 32.3 were between 31 and 40 years, 13.2% were in age group between 41 and 50 years and 23.% were Above 50 years, 45.5% were in the Lower level management, 35.9% were in Middle level management and remaining 18.6% were in Top level management

Furthermore, it is identified that 58.7% were living in nuclear family and remaining 41.3% were living in joint family, 46.1% of the sample population have completed under graduation course, 23.4% have completed post graduation course, 17.4% have completed professional course and remaining 13.2% have done other courses. Lastly 26.9% were having experience of little less than 5 years..

12.3.2 RELIABILITY ANALYSIS

The next step in the analysis is to test whether the data is reliable and valid, for this purpose Cronbach alpha is used. The researcher considers four key independent variables: Efficient Routing Management; Data driven Decision Making; Better Collaboration and Integration and Protection of Environment, whereas the dependent variable is Sustainable SCM

TABLE 12.2 Test of Reliability.

Variables	Cronbach's alpha
Efficient routing management	0.859
Data driven decision making	0.853
Better collaboration and integration	0.833
Protection of environment	0.813
Sustainable SCM	0.842

From the above table it is noted that the value of Cronbach's alpha is more than 0.700 hence it can be stated that the data is highly reliable and valid.

12.3.3 CORRELATION ANALYSIS

The researcher is then poised to understand the nature of relationship between independent variables and dependent variable for this purpose correlation analysis is applied

TABLE 12.3 Correlation Analysis.

Correlations	Efficient routing management	Decision making	Collaboration	Environment protection	Sustainable SCM
Efficient Routing Management	1	.893**	.834**	.948**	.870**
Decision Making	.893**	1	.859**	.944**	.886**
Collaboration	.834**	.859**	1	.895**	.834**
Environment Protection	.948**	.944**	.895**	1	.900**
Sustainable SCM	.870**	.886**	.834**	.900**	1

Based on Table 12.3 of correlation analysis, it is noted that all the independent variables possess significant positive correlation towards the dependent variable. It is further noted that environment protection possess high positive correlation towards sustainable supply chain management with the coefficient value of 0.900, followed by decision making with nearly 0.886, efficient routing management possess a coefficient of 0.870 towards sustainable supply chain management, lastly, collaboration and integration possess a coefficient of 0.834 towards the dependent variable : sustainable supply chain management.

12.3.4 CHI SQUARE ANALYSIS

This section is involved in testing the hypothesis.

12.3.5 HYPOTHESIS 1

Null: There is no significant difference between Efficient Routing Management and Industry 4.0 Software tools for Sustainable supply chain management

TABLE 12.4 Chi Square Analysis Between Efficient Routing Management and Industry 4.0 Software Tools for Sustainable Supply Chain Management.

Efficient routing management	Value	df	P Value
Pearson Chi-Square	312.972a	16	0.00
Phi	1.369		0.00
Cramer's V	0.684		0.00

The p value is 0.00. Furthermore, the value of Phi is 1.36 which states that the variables possess positive relationship, also the value of Cramer's V is 0.684, usually the value ranges between 0 (no association) to 1 (perfect association). Since the value is nearly 0.684, it can be stated that the association is strong among the variables hence it can be concluded that there is a significant difference between Efficient Routing Management and Industry 4.0 Software tools for Sustainable supply chain management.

12.3.6 HYPOTHESIS 2

Null: There is no significant difference between Data driven Decision Making and Industry 4.0 Software tools for Sustainable supply chain management

TABLE 12.5 Chi Square analysis between Data driven Decision Making and Industry 4.0 Software tools for Sustainable supply chain management.

Data driven decision making	Value	df	P Value
Pearson Chi-Square	254.739a	16	0.00
Phi	1.235		0.00
Cramer's V	0.618		0.00

Based on table, it is noted that the p value of chi square is 0.00, hence null hypothesis is rejected and alternate hypothesis is accepted. Furthermore, the value of Phi is 1.23 which states that the variables possess positive relationship, also the value of Cramer's V is 0.618, usually the value ranges between 0 (no association) to 1 (perfect association). Since the value is nearly 0.618, it can be stated that the association is strong among the variables hence it can be concluded that there is a significant difference between Data driven Decision Making and Industry 4.0 Software tools for Sustainable supply chain management.

12.3.7 HYPOTHESIS 3

Null: There is no significant difference between Better collaboration and Integration and Industry 4.0 Software tools for Sustainable supply chain management

TABLE 12.6 Chi Square Analysis Between Better Collaboration and Integration and Industry 4.0 Software Tools for Sustainable Supply Chain Management.

Better collaboration and integration	Value	df	P Value
Pearson Chi-Square	216.982a	16	0.00
Phi	1.14		0.00
Cramer's V	0.57		0.00

Based on table, it is noted that the p value of chi square is 0.00, hence null hypothesis is rejected and alternate hypothesis is accepted. Furthermore, the value of Phi is 1.14 which states that the variables possess positive relationship, also the value of Cramer's V is 0.570, usually the value ranges between 0 (no association) to 1 (perfect association). Since the value is nearly 0.570, it can be stated that the association is strong among the variables hence it can be concluded that there is a significant difference between Better collaboration and Integration and Industry 4.0 Software tools for Sustainable supply chain management.

12.3.8 HYPOTHESIS 4

Null: There is no significant difference between Protection of environment and Integration and Industry 4.0 Software tools for Sustainable supply chain management

TABLE 12.7 Chi Square Analysis Between Protection of Environment and Industry 4.0 Software Tools for Sustainable Supply Chain Management.

Protection of environment	Value	df	P value
Pearson Chi-Square	379.606a	16	0.00
Phi	1.508		0.00
Cramer's V	0.754		0.00

Based on table, it is noted that the p value of chi square is 0.00, hence null hypothesis is rejected and alternate hypothesis is accepted. Furthermore, the value of Phi is 1.50 which states that the variables possess positive relationship, also the value of Cramer's V is 0.754, usually the value ranges between 0 (no association) to 1 (perfect association). Since the value is nearly 0.754, it can be stated that the association is strong among the variables hence it can be concluded that there is a significant difference between Protection of environment and Industry 4.0 Software tools for Sustainable supply chain management.

12.4 IMPLICATIONS

Industry 4.0 is bringing a variety of benefits to businesses thanks to the digitization of activities involved in supply chains. It's possible that the findings of this analysis will be beneficial to researchers, lawmakers, and the administration of corporations. According to the published research, the SC process is still being automated, and the vast majority of businesses, especially SMEs, are resistant to change. In order to assist companies in making the transition from a traditional to a digital supply chain, managers are required to provide guidance and instruction to their task forces, employees, and workers. Companies should collaborate with educational institutions such as universities and research institutes in order to get knowledge about the possible technological breakthroughs that may make SC processes viable. This report should be read in its entirety if Industry 4.0 has not yet been implemented at your organisation. This article provides a framework that managers and policymakers may use to understand the purpose of technology related to Industry 4.0 at different points throughout the supply chain.

12.5 CONCLUSIONS

Consolidating sustainable supply chains requires management in which public-private support mechanisms are reflected in territorial and individual-level policies and financing options, as well as a better understanding of the benefits of technological applications related to Industry 4.0 and the significance of exchange and collaboration for more efficient utilisation of the capabilities and resources of the various actors. In addition, a better understanding of the benefits of Industry 4.0 technological applications is required. A sustainable supply chain can improve its economic, environmental, and social performance by enhancing its coordination, delivery, error reduction, and waste prevention, as well as by developing ethical practises in which transparency, collaboration, and data traceability are prioritised, and by incorporating Gap Aware practises. The use of technology 4.0 into the process of managing the sustainability of supply chains highlights a distinction.

12.6 FUTURE STUDIES

In spite of the fact that it is helpful, a systematic evaluation of the relevant literature has critical limitations that need to be taken into consideration. The academic journals were the only sources that were considered for the literature review in this work; however, the research may have also included conference papers and books. In addition, the scope of this inquiry is limited to only five different breakthroughs related to Industry 4.0. A wide array of resources, such as the online databases ScienceDirect, IEEE Explore, and Scholar, are used to compile the data that is used in this study. Yet, there is a possibility that significant articles were missed since they were not included in the database search. This might have been a significant oversight. The selection of keywords used in the publication is another shortcoming, since it may have required researchers to limit the scope of their search. Other criteria for the selection of keywords may be used to future study in order to locate material that is both more comprehensive and relevant. The gathering of manuscripts may also make use of several other databases, such as Scopus and Web of Sciences. It's possible that the amount of time spent on literature reviews by future researchers will be a role in driving this process. Big data, blockchain, and RFID are three other examples of Industry 4.0 technologies that have the potential to be used in the supply chain in the near future. Developing countries, where small and medium-sized firms (SMEs) represent the backbone of the economy, may be the focus of future research that investigates the framework in context and looks at context-specific applications. We have shown that proprietors of small and medium-sized companies do not consider Industry 4.0 to be an indication of long-term prosperity.

KEYWORDS

- sustainable supply chain management
- data driven decision making
- routing management
- chi square analysis
- conceptual mode

REFERENCES

Bag, S.; Telukdarie, A.; Pretorius, J.; Gupta, S. (2018). Industry 4.0 and supply chain sustainability: Framework and future research directions. *Benchmarking Int. J.* **2018**, 28, 1410–1450

Bai, C.; Dallasega, P.; Orzes, G.; Sarkis, J. Industry 4.0 Technologies Assessment: A Sustainability Perspective. *Int. J. Prod. Econ.* **2020**, *229*, 107776.

Bezai, N. E.; Medjdoub, B.; Al-Habaibeh, A.; Chalal, M. L.; Fadli, F. Future Cities and Autonomous Vehicles: Analysis of the Barriers to Full Adoption. *Energy Built Environ.* **2021**, *2*, 65–68.

Chalmeta, R.; Santos-Deleón, N. J. Sustainable Supply Chain in the Era of Industry 4.0 and Big Data: A Systematic Analysis of Literature and Research. *Sustainability* **2020**, *12*, 4108.

Culot, G.; Nassimbeni, G.; Orzes, G.; Sartor, M. Behind the Definition of Industry 4.0: Analysis and Open Questions. *Int. J. Prod. Econ.* **2020**, *226*, 107617.

Feng, L. Integration of Industry 4.0 Related Technologies in Construction Industry: A Framework of Cyber-Physical System. *IEEE Access* **2020**, *8*, 122908–122922.

Govindan, K.; Rajeev, A.; Padhi, S. S.; Pati, R. K. Supply Chain Sustainability and Performance of Firms: A Meta-Analysis of the Literature. *Transp. Res. Part E Logist. Transp. Rev.* **2020**, *137*, 101923.

Gupta, R.; Tanwar, S.; Kumar, N.; Tyagi, S. Blockchain-Based Security Attack Resilience Schemes for Autonomous Vehicles in Industry 4.0: A Systematic Review. *Comput. Electr. Eng.* **2020**, *86*, 106717.

Legenvre, H.; Henke, M.; Ruile, H. Making Sense of the Impact of the Internet of Things on Purchasing and Supply Management: A Tension Perspective. *J. Purch. Supply Manag.* **2020**, *26*, 100596.

Manavalan, E.; Jayakrishna, K. A Review of Internet of Things (IoT) Embedded Sustainable Supply Chain for Industry 4.0 Requirements. *Comput. Ind. Eng.* **2019**, *127*, 925–953.

Mangla, S. K.; Luthra, S.; Rich, N.; Kumar, D.; Rana, N. P.; Dwivedi, Y. K. Enablers to Implement Sustainable Initiatives in Agri-Food Supply Chains. *Int. J. Prod. Econ.* **2018**, *203*, 379–393

Mani, V.; Gunasekaran, A.; Delgado, C. Enhancing Supply Chain Performance Through Supplier Social Sustainability: An Emerging Economy Perspective. *Int. J. Prod. Econ.* **2018**, *195*, 259–272.

Meneghello, F.; Calore, M.; Zucchetto, D.; Polese, M.; Zanella, A. Internet of Threats? A Survey of Practical Security Vulnerabilities in Real IoT Devices. *IEEE Internet Things J.* **2019**, *6*, 8182–8201.

Osterrieder, P.; Budde, L.; Friedli, T. The Smart Factory as a Key Construct of Industry 4.0: A Systematic Literature Review. *Int. J. Prod. Econ.* 2020, 221, 10747.

Palladino, R.; Hassan, R.; Escobar, O. Artificial Intelligence and Business Models in the Sustainable Development Goals Perspective: A Systematic Literature Review. *J. Bus. Res.* **2020**, *121*, 283–314.

Palmaccio, M.; Dicuonzo, G.; Belyaeva, Z. S. The Internet of Things and Corporate Business Models: A Systematic Literature Review. *J. Bus. Res.* **2021**, *131*, 610–618.

Raj, A.; Dwivedi, G.; Sharma, A.; Jabbour, A. B. L. D. S.; Rajak, S. (2020). Barriers to the Adoption of Industry 4.0 Technologies in the Manufacturing Sector: An Inter-Country Comparative Perspective. *Int. J. Prod. Econ.* **2020**, *224*, 107546.

Sony, M.; Naik, S. Industry 4.0 Integration with Socio-Technical Systems Theory: A Systematic Review and Proposed Theoretical Model. *Technol. Soc.* **2020**, *61*, 101248.

Wang, J.; Lim, M. K.; Zhan, Y.; Wang, X. An Intelligent Logistics Service System for Enhancing Dispatching Operations in an IoT Environment. *Transp. Res. Part E Logist. Transp. Rev.* **2020**, *135*, 101886.

Weking, J.; Stöcker, M.; Kowalkiewicz, M.; Böhm, M.; Krcmar, H. Leveraging Industry 4.0—A Business Model Pattern Framework. *Int. J. Prod. Econ.* **2020**, *225*, 107588.

Yadav, G.; Luthra, S.; Jakhar, S. K.; Mangla, S. K.; Rai, D. P. A Framework to Overcome Sustainable Supply Chain Challenges Through Solution Measures of Industry 4.0 and Circular Economy: An Automotive Case. *J. Clean. Prod.* **2020**, *254*, 120112.

Yavas, V.; Ozkan-Ozen, Y. D. Logistics Centers in the New Industrial Era: A Proposed Framework for Logistics Center 4.0. *Transp. Res. Part E Logist. Transp. Rev.* 2020, *135*, 101864.

CHAPTER 13

Green Supply Chain Management in the Hospitality Industry

FATAWU ALHASSAN[1], SHERIFATU ABAS[1], STANLEY COWTHER[1], and SUSSANA ANTWI-BOASIAKO[2]

[1]*Tamale Technical University, Tamale, Ghana*

[2]*Accra Technical University, Accra, Ghana*

ABSTRACT

Green Supply Chain Management (GSCM) is becoming increasingly important in today's highly competitive hospitality industry as it enables hotels to offer individualized service to their guests and improves overall performance and coordination among a group of hotels. The goal of this chapter is to explain green supply chain management from a hospitality industry perspective. GSCM practices, such as green distribution, green design, green procurement/purchasing, green packaging, reverse logistics, green logistics, and green waste management, were found to have the ability to save money and give a business an edge. Due to the growing need for information on how to make people healthier, this chapter could change society by teaching hotel managers how to improve environmental conservation while lowering harmful environmental effects like air pollution. Some of the things that might happen when GSCM is put into place are less air pollution, less solid trash, and less use of toxic materials. Hence, GSCM is key for hotels to practice to achieve a competitive advantage.

13.1 INTRODUCTION

The tourism industry helps achieve all 17 of the United Nations' Sustainable Development Goals but especially goals 8, 12, and 14. Sustainable tourism is central to the UN's post-2015 developmental goals, which has pushed for a more defined strategy for its execution (United Nations World Tourism Organization, 2021). While some of the most prominent hotel chains do make contributions to the SDGs, the success of these efforts requires closer scrutiny from tourist and hospitality experts (Jones and Comfort, 2019). Because of this, economic activity as a whole is boosted because jobs can be created and earnings can be made. Due to globalization, competition has intensified locally in the hospitality sector as multinational corporations have expanded into new markets (Mahammad, 2022). As consumers shift toward eating more natural, sustainably produced foods, there has been a corresponding rise in the demand for sustainable and hygienic food goods and services (Baloch and Rashid, 2022; Ayaz, 2022). Growing public and governmental pressure to safeguard ecosystems of all types is a direct result of rising environmental consciousness (Alreahi et al., 2023). More regulations and laws have been announced with the goal of reducing negative effects on the environment, which is a direct reflection of governments' fears and concerns about the environment (Robertson et al., 2017). Therefore, institutions of every stripe feel pressured to take environmental practices more seriously and effectively and to gain knowledge and training in addressing the wide range of environmental problems they may encounter. Green supply chain management (GSCM) is the practice of incorporating environmental considerations into conventional supply chain management by means of material reuse, material reduction, and material reprocessing (Yan et al., 2016). Businesses that want to implement green supply chain management must first ask their suppliers and distributors to help them save money and improve efficiency by using more environmentally friendly methods of production and delivery. Miroshnychenko et al.'s (2017) findings lend credence to the idea that corporate environmental responsibility plays a major role in sustainable development that places a premium on ecological sustainability. Businesses are interested in going green because it can help them save money and lessen their negative influence on the planet (Ali, 2022). More advantages accrue to hotels that go green than to those that do not (Chen et al., 2021). The hospitality industry is increasingly recognizing the strategic importance of green supply chain management in maintaining and expanding its competitive edge (Cingoski and Petrevska, 2018). Green supply chain management has been shown to improve financial, logistical, and ecological outcomes (Masa'deh et al., 2017). Some business executives in the manufacturing sector are ignoring the proven effectiveness of GSCM in boosting bottom-line results (Ater et al., 2018). 70% of company executives said they do not incorporate GSCM strategies into their operational initiatives, despite the fact that industry leaders have raised awareness of GSCM in emerging markets (Geng et al., 2017). Business managers can boost their company's economic advantage, cut expenses, and attract new clients and vendors by adopting a GSCM strategy (Daddi et al., 2016; Rahim et al., 2016).

Hotel green supply chain management strategies, such as those examined in hotel best practices in green strategy studies, are still in their infancy compared to other fields of study (Cingoski and Petrevska, 2018) and have not thoroughly looked into all the procedures involved in the lodging supply chain's upstream, intermediate, and final stages (Galeazzo et al., 2021). In addition, few studies have looked into the full effect of these practices on benefits (Filimonau and Tochukwu, 2020). While the idea of sustainability is not novel, many businesses lack the expertise to put it into practice or evaluate its results (Kalender and Vayvay, 2016). Therefore, the purpose of this chapter is to detail the GSCM procedures used by motels and the advantages of GSCM in the hospitality industry. The need for a healthier population is addressed in this chapter by providing hotel managers with information on how to implement practices that optimize environmental conservation and minimize negative ecological effects like air pollution. Some of the anticipated results of implementing GSCM include a decrease in air emissions, effluent waste, solid waste, and the use of toxic materials. Insights into GSCM strategies that can boost competitive advantage at hotels may be found in this volume. Green supply chain management (GSCM) practices, such as green purchasing, green design, green distribution, green packaging, and green waste management, were found to have the potential to provide both a cost savings and a competitive edge. In light of the growing demand for information on how to promote a healthier population, this chapter has the potential to affect societal change by educating business managers on methods that improve environmental conservation while reducing harmful ecological impacts like air pollution. Some of the anticipated results of implementing GSCM include a decrease in air emissions, effluent waste, solid waste, and the use of toxic materials.

13.2 LITERATURE

13.2.1 GSCM

Supplying goods and services from vendors, producers, and final customers via material movement, communication of information, and revenue generation in the backdrop of environmental concerns is the focus of Green Supply Chain Management. Storage administration, vendor and consumer relations, product development, manufacturing, and distribution are all aspects of the supply network that fall under the purview of SCM (Ikram et al., 2018). By fostering measures to improve the ecological sustainability of goods and calculating the expenses related to waste in operational processes, businesses can accurately gauge their providers' environmental sustainability through green supply chain management (GSCM) practices (Kot and Kozicka, 2018). This includes everything from repurposing and reproduction to ecologically responsible buying and a connected distribution system that involves vendors, manufacturers, and consumers (Husaini, 2020; Pirzada and Saiful, 2020). Global supply chain management, or GSCM, is the practice of considering environmental impacts at every stage of the supply chain, from initial ideation to ultimate disposal. This includes everything from the choice of the raw materials to the production procedure to the logistics of getting finished products to consumers (Aslam et al. 2019; Waseem and Khurram, 2019; Vazquez-Brust, 2019). The Green Supply Chain (GSC) emphasizes business ideals and ethical business practices while also being mindful of the environment. Reverse logistics consists of environmentally friendly manufacturing, sourcing, buying, shipping, and planning (Husaini et al., 2018). The food and beverage and hotel sectors are just two examples where green supply chain management (GSCM) has proven to be essential. Additionally, businesses cannot go green without GSCM. In light of the complicated makeup of managerial interactions with those involved, GSCM implementation is challenging and requires buy-in from all parties engaged in order to yield the desired management outcomes (Sarkis and Duo, 2018). Effective strategies applied via the many "R"s (reduce, reuse, rework, refurbish, reclaim, recycle, remanufacture, and reverse logistics) are also within the purview of GSCM (Arora, 2020; Jumady and Fajriah, 2020). Lean manufacturing is one approach to GSCM. Lean manufacturing is reducing inefficiencies throughout the production process. Lean manufacturing is an approach to production that seeks to maximize efficiency and cut down on waste (Rao and Holt, 2005). Having clear lines of contact at every stage of the supply chain helps get products to customers more quickly (MacCarthy et al., 2016). Renewable resources are threatened by reckless use, and wasteful practices have negative effects on the ecosystem (Montabon et al., 2016). An abundance of resources exists to assist managers in making the most of their GSCM efforts. Multinational companies can reap many financial benefits from obtaining ISO 14001 accreditation, including improved operational efficiency, product/brand recognition on a global scale, marketing benefits, increased competitiveness, and lower handling of waste costs (Cherrafi et al., 2016). Using GSCM, leaders have cut down on waste and the consumption of nonrenewable resources while simultaneously expanding their opportunities for recuperation in the hereafter (Nasir et al., 2017). By taking a life cycle view of product development, material selection, production, distribution, and disposal, GSCM seeks to optimize ecological profit (Sajid et al., 2016). Managers' use of GSCM allows for the creation and implementation of sustainable development methods, leading to vast improvements in business processes (Kirchoff et al., 2016). The economic, environmental, and social success of a company can be affected by eight different GSCM dimensions, as stated by Yildiz Ankaya and Sezen (2019). Green buying, green production, green distribution, environmentally conscious packaging, green marketing, awareness of the environment, corporate environmental oversight, and recovery of investments are the eight pillars that Yildiz Ankaya and Sezen (2019) discussed.

13.2.2 HOTELS AND GSCM

For hotels to meet their profit, effectiveness, and customer base goals while also lowering their impact on the environment through exposure and effect, green supply chain management (GSCM) has become an increasingly important new strategy (Alreahi et al., 2023). Ecological actions, laws, and issues have sprung up suddenly over the past decade, leading to a growing consensus that supply chain management and environmental protection should work together to combat the pollution that comes with industrial development (Masa'deh et al., 2017). Resources like beginning materials, semimanufactured finished items, supplies, cash products, and services are essential to the hospitality sector's ability to operate. It takes work to negotiate and coordinate each of these factors. Inefficient use of scarce resources is possible if these factors are not coordinated properly. This has the potential to significantly impact the revenue (or variety) of services offered by motels and other establishments (Alreahi et al., 2023). Supplier leaders must maintain a fine equilibrium between employees, procedures, and technology across the entire supply chain, from research and development to marketing and sales to strategic management, to guarantee that their products and services meet the needs of their clientele.

13.2.3 GREEN SCM PRACTICES IN HOTELS

Supply chain management (SCM) practice refers to the internal operations of a company aimed at improving SCM effectiveness. In the near term, SCM aims to boost earnings and cut down on stockpiles and turnaround times, while in the long run, SCM aims to expand its customer base and streamline the supply chain (Koh et al., 2007).

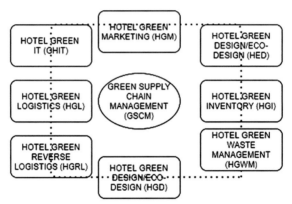

FIGURE 13.1 Green supply chain management (GSCM) practices.

Source: Authors.

13.2.4 HOTEL GREEN WASTE MANAGEMENT

Khan et al. (2019) propose a multiobjective location–allocation model backed by planning heuristics for the entire solid refuse management system (collection, transportation, incineration, composting, recycling, and disposal). Schöggl et al. show a decision support system for regional urban waste management that can help assess broad collection policies and pinpoint prime locations for waste treatment and disposal facilities (2017). To decide the optimal placement of waste disposal and treatment centers within a transportation network, Giannikos (1998) employs a multiobjective model. Schöggl et al. (2017) apply different quantitative modeling strategies to the field of waste administration.

13.2.5 GREEN HOTEL PROCUREMENT

This is also dubbed hotel ecofriendly procurement. When it comes to environmental buying, "green" means actively engaging in practices like material reduction, material reuse, and material recycling. Selecting products and services that are better for the climate is part of the purchasing process. Green purchasing is a strategy for favoring products and services that do not negatively affect the ecosystem (Arora, 2020; Sarkis and Duo, 2018). In addition to being an answer for ecoconscious and frugal businesses, "green procurement" is the practice of buying goods and services that have a low ecological footprint (Khan et al., 2019). Environmental requirements for purchased items should be specified in the design specification provided to suppliers, and the company should work together with its suppliers to achieve its environmental goals, conduct environmental audits of the supplier's internal management, and be ISO 14001 certified. It also aids in raising awareness among consumers about environmental issues (Arora, 2020). Buying biodegradable paper is a good illustration. Sustainable buying is a vital part of green supply chain management. Buying has recently been seen as only a financial consideration; however, new studies on buying practices show that it is also intrinsically linked with environmental management (Ananda et al., 2018). Improvements in organizational performance, as well as monetary and ecological considerations, have been found to be positively impacted by environmentally conscious buying practices (Liobikiene et al., 2016). Many businesses now use ecofriendly buying practices. The strategies range in scope and purpose, and their effects on the ecological habits of service suppliers vary. It emphasizes goods that are better for the environment. Customers who value sustainability are likely to reward the company with increased market share if given the option between conventional and ecofriendly options (Khoiruman and Haryanto, 2017).

13.2.6 HOTEL GREEN INVENTORY

Effective ordering and the maintenance of a wide variety of goods and supplies are facilitated by the stock control strategies that hotels employ. In addition to reconciling or adjusting inventory after actual counts, inventory management systems are also used to generate reports on which suppliers and vendors have the best prices (Khan and Qianli, 2017). Popular inventory management tools today, such as those created by Motorola, can scan bar codes to provide instant visibility into stock upon delivery and instantaneous order reconciliation, greatly streamlining the stocking and receiving processes. As a result, we now have access to up-to-the-minute data that can prevent waste, solve stock-out problems, and improve precision (Motorola Solutions, 2012).

13.2.7 HOTEL ECOFRIENDLY/GREEN DESIGN

When companies design their manufacturing processes with the environment in mind, they are said to practice ecodesign (Kuo et al., 2018). The term "Green Design" refers to the method employed to create goods and services that are gentler on the planet. Alternative names for "green design" include ecodesign, design for the ecosystem, and life cycle design. The essence of green design is the creation of goods that are recyclable, reusable, and harmless to the natural world (Arora, 2020). The term "green design" has been widely used to refer to product development that takes environmental factors into account and new product and process creation that takes environmental and health safety concerns into account throughout the design process (Machogu, 2014). Ecodesign practices that mitigate the manufacturing process's environmental impacts improve businesses' effectiveness and output. One example of these measures is the increased output of businesses that make use of renewable energy sources in their production processes (Aziziankohan et al., 2017). Its scope extends to a wide range of fields, such as pollution prevention, resource-saving, waste management, and product safety. It is a common practice to find an alternative to a possibly dangerous material or process. The rapid depletion of a scarce resource or the increased extraction of other environmentally problematic materials may be unintended consequences of this apparently reasonable action. Khan and Qianli give multiple instances of such ambiguous proposals (2017). Principle and method can both be used to describe ecodesign. The standards for environmental safety are placed ahead of the product's or service's useful lifespan. Ecodesigns are based on the principle of reducing or eliminating environmental impacts during product development, use, and removal. Ecodesign can be implemented at each stage of a product's life cycle, beginning with the procurement of raw materials and continuing through production, distribution, and ultimately consumption by end users (Jumady and Fajriah, 2020). The hotels have implemented an ecodesign methodology that begins with the procurement of raw materials and extends to wholesalers, manufacturers, service providers, and ultimately, guests. Ecodesign incorporates the entire value chain operations of the product (Arshad Ali et al., 2020).

13.2.8 HOTEL GREEN LOGISTICS

Kusuma et al. (2022) say that in the process of purchasing a product for operational reasons, every logistics activity considers the following factors: (a) Green Packaging refers to the practice of buying products while also giving thought to their packaging, which can be done by using recyclable plastic, natural packaging, and so on. (b) Delivery and Transportation of Products Process ensures that the ordered products arrive safely by using a proper method and a suitable vehicle. (c) Storage areas that follow a FIFO (First In, First Out) or FEFO (First Everything, First Out) system (First Expired, First Out). In order to preserve the high standards of the products bought within a predetermined time frame, both of these warehouse systems are employed depending on the characteristics of the goods to be stored (Jia and Wang, 2019).

13.2.9   GREEN HOTEL REVERSE LOGISTICS

While traditional logistics deals with the upward movement of raw materials, reverse logistics is concerned with the management of their backward movements. Simply put, reverse logistics entails transporting used items back to their original manufacturer for refurbishment, refilling, recycling, or destruction (Arora, 2020). Some universal features of reverse logistics networks include a need for coordination between two marketplaces, unpredictability in supplies, choices in how returns are to be handled, delays, and speculation. For a truly sustainable delivery system, green packaging and logistics are essential. Size, shape, and material choices in packaging all affect how practical the product is to move and, thus, how widely it can be dispersed. By improving packaging and rearranging loading patterns, we can save on storage and transportation costs, as well as cut down on labor hours spent on material processing.

13.2.10   GREEN HOTEL INFORMATION TECHNOLOGY

When it comes to IT, best practices center on data collected and stored in the GSCM. Hotels can save money by integrating and electronically distributing information about customer orders across multiple platforms (Shevchuk and Oinas-Kukkonen, 2016). Supply chain managers can maintain an edge in today's rapidly evolving business climate through strategic data collection and analysis (Su et al., 2014). Holsapple et al. (2015) argue that knowledge is one of the most significant sources of long-term competitive advantage. Therefore, it is crucial for supply chain managers to learn about GSCM tactics. Information technology has altered the traditional supplier–customer relationship. Companies have seen improvements in cycle time, order fill rates, inventory at the appropriate safety stock level, and customer service as a result of the integration of various information systems, such as Point of Sale, to aid in forecasting data, monitor inventory levels, and track sales trends (Shevchuk and Oinas-Kukkonen, 2016). Green information systems became an important part of green supply chain management as a means to eradicate environmental problems. The processes, software, and other associated technologies that contribute to a green information system's ability to aid in a company's sustainable performance and support its individual, organizational, social, and environmental aims are all part of environmental sustainability (Recker, 2016). In green information systems, data plays a crucial role. The study of product life cycles, environmental management, and the development of environmentally friendly procedures all benefit from green data. The success of environmentally conscious information systems is highly dependent on the company's information technology resources (Anthony, 2016).

13.2.11 HOTEL GREEN MARKETING

When offering a product or service, green marketers highlight its positive impact on the planet. Sustainable business practices, environmentally friendly goods and packaging, clear explanations of those benefits, etc. are all part of it (Emeritus, 2022). In green marketing, consumers' wants are met while causing minimal damage to the ecosystem (Hanif et al., 2019). According to Yildiz et al. (2019), "green marketing" is the process of making ecofriendly decisions at every stage of the product life cycle. The focus of this research is on green marketing as a form of advertising. Businesses that prioritize environmental protection and long-term sustainability by investing in green marketing see increased customer loyalty and a good brand reputation as side effects. However, this is only the beginning. Businesses looking to make a change and expand their reach, particularly among their ideal customers, have a lot to gain from embracing green marketing strategies. While some companies attempt to greenwash their way to success, others who are environmentally conscious for real often fail to connect with customers despite bearing the additional costs associated with doing so. Companies that are conscious of their impact on the climate must improve their ability to persuade others through their words. Using ecofriendly advertising techniques, businesses can reach a wider customer base. Concern about the impact of multinational companies on the environment is rising among consumers (Indeed, 2023).

Green marketing is especially effective for pioneering businesses that are the first in their field to provide an environmentally friendly option. As more and more consumers become environmentally conscientious, they actively search for businesses that make sustainable claims. As a result, companies can increase sales and customer loyalty by repositioning their products using green marketing strategies (Indeed, 2023). Companies that care about their clients' preferences have started making ecofriendly products. Businesses must make wholesale changes to their supply chains if they are to respond to green marketing. Consumers are more likely to consider the environmental effects of their purchasing decisions if prominent companies demonstrate responsible practices (Emeritus, 2022).

13.2.12 BENEFITS OF GSCM IN HOTELS

Hotel chains are frequently reluctant to implement environmentally friendly procedures as they worry it will happen at the cost of the business's bottom line. It is still the most important concern for businesses. Going green often requires investing more money upfront to make necessary adjustments and runs the risk of reducing efficiency. However, you can make your vendor network more environmentally friendly by using a variety of low-cost, relatively safe methods. Taking steps to reduce environmental impact does not require an immediate transition to driverless vehicles and a halt in business. In order to control costs, oversee and minimize risks, and correctly push these modifications in guests and collaborators, hotel managers can apply them incrementally.

The provider and the hotel both gain from the streamlined processes of the supply chain. Skilled management, in the form of the creation of sound buying policies, helps to fortify ties between the hotel and its suppliers (Sarkis and Duo, 2018). As a corollary, this may cause businesses to prioritize a select group of reliable vendors over an expansive network of less-effective ones. Finding new, more effective vendors is possible, which would boost productivity. It aids in the constant assessment and enhancement of the purchasing procedure and results in significant cost savings. An intense market study could either result in a broader selection of products or a slimmed-down catalog or a better preparation for the future with updated managerial data. Customers are attracted to businesses with sustainable supply chains, and businesses have more chances to work together and form partnerships as a result. Today's companies plan their partnerships with great care. Companies that follow ISO 14001 and other worldwide sustainability standards are therefore often preferred (The international standard for environmental management systems). Implementing a sustainability strategy is a great way to increase your customer base as many contemporary customers will simply refuse to buy your goods if they go against their personal environmental values. Sustainable hotel practices span the entire supply chain, from partnering with environmentally aware suppliers to using recyclable or biodegradable containers.

Supply chain sustainability goes beyond mere natural concerns. Despite its importance, there is another growing contributor: supply chain resilience. Your supply chain can not only endure but thrive, over decades of difficulties, if you optimize it to achieve more environmentally sustainable practices. Gaining insight into how hotels manage their operations sustainably can help you avoid many possible pitfalls and improve your productivity. Businesses should conduct supply chain risk assessments to identify any possibly harmful practices before they have an adverse effect on workers, customers, or the environment. This is the foundational first step in eliminating those dangers. Since logistics and supply chain processes use so much fuel and move products from place to place, resulting in a great deal of greenhouse gas emissions, they have a duty to reduce the negative effects of their operations on the environment. Streamlining logistics reduces the number of miles that various modes of transportation have to travel, which in turn reduces the likelihood that the company will incur fines for violating environmental laws. Another benefit of sustainability is the ability to ship large quantities of products over great distances.

Local and national governments (and their constituents) are joining consumers in pressing companies to do more to improve the environment. If these parties ever have a need for the services of a logistics provider, they may look favorably upon your business if your logistics and supply chain procedures are environmentally friendly (Joloda, 2023).

13.3 DISCUSSIONS

This centralized study deepens our familiarity with the connection between GSCM's many facets and the positive effects the practice has on lodgings. There are not many studies that look at GSCM practices, so this one is significant because it examines eight aspects of GSCM applications and how they affect hotels. One can sum up the environmentally friendly methods that make up Green Supply Chains as follows: environmentally friendly purchasing, green distribution and warehousing, green transportation via the use of biofuels, green manufacturing processes, and finally, green end-of-life management. Green Supply Chain Management (GSCM) seeks to implement strategies for sustainable development by balancing economic benefits with environmental performance in the face of rising community and customer pressure, stricter laws and regulations, and the possibility of cost savings in energy consumption and administrative overhead. In light of the rising cost of doing business in today's global economy, GSCM has emerged as a leading cost-cutting strategy (Sarkis and Dou, 2018). In order to boost competitiveness strategies across all industries, GSCM mandates that businesses strike a better balance between performance and environmental issues that give birth to new problems, such as lowering energy consumption and pollution levels (Jumady and Fajriah, 2020). Since the competitive character of businesses has shifted from organizational to supply chain bases, measuring supply chain implementation has received more attention, as stated by Montabon et al. (2016). By increasing resource-saving, decreasing hazardous materials, and employing product recycling procedures, the green supply chain seeks to lessen a product's ecological impact over the course of its entire lifecycle (Sezen and Ankaya, 2016). Businesses that implement GSCM may see an increase in their fundamental viability and a subsequent boost to economic growth (Zhuo and Wei, 2017). The term "Green Supply Chain Management" refers to a relatively new approach to business management that emphasizes the conservation of natural resources and the reduction of operational waste (Jia and Wang, 2019). GSCM has risen to the forefront of business cost efficiency in today's increasingly competitive market because of its importance in helping hotels strike a balance between economic benefits, environmental performance, and potential benefits from energy savings or reduced management costs. Thus, in the evolution of the lodging industry, green products, green design, green material management, green manufacturing processes, green distribution and marketing, and reverse logistics are all elements of green supply chain management, as described by Ghobakhlo (2013). As part of an initiative to support green hotel policies, the purchasing process itself must be executed in the correct location, a purchasing concept related to environmentally friendly product design. Suppliers are selected for the green procurement system, and suppliers are only considered if they are ISO 14000 certified and have certificates related to achievements in the green concept. Materials are only purchased from "green partners" who have environmental quality standards and pass the audit process. Kusuma et al. (2022) backed up the claims made by Khan et al. (2019) and defined green logistics as the following: "the process of acquiring a product for operational purposes, wherein all logistics activities take into consideration the following elements: Green Packaging, Delivery and Transportation, and Warehousing". Enterprise managers can improve their companies' ecofriendly actions and waste diversion rates by employing efficient GSCM practices, as stated by Mirghafoori et al. (2017). However, business managers still lacked an understanding of how GSCM methods affect productivity. Zhuo and Wei (2017) state that when GSCM is put into action, both the economy and the environment gain. Businesses that implement GSCM may see an increase in their fundamental viability and a subsequent boost to economic growth (Zhuo and Wei, 2017).

13.4 IMPLICATIONS

The study's results provided information that could be used by GSCM managers to zero in on the most effective methods of GSCM for gaining an edge in the hotel industry. The hotel business can gain a sustainable competitive advantage for individual hotel companies through the implementation of a widely recognized supply chain management and logistics system. In order to comply with international regulations concerning the reduction of releases, garbage, efficient use of resources, and general environmental preservation, the management of hotels should implement ISO 14001 environmental norms. Effective transportation and supply chain management can boost the hotel's service and standards while also reducing expenses. In order to provide better service to customers, it is essential for workers in this business to establish reliable relationships with their suppliers and use an efficient ordering system. Customers are of utmost significance to the hotel business, and guest satisfaction is a top priority. In order to achieve a healthy balance between immediate achievement (as measured by financial parameters) and long-term success (as determined by nonfinancial factors), hotel managers should implement BSC to translate competitive strategies into key performance indicators (KPIs). The hospitality business places a premium on customer-facing functions like food and beverage preparation and service, maintenance, and front desk administration. Accounting, buying, supply chain management, income recording, and similar back-office tasks are neglected. In order to gain a competitive edge, businesses should implement GSCM practices across their supply chains, engaging not only their own employees but also their suppliers and customers. Hotel executives should focus on green buying, production, distribution, wrapping, marketing, learning about the environment, internal environmental management, investment recovery, and external environmental management. Finally, hotel managers should create a comprehensive framework that includes policies, procedures, and role definitions for every staff member communicating with the operational and strategic implementation of green practices.

13.5 CONCLUSIONS

The way things are going in the industrial and service sectors right now is bad for the planet, and one day the harm will be permanent. Since GSCM is essential for maintaining a sustainable planet, it follows that the right approach can be taken by businesses and services to lessen their negative impact. The provider and the hotel both gain from the streamlined processes of the supply chain. Supply chain management that is both efficient and cost-effective reduces those three factors. Just-in-time supply chains, in which rising demand at stores triggers immediate production, have become the norm. Through the implementation of sound purchasing policies, expert management helps strengthen the bond between the hotel and its suppliers. As a corollary, this may cause businesses to prioritize a select group of reliable vendors over an expansive network of less-effective ones. Hotels would benefit from the discovery of new, more effective vendors. Significant savings can be realized, and the process of purchasing lodging and meals can be evaluated and refined in an ongoing manner. An intense market study could either result in a broader selection of products or a slimmed-down catalog or more accurate forecasts of the hotel's and guests' needs for the future. Through the design phase, supplier phase, distribution phase, packaging phase, warehousing phase, and reuse of a product that is a concern in product selection, GSCM is integrated with green hotel policies implemented in environmentally friendly business practices from the very beginning. Products that have a positive influence on human health, the environment, and the efficiency and cost-effectiveness of their use, like vegetable foods and an aerated atmosphere, have been successful. This is due to the fact that a green supply chain has the potential to cut down on pollution and production costs while simultaneously stimulating economic growth, creating competitive advantage through increased customer satisfaction, enhancing the company's public image, and giving exporters a leg up on the international market. Corporate social responsibility, green manufacturing, waste reduction, recycling, and remanufacturing are all examples of environmentally responsible practices that contribute to a more comprehensive understanding of what it means to be green.

KEYWORDS

- **GSCM**
- **green distribution**
- **green design**
- **green procurement/purchasing**
- **green packaging**
- **reverse logistics**
- **green logistics**
- **green waste management**

REFERENCES

Abdul-Rashid, S. H.; Sakundarini, N.; Ghazilla, R. A. R.; Thurasamy, R. The Impact of Sustainable Manufacturing Practices on Sustainability Performance: Empirical Evidence from Malaysia. *Int. J. Oper. Prod. Manag.* **2017**, *37*, 182–204. DOI: 10.1108/IJOPM-04-2015-0223

Ahmad, A.; Ikram, A.; Rehan, M. F.; Ahmad, A. Going Green: Impact of Green Supply Chain Management Practices on Sustainability Performance. *Front. Psychol.* **2022**, *13*, 973676. DOI: 10.3389/fpsyg.2022.973676

Ali, S. B. Industrial Revolution 4.0 and Supply Chain Digitization. *SA J. Soc. Rev.* **2022**, *1* (1), 21–41.

Alreahi, M.; Bujdosó, Z.; Dávid, L. D.; Gyenge, B. Green Supply Chain Management in Hotel Industry: A Systematic Review. *Sustainability* **2023**, *15*, 5622. https://doi.org/10.3390/su15075622

Ananda, A. R. W.; Astuty, P.; Nugroho, Y. C. Role of Green Supply Chain Management in Embolden Competitiveness and Performance: Evidence from Indonesian Organizations. *Int. J. Supp. Chain Manag.* **2018**, *7*, 437–442.

Anthony, B. J. Green Information Systems Integration in Information Technology Based Organizations: An Academic Literature Review. *J. Soft Comput. Decis. Supp. Syst.* **2016**, *3*, 45–66.

Arora, K. Green Supply Chain Management: Need, Advantages and Challenges. LinkedIn, 2 Feb 2020. https://www.linkedin.com/pulse/green-supply-chain-management-need-advantages-challenges-keshav-arora

Arshad Ali, A.; Mahmood, A.; Ikram, A.; Ahmad, A. Configuring the Drivers and Carriers of Process Innovation in Manufacturing Organizations. *J. Open Innov.* **2020,** *6*, 154. DOI: 10.3390/joitmc6040154

Arshad Ali, A.; Mahmood, A.; Ikram, A.; Ahmad, A. Configuring the Drivers and Carriers of Process Innovation in Manufacturing Organizations. *J. Open Innov.* **2020,** *6*, 154. DOI: 10.3390/joitmc6040154

Aslam, M. M. H.; Waseem, M.; Khurram, M.; Impact of Green Supply Chain Management Practices on Corporate Image: Mediating Role of Green Communications. *Pak. J. Comm. Soc. Sci.* **2019,** *13* (3), 581–598.

Awan, U.; Kraslawski, A.; Huiskonen, J. Understanding the Relationship Between Stakeholder Pressure and Sustainability Performance in Manufacturing Firms in Pakistan. *Proc. Manuf.* **2017,** *11*, 768–777. DOI: 10.1016/j.promfg. 2017.07.178

Ayaz, J. Relationship between Green Supply Chain Management, Supply Chain Quality Integration, and Environmental Performance. *SA Manag. Rev.* **2022,** *1* (1), 22–38.

Aziziankohan, A.; Jolai, F.; Khalilzadeh, M.; Soltani, R.; Tavakkoli Moghaddam, R. Green Supply Chain Management Using the Queuing Theory to Handle Congestion and Reduce Energy Consumption and Emissions from Supply Chain Transportation Fleet. *J. Ind. Eng. Manag.* **2017,** *10*, 213–236. DOI: 10.3926/ jiem.2170

Baloch, N.; Rashid, A. Supply Chain Networks, Complexity, and Optimization in Developing Economies: A Systematic Literature Review and Meta-Analysis. *South Asian J. Operat. Logist.* **2022,** *1* (1), 1–13.

Chen, M. H.; Wei, H.; Wei, M.; Huang, H.; Su, C. H. J. Modeling a Green Supply Chain in the Hotel Industry: An Evolutionary Game Theory Approach. *Int. J. Hosp. Manag.* **2021,** *92* (1), 102716–102727. https://doi.org/10.1016/j.ijhm.2020.102716

Cingoski, V.; Petrevska, B. Making Hotels More Energy Efficient: The Managerial Perception. *Econ. Res.—Ekonomska istraživanja* **2018,** *31* (1), 87–101. https://doi.org/10.1080/1331 677X.2017.1421994

Emeritus. How Green Marketing Helps Brands Build Loyalty While Saving the Plane, 9 Dec 2022. https://emeritus.org/blog/sales-and-marketing-green-marketing/#:~:text=Green%20 marketing%20focuses%20on%20selling,benefits%20of%20the%20product%2C%20etc.

Filimonau, V.; Tochukwu, C. O. Exploring Managerial Approaches to Mitigating Solid Waste in Hotels of Lagos, Nigeria. *J. Clean. Prod.* **2020,** *270* (1), 122410–122418. https://doi.org/10.1016/j.jclepro.2020.122410

Galeazzo, A.; Ortiz-de-mandojana, N.; Delgado-Ceballos, J. Green Procurement and Financial Performance in the Tourism Industry: The Moderating Role of Tourists' Green Purchasing Behavior. *Curr. Iss. Tour.* **2021,** *24* (5), 1–17. https://doi.org/10.1080/1368350 0.2020.1734546

Hanif, H.; Rakhman, A.; Nurkholis, M.; Pirzada, K.; Intellectual Capital: Extended VAIC Model and Building of a New HCE Concept: The Case of Padang Restaurant Indonesia. *Afr. J. Hosp. Tour. Leisure* **2019,** *8*, 1–15.

Husaini, Pirzada, K.; Saiful, Risk Management, Sustainable Governance Impact on Corporate Performance. *J. Secur. Sustain. Iss.* **2020,** *9* (3), 993–1004.

Ikram, A.; Su, Q.; Fiaz, M.; Rehman, R. U. Cluster Strategy and Supply Chain Management: The Road to Competitiveness for Emerging Economies. *Benchmarking* **2018,** *25*, 1302–1318. DOI: 10.1108/BIJ-06-2015-0059

Indeed. What Is Green Marketing? Definition, Benefits and Strategies, 4 Feb 2023. https://www.indeed.com/career-advice/career-development/green-marketing

Joloda. 2023. https://www.joloda.com/news/the-benefits-of-sustainable-logistics/

Khan, S. A. R.; Qianli, D. Impact of Green Supply Chain Management Practices on Firms' Performance: An Empirical Study from the Perspective of Pakistan. *Environ. Sci. Pollut. Res.* **2017**, *24*, 16829–16844. DOI: 10.1007/s11356-017-9172-5

Khan, S. A. R.; Jian, C.; Yu, Z.; Golpîra, H.; Kumar, A. Impact of Green Practices on Pakistani Manufacturing Firm Performance: A Path Analysis Using Structural Equation Modeling Computational Intelligence and Sustainable Systems. In *Computational Intelligence and Sustainable Systems*; Springer, 2019; pp 87–97. DOI: 10.1007/978-3-030-02674-5_6

Khoiruman, M.; Haryanto, A. T. Green Purchasing Behavior Analysis of Government Policy About Paid Plastic Bags. *Indonesian J. Sustain. Account. Manag.* **2017**, *1*, 31–39. DOI: 10.28992/ijsam.v1i1.25

Kot, S.; Kozicka, K.; Supply Chain Management Evidence from Tourism Industry in Greece. *J. Environ. Manag. Tour.* **2018**, *9* (4), 683–693.

Kuo, T. C.; Tseng, M.-L.; Lin, C. H.; Wang, R.-W.; Lee, C.-H. Identifying Sustainable Behavior of Energy Consumers as a Driver of Design Solutions: The Missing Link in Eco-Design. *J. Clean. Prod.* **2018**, *192*, 486–495. DOI: 10.1016/j.jclepro.2018.04.250

Kusuma, K. A. W. A.; Mandravickait'e, J.; Bernatonien'e, J. Green Supply Chain Management as Competitive Advantage at Discovery. Repository Politeknik Negeri Bali, 2022. https://repository.pnb.ac.id

Liobikiene, G.; Mandravickait e, J.; Bernatonien e, J. Theory of Planned Behavior Approach to Understand the Green Purchasing Behavior in the EU: A Cross-Cultural Study. *Ecol. Econ.* **2016**, *125*, 38–46. DOI: 10.1016/j.ecolecon.2016. 02.008

Machogu, W. N. Factors Influencing the Adoption of Green Supply Chain Management Strategy in Industries: A Case of Delmonte Company. *Int. Acad. J. Inf. Sci. Project Manag.* **2014**, 1 (2), 1–21.

Masa'deh, R.; Alananzeh, O.; Algiatheen, N.; Ryati, R.; Albayyari, R.; Tarhini, A. The Impact of Employee's Perception of Implementing Green Supply Chain Management on Hotel's Economic and Operational Performance. *J. Hosp. Tour. Technol.* **2017**, *8* (3), 395–416. https://doi.org/10.1108/JHTT-02-2017-0011

Mirghafoori, S. H.; Andalib, D.; Keshavarz, P. Developing Green Performance Through Supply Chain Agility in Manufacturing Industry: A Case Study Approach. *Corp. Soc. Respons. Environ. Manag.* **2017**, *24*, 368–381. https://doi.org/10.1002/csr.1411

Motorola Solutions 2012. Inventory Management Solution for the Hospitality, 2012. http://www.motorola.com/Business/USEN/Business+Solutions/Industry+Solutions/Hospi tality/Inventory+Management+Solutions+for+Hospitality_US-EN

Muhammad, A. H. Importance of Green Supply Chain Management in Hospitality Business. *SA J. Operat. Logist.* **2022**, *1* (2), 1–15. DOI: 10.57044/SAJOL.2022.1.2.2206

Rao, P.; Holt, D. Do Green Supply Chains Lead to Competitiveness and Economic Performance? *Int. J. Operat. Prod. Manag.* **2005**, *25*, 898–916. DOI: 10.1108/01443570510613956

Recker, J. Toward a Design Theory for Green Information Systems. Paper presented at the 2016 49th Hawaii International Conference on System Sciences (HICSS); IEEE: Koloa, 2016. DOI: 10.1109/HICSS.2016.556

Robertson, J.; Barling, L.; Toward, J. New Measure of Organizational Environmental Citizenship Behavior. *J. Bus. Res.* **2017**, *75*, 57–66.

Schöggl, J.-P.; Baumgartner, R. J.; Hofer, D. Improving Sustainability Performance in Early Phases of Product Design: A Checklist for Sustainable Product Development Tested in the Automotive Industry. *J. Clean. Prod.* **2017**, *140*, 1602–1617. DOI: 10.1016/j. jclepro.2016.09.195

Seethamraju, R. C.; Frost, G. Deployment of Information Systems for Sustainability Reporting and Performance. 25th Americas Conference on Information Systems, AMCIS 2019, Cancún, Mexico, August 15–17, 2019, Atlanta, GA,

Seles, B. M. R. P.; de Sousa Jabbour, A. B. L.; Jabbour, C. J. C.; Dangelico, R. M. The Green Bullwhip Effect, the Diffusion of Green Supply Chain Practices, and Institutional Pressures: Evidence from the Automotive Sector. *Int. J. Prod. Econ.* **2016**, *182*, 342–355. DOI: 10.1016/j.ijpe.2016.08.033

Shevchuk, N.; Oinas-Kukkonen, H. Exploring Green Information Systems and Technologies as Persuasive Systems: A Systematic Review of Applications in Published Research. In: *CIS 2016 Proceedings*; Dublin, 2016.

Yan, M. R.; Chien, K. M.; Yang, T. N. Green Component Procurement Collaboration for Improving Supply Chain Management in the High Technology Industries: A Case Study from the Systems Perspective. *Sustainability* **2016**, *8*, 105. https://doi.org/10.3390/su8020105

Yildiz Çankaya, S.; Sezen, B. Effects of Green Supply Chain Management Practices on Sustainability Performance. *J. Manuf. Technol. Manag.* **2019**, *30*, 98–121. https://doi.org/10.1108/JMTM-03-2018-0099

Zhao, R.; Liu, Y.; Zhang, N.; Huang, T. An Optimization Model for Green Supply Chain Management by Using a Big Data Analytic Approach. *J. Clean. Prod.* **2017**, 142, 1085–1097. https://doi.org/10.1016/j.jclepro.2016.03.006

Zhuo, H.; Wei, S. Gaming of Green Supply Chain Members Under Government Subsidies—Based on the Perspective of Demand Uncertainty. In: *Proceedings of the Tenth International Conference on Management Science and Engineering Management*; 2017; pp 1105–1116. https://doi.org/10.1007/978-981-10-1837-4_91

CHAPTER 14

Green Procurement

FATAWU ALHASSAN[1], SHERIFATU ABAS[2], STANLEY COWTHER[1], and SUSSANA ANTWI-BOASIAKO[2]

[1]Tamale Technical University, Tamale, Ghana

[2]Accra Technical University, Accra, Ghana

ABSTRACT

Since more and more people are opting to buy ecological products, green has become the color of the day. For instance, switching to nonhazardous cleaning supplies can lessen the number of cases of asthma, allergies, burns, eye damage, and even cancer that have been linked to the dangerous compounds found in many conventional cleaners. Incorporating green buying practices into an organization's operations is an example of a system-wide workflow improvement that adds up to a smaller environmental impact. Rather than taking on their providers' economic and ecological risks, businesses can mitigate them through green buying. Or, businesses can work with their suppliers right from the start of the planning process, or they can establish a system to identify and select only providers who practice sustainable business practices. Organizations can benefit from assessments and comparisons in this regard. Risk reduction, ecoefficiency, improved relationships with suppliers, and enhanced environmental performance are just a few of the ways in which green purchasing can help its users.

14.1 INTRODUCTION

The term "green procurement" has become popular among industrial companies as a means to influence their entire supply chain in a more environmentally friendly direction (Mosgaard, 2015). The term "green procurement" is used to describe the practice of buying products and services that have a negligible effect on the environment. Ecofriendly company practices are on the rise as a result of rising consumer demand for ecofriendly goods like recyclables, energy-efficient infrastructure, and ecofriendly fuels and technologies. For businesses to make informed decisions about the products, supplies, and services they use, a green purchasing or green procurement (GP) strategy is implemented to serve as a guide. When it comes to purchasing goods and services, the way businesses are thinking is changing drastically, and green buying is a major factor in this shift (Bohari, 2017; Skitmore, 2017; Xia and Teo, 2017; Kaur and Singh, 2017). One possibility is for businesses to incorporate social health and environmental concerns into supply chain practices and processes to lessen the impact they have on the environment, particularly with regard to pollution in the air and in buildings, as well as the impact they have on greenhouse gas emissions and energy use (Rebelo, 2016; Santos and Silva, 2016). The word "green purchases" refers to acquisitions that are less harmful to the environment due to their materials and manufacturing processes. The consumption and ultimate disposal of purchased items are also taken into account during the green procurement process. The triple bottom line (TBL) is a paradigm for doing business that emphasizes the interconnectedness of environmental, social, and financial well-being. Purchasing with an eye toward sustainability is called "green," and it aims to save money and resources in the long run while still providing for the needs of a business, its clients, and the community at large. The full product life cycle is considered here, from the initial purchase price to decommissioning fees. Environmental sustainability practices, including fair commerce, ethical employment, and health and safety, are also crucial (Shen et al., 2017a, 2017b). So, the researcher set out to examine the impact of green buying on business operations.

14.2 LITERATURE REVIEW

14.2.1 PROCUREMENT

Acquisition is the method or action of acquiring products or services for an organization. Since businesses typically have largescale needs for both goods and services, the term "procurement" is most often linked with commercial settings. These products and services are essential to the functioning of the company. When properly planned and executed, procurement can help guarantee increased profits for any company. Therefore, it is crucial to regularly inspect and analyze the purchasing procedure, fix any problems discovered, and shore up any vulnerable spots (Rostamzadeh et al., 2015). The acquisition of goods, services, or construction from an outside source, typically through a bid or tendering procedure, is known as procurement. By comparing factors like quality, quantity, time, and location, this method ensures that the buyers get the best value for their money.

14.2.2 GREEN PROCUREMENT/PURCHASING/BUYING

Green buying refers to environmentally responsible purchasing practices like waste minimization, product repurposing, and material recycling. In addition to being an answer for ecoconscious and frugal businesses, "green procurement" is the practice of buying goods and services that have a low ecological footprint (Salam, 2008). Key factors for green purchasing were identified by Sievo (2023) in a global study. These factors include communicating environmental requirements for purchased items to suppliers in advance, working together with suppliers to achieve shared goals, conducting environmental audits of their internal management, and requiring suppliers to be ISO 14001 certified. Green purchasing is a well-known idea in the world of procurement, but it lacks a universally accepted definition. Companies considering the environmental performance of their suppliers' goods and processes is one definition often cited. When a company engages in green procurement, it takes into account nonfinancial measures such as social and economic impact in addition to traditional financial ones such as price and quality. In the past, when a company's budget was tight, cutting costs wherever possible and complying with procurement rules were top priorities. When a company practices "procurement with purpose," it directs a portion of its budget toward solving a global problem. Green purchasing is defined by Carter and Carter (1998) as follows: the purchasing department is actively involved in all aspects of supply chain management and makes every effort to buy recycled or previously owned materials whenever feasible. Green purchasing, as described by Zsidisin and Siferd (2001), entails adhering to a set of principles and methods that are predicated on taking into account the complete effect on the environment. According to Zhu and Geng (2002), "green purchasing" is when "every department in the company consults decision-making to improve business performance by decreasing the use of materials and end treatment costs, protecting resources, enhancing the enterprise image, etc." The elimination of waste was identified by Martha and Houston (2010) as a possible goal of green procurement, and it is expected that the purchasing department will prioritize value by taking into account the full cost of waste elimination. In most cases, preventing waste at the beginning of the supply chain can result in greater savings than doing so at the conclusion. The first step in reducing waste is the buying process, making the state of the company's recycling and reusing programs a crucial factor in the success of green purchasing. Reducing emissions from vehicles, factories, wastewater treatment plants, and other sources was suggested as a key strategy for advancing green procurement by Montalban et al. (2017). Both the technology, equipment, and facilities of waste separation, as well as the purchasing practices of businesses, can be affected by the types of resources available to them. Green purchasing, according to Stock (1992), can boost a company's bottom line by cutting expenses in areas such as disposal and liability while simultaneously preserving resources and enhancing the brand's reputation. The evaluation of second-tier suppliers' environmentally friendly practices was ranked as the second most significant of the ten top environmental supplier evaluation criteria proposed by Nutburn (2019). In addition, major buyers have pushed their vendors to improve environmental performance, which has increased the incentive for suppliers to work together with buyers to achieve environmental goals (Nutburn, 2019). Bristol-Myers Squibb, IBM, and Xerox, to name a few, have all urged or mandated that their Chinese vendors implement ISO 14001-compliant environmental management systems. Ford, General Motors, and Toyota have taken a similar tack (Klufallah et al., 2019). According to research by Min and Galle (1997), the highest-ranked barriers to adopting green purchasing were financial. It is inevitable that the enterprise will incur additional costs associated with green procurement, such as those associated with investing in equipment, training employees, communicating with suppliers, etc., which will result in the company foregoing alternative investment possibilities (Klufallah et al., 2019). These additional expenditures and costs will be categorized as company environmental management expenses in this analysis. It was discovered through a study conducted by Montalban et al. (2017) that suppliers' stress had a greater impact on the implementation of the green supply chain.

14.3 GREEN PROCUREMENT METHODS

14.3.1 LEAN SUPPLY

Lamming (1996) coined the term "lean supply" as a consequence of his study of Japanese supply chain management practices. The Japanese method centered on streamlining their supply chains so they could devote more energy to things like R&D and service expansion. There have been new shifts in how lean supply is implemented in businesses. In order to stay relevant, many businesses are banking on the benefits of implementing lean attributes throughout their supply chains. Lean supply, as defined by Lamming (1996), is an effort to streamline the supply chain such that only value moves through and all resources are used to their full potential. In order to achieve results that are up to par with what the company expects, this process is subjected to constant development.

14.3.2 CLOSED-LOOP SUPPLY CYCLE (CLSC)

The goal of a closed-loop supply cycle (CLSC) is for businesses to behave sustainably throughout the entire lifespan of a product. To lessen their environmental footprint, businesses can purchase goods from vendors who make use of recycled or reused materials. In addition, many companies have repair or recycling programs to help customers extend the life of their goods or responsibly dispose of their leftovers (Dryden, 2021).

14.3.3 TRIPLE-BOTTOM LINE (TBL)

Procurement experts use TBL criteria—including ecological, social, and economic considerations—to evaluate and pick appropriate procurement strategies. By pooling the expertise of various buying groups, we hope to identify a strategy that will minimize the business's financial and social impacts (Dryden, 2021).

14.3.4 E-PROCUREMENT

Business organizations can save time, money, and human error by using the internet for e-procurement, or electronic purchasing, which entails the automation of previously manual tasks like planning, source selection, order processing, payment, and evaluation following the purchase (Klufallah et al., 2019). E-procurement makes it easier to execute profitable business strategies. In the same manner, it has facilitated the adoption of green procurement strategies by doing away with the need for paper and printing solvents (Klufallah et al., 2019). With the help of e-procurement, system integration with suppliers, and a solid customer connection, Garca-Rodrguez (2013) found that the value stream was able to become waste-free by employing measures like repurposing and material reuse.

14.3.5 ETHICAL PROCUREMENT

In order to achieve their own objectives, procurement teams can benefit from engaging in ethical procurement by monitoring and assessing the suppliers' ethical practices. In the event that a supplier's policies, such as those related to conditions at work or misconduct within the business, conflict with the procurement team's ethical goals, the team may look elsewhere for a supplier. Responsible purchasing may be contingent on factors such as adherence to labor and human rights policies (Dryden, 2021).

14.3.6 REVERSE SUPPLY CHAIN (RSC)

The CLSC includes a specialized cycle known as the "reverse supply chain," in which goods are sent back to the manufacturer for maintenance or recycling. Organizations that employ a reverse supply chain advocate for consumers to instead invest in repairs rather than dispose of broken goods. They also ask customers to send back unwanted goods so that less waste ends up in landfills (Dryden, 2021).

14.4 BARRIERS OF GREEN PROCUREMENT

14.4.1 ECOLOGICAL GOODS ARE VIEWED AS MORE EXPENSIVE

Numerous government agencies have named the difficulty of influencing buying department culture as a major obstacle. Choosing between offers based on purchase price alone, rather than considering the total cost of ownership, can discourage the adoption of environmentally friendly options. Adopting ecofriendly purchasing policies may result in slightly higher rates at the register, but in the long run, businesses save money because they spend less on energy, water, and other resources thanks to the reduced need for repairs and replacements. There may be a price premium associated with ecofriendly buying practices. This is because there is a correlation between the price of green goods and their positive impact on the environment or because of the extra steps required to manufacture them. Green purchasing may be more costly than regular purchasing at first. It is important for businesses to know that the savings they will see in the long run from green purchasing will more than compensate for any upfront expenses (European Commission, 2006).

14.4.2 OUTCOMES ARE HARD TO ASSESS

Measuring the environmental advantages of green procurement can be challenging due to the intangible nature of reduced emissions and waste. Because of this, it can be hard to tell if green buying is actually helping.

14.4.3 EXTENSIVE AND TIME-CONSUMING

Buying sustainably can be a time-consuming and difficult process. It is important to be able to tell which vendors a firm can trust and evaluate the ecological credentials of their goods. This can be a time-consuming ordeal.

14.4.4 INADEQUATE KNOWLEDGE OF ENVIRONMENTAL LAWS

It is unreasonable to assume that all purchasers in the public sector are fully aware of the full range of environmental and social impacts of any given transaction. There are still situations in which buyers have difficulty articulating what it means to acquire an "environmentally and/or socially preferable" good or service and how to incorporate the necessary criteria for doing so into the bidding process. It is also difficult to evaluate and confirm the validity of the data submitted by bidders according to environmental criteria.

14.4.5 INADEQUATE INSTRUCTION

In some cases, employees tasked with certain duties lack the necessary expertise or receive inadequate instruction. Procurers need training on the legal and technical aspects of GP implementation, as well as the idea of life-cycle costing, and end-users need training on the green use of products.

14.4.6 ABSENCE OF COOPERATION BETWEEN GOVERNMENT AGENCIES

Worldwide, there has been little in the way of coordinated efforts to adopt GP, with most government agencies instead proceeding largely independently and sometimes on their own initiative. In order to improve GP, we need to see a rise in both informal and official cooperation. One thing holding back wider GP adoption is a dearth of authorities talking to each other and sharing what works (European Commission, 2006).

14.4.7 ECONOMIC

Montalban et al. (2017) state that monetary constraints are one of the most significant barriers to sustainable procurement around the globe. The application of green procurement is hampered by financial concerns for contractors and developers. One common misconception is that investing in long-term sustainability will break the bank. This medium exists because the approach to building and the selection of elements differ from the norm. Capital expenditures need not rise to accommodate sustainable building procurement.

14.4.8 LACK OF STANDARDS FOR GREEN PRODUCTS

In order to incorporate environmental considerations into tendering while meeting the requirements of the Procurement Directives and other sources of procurement legislation, public authorities need access to clear and verifiable criteria for many product and service groups (European Commission, 2006).

14.4.9 LACK OF AWARENESS

It has been my experience that many businesses do not understand the environmental implications of their purchases. When this happens, companies may make purchases without considering the long-term effects of their decisions on the atmosphere (European Commission, 2006).

14.4.10 REDUCED SUPPLY CHOICES

The accessibility of green goods may be a barrier to environmentally responsible purchasing. This may occur when there is no other option or when certain ecofriendly products are in short supply. Sometimes, vendors just do not have enough ecofriendly options to satisfy businesses' demands. There is also the possibility that vendors do not have what it takes to adhere to a firm's stringent environmental measures (European Commission, 2006).

14.4.11 ENVIRONMENTAL

Rais et al. (2018) state that the biggest barrier to enacting green procurement is a lack of stakeholder comprehension. According to Khan et al. (2018), this channel was chosen because many professionals think that developers are unfamiliar with green procurement and do not grasp its meaning or its significance in the building industry. Managers are unsure of how to integrate sustainability concerns into the purchasing procedure. According to Buniamin et al. (2016), there is still a lack of qualified personnel to manage green buying.

14.4.12 SOCIAL

Green procurement faces significant challenges, including reluctance to change, as stated by Bohari and Bo (2015) and Buniamin et al. (2016). Customers and other project stakeholders show less interest in the structure as a result of this resistance to change, which has a negative effect on supply. Demand from consumers and their preparedness to make green purchases are two crucial drivers of this sector's expansion. The growing awareness among consumers about the importance of sustainable business practices is a major motivator for change. Many people have set ways that they always do their jobs, and it can be challenging to get them to consider new ways of doing things, especially when it comes to more common practices like using older, more conventional building methods and tools (Klufallah et al., 2019).

14.4.13 BENEFITS OF GREEN PROCUREMENT

In addition to lessening negative effects on the natural world, green purchases can improve people's quality of life in other ways, such as their financial stability.

14.4.14 ALLIANCE FORMATION IS A DISTINCT POSSIBILITY

This one might not be as clear-cut. Many other businesses will be more interested in forming partnerships with a company that has a green supply network. The ethical credibility of the company will probably mesh with the ethics of another brand. As a result, doors for future collaboration have opened (Nutburn, 2019).

14.4.15 REPUTATION ENHANCEMENT

More and more consumers are showing a preference for environmentally and socially conscious companies, so adhering to a green procurement strategy can only help a firm's brand's public image. By using a GP, a firm's company can be open and honest about the goods and services it purchases, the vendors it backs, and its spending habits with its customers, workers, and other stakeholders (Soto, 2021). The introduction of a doctor is yet another demonstration of the firm's dedication to environmental and social responsibility.

14.4.16 POSITIVE EFFECTS ON THE EARTH

Climate change, unsustainable consumption of primary resources, deforestation, air, water, and soil pollution, waste generation, and packaging waste are just a few of the environmental issues that green buying policies aim to address. The goal is to lessen the environmental damage caused by manufactured goods. Incorrect assumptions circulate that minimizing a company's negative effects on the environment will force them to fork over more money. Money can be saved as a result. Quick payoffs are possible through waste reduction and efficiency improvements to infrastructure like buildings, vehicles, and equipment (Slovenska and Prostredia, 2014). Green procurement, as defined by Sievo (2023), aims to help the environment in a variety of ways including, but not limited to, the following: lowering greenhouse gas emissions; increasing energy efficiency and resource usage; decreasing air, water, and soil pollution; eliminating toxic substances from the manufacturing process; decreasing waste and effluent; eliminating unnecessary processes or packaging; and/or establishing requirements for reuse and recycling.

14.4.17 STRENGTHEN THE AVAILABILITY OF RESOURCES

The supply network should be diversified so that the company is not dependent on any one vendor. Many instances have occurred throughout history in which a provider failed to deliver on a service or product, causing repercussions for other companies (Nutburn, 2019). Having multiple suppliers in various locations helps ensure that a company's products and services are consistently delivered, minimizing the risk of interruptions that could be both financially and strategically disastrous.

14.4.18 MANAGEMENT OF RISK AND MITIGATION OF RISK

The use of harmful products or collaboration with unethical providers can put a company at risk of violating corporate laws, but a GP can help mitigate this risk. A firm will keep the support of the people and protect itself from potential legal trouble (Soto, 2021). This is the situation that led to allegations of child labor against these chocolate business behemoths. Do some serious threat and opportunity analysis for economic, legal, environmental, and societal sustainability, and come up with plans to deal with them (World Bank, 2019).

14.4.19 ACCOUNTING FOR CUSTOMERS

Any business can reap the rewards of turning green by retaining and satisfying the unique demands of its clientele, boosting resource efficiency, and rearranging its value chain (Ford and Despeisse, 2016; Stindt, 2017). According to Pazirandeh and Jafari (2013), small and medium-sized enterprises (SMEs) can reap long-term benefits in the form of increased market share and better profit margins by incorporating green practices into their procurement and supply chain processes. This has led to a rise in the number of environmentally conscious companies around the world, particularly in advanced countries, which aim to provide a higher value to their clientele (Fritz et al., 2017; Rajeev et al., 2017). Therefore, green business is a competitive strategy for managing and generating value for the organization and its clients, much like globalization and cutting-edge technology.

14.4.20 ATTRACTIVENESS

Depending on how well a borrower or project does in terms of social responsibility and sustainability, it could improve the borrower's or project's reputation, increase competition, and give groups an edge. Green buying has the potential to entice additional financial investors, strengthen labor markets, draw in the most competitive bidders, and propel development objectives (World Bank, 2019).

14.4.21 ASSURANCE OF HIGH-QUALITY MATERIALS

The term "green procurement" refers to the practice of purchasing products and services from third parties in a way that minimizes negative impacts on the environment. Everything from sourcing raw materials to recycling finished goods requires high-quality data to aid management in making informed decisions and providing for transparent operations at every stage of the supply chain, from procurement to disposal (Fiorini and Jabbour, 2017; Wu et al., 2017; Han et al., 2017; Wang and Naim, 2017). Effective information quality is a key predictor and enabler of green buying, as stated by De Corbière, Rowe, and Habib (2016). The importance and benefits of high-quality information for green buying processes' transparency and efficiency have been acknowledged (Li and Lin, 2006; Omar, Ramayah et al., 2010; Mafini and Muposhi, 2017).

14.4.22 REVERSE SUPPLY NETWORK

The use of a reverse supply chain is also essential to the success of green buying in SMEs. For a company to maximize its long-term profitability, it must effectively manage its "reverse supply chain," which entails the flow of goods, demand information, and money in the opposite direction of the primary logistics flow; a decrease in waste production; and the collection, transportation, disposal, and recycling of hazardous and nonhazardous waste (De Villiers et al., 2017; Nieman and Niemann, 2017).

14.4.23 HEALTH AND SOCIAL ADVANTAGES

Spending in a more environmentally responsible manner enhances public services and, by extension, people's standard of living. Green buying helps make for cleaner commercial transportation by lowering emissions and pollution (Nutburn, 2019). Cleaning items with fewer toxic chemicals means a healthier workplace (Carrol, 2015). To make a structure safer for its occupants, it should only be constructed with materials that do not include any potentially harmful elements. To quote Sievo (2023), green purchasing has positive societal effects because it encourages businesses to do the following: give back to the neighborhoods where they operate; ensure their workers are paid a fair salary; get their employees involved in community service; and fund initiatives that boost local residents' quality of life.

14.4.24 PARTICIPATION OF WORKERS

By rolling out a GP, a firm can help its staff stay informed about the green practices they should adopt and about the company's bigger sustainability goals. Building a green work ethic and encouraging green behavior outside of work can be accomplished by increasing employees' exposure to and participation in green purchasing (Soto, 2021).

14.4.25 INNOVATION

Sustainable purchasing necessitates an ingenious assessment of present goods and procedures. It is possible that going green with a firm's purchases and vendors will force a firm to reevaluate and revamp some of the firm's business practices. Brands like these are making shoes that are durable and comfortable while still being environmentally friendly by using recycled and biodegradable materials and procuring sustainably (Soto, 2021). Make it a policy to listen to suggestions for improving the firm's environmental performance from employees at all levels and in all divisions. One must always be open to new ideas and inventive approaches.

14.4.26 GAINS TO THE ECONOMY

When the total cost of ownership is calculated, including not only the initial outlay for the product but also its use and eventual disposal, green buying can be cost-effective. Farrell and Shapiro found that consumers valued price information highly (Farrell and Shapiro, 2010). By encouraging environmentally responsible purchases, we can help spur the manufacturing sector's growth, spur the creation of new green technologies, and support the commercialization of these goods. It is possible for environmentally friendly goods and services to rise in popularity as more people make purchases (Slovenska and Prostredia, 2014). A TC strategy for life-cycle costing allows for cost-control, which is one of the many financial benefits of green procurement, as stated by Sievo (2023).

14.4.27 EFFECTIVE USE OF MATERIALS AND LABOR

Increasing resource productivity is as simple as buying green goods and services. General practitioners frequently advise companies to switch to more resource-efficient goods like low-flow faucets and energy-efficient light bulbs (Soto, 2021). A firm's contribution to landfills can be diminished further if it sources its goods from companies that provide them in recyclable or otherwise waste-free packaging. As a result of these efficiencies, the firm's company will save money, and the environment will benefit from less waste (Soto, 2021). Having a GP also boosts productivity because it specifies which environmentally friendly goods everyone should be on the lookout for, and this applies to all facets of the company. Businesses can make trustworthy green purchases with ease when they have access to comprehensive information on their GP needs and product standards (Soto, 2021).

14.4.28 PREVENTING IRREPARABLE HARM TO ONE'S GOOD NAME

A firm's company's supply chain has an impact on its brand reputation because of the open accessibility of information online. Keeping a company's good name intact is crucial to its success (Nutburn, 2019). See to it that the company's approach to sustainability improves the quality of life for all employees. This entails doing things like reducing waste and limiting the negative effects of operations on the earth. Workers should never be exposed to danger. Apple's Chinese factory has been under scrutiny for its poor working conditions in recent years. Some were worried that the new, more affordable iPhone was being made in deplorable conditions.

14.4.29 EMPLOYEE HEALTH AND SAFETY IMPROVED

The health, safety, and well-being of the firm's staff are direct results of the firm's company's commitment to environmentally responsible purchasing practices. If a firm wants to protect itself and its coworkers from harsh, sometimes toxic chemicals, it should use only approved ecofriendly cleaners in the office (Soto, 2021). Investing in locally produced, organic, and environmentally friendly food choices is likely to benefit the health and well-being of the firm's workforce, leading to increased productivity.

14.4.30 BOOSTING THE ECOLOGICALLY SOUND INDUSTRY

Green markets are gaining traction in economies around the globe, and consumers can help foster their growth by continuing to buy truly ecofriendly products and supporting other green businesses. There has never been a better time to buy a product that is good for the environment as there are so many options available (Soto, 2021). The widespread greenwashing in the market can be combated, however, by employing a GP who ensures that only goods that adhere to stringent standards and certifications are purchased. One of the most important aspects of green purchasing is the accessibility of ecofriendly options on the market. A firm's goal should be to locate both domestic and international sources for the goods it intends to purchase. The organization's green procurement strategy should be reflected in the tendering process in order to encourage suppliers to provide environmentally preferable options.

14.4.31 SUCCESSFUL BUSINESS RESULTS IN MORE MONEY

Sustainable purchasing has many potential profit-boosting outcomes. Green purchasing not only attracts and retains customers but also saves money through improved energy economy and less waste. In spite of the fact that many ecofriendly goods are more costly, many are eligible for discounts (Soto, 2021). As was previously stated, using a GP makes ecofriendly shopping much easier. The effort a firm once put into making sense of a crowded marketplace is now free to be applied elsewhere.

14.5 DRIVERS FOR GREEN PROCUREMENT

14.5.1 COST REDUCTION

Reducing the overall cost of ownership is one of the many benefits of adopting environmentally responsible purchasing policies and procedures. This is accomplished through savings in areas such as electricity, overspecification, consumption, and social and environmental compliance expenses.

14.5.2 RISK

Depending on the nature of the danger, various departments and initiatives may need to be implemented. Companies now have a set of rules and guidelines to work within and report against, thanks to the spread of laws and standards (Greenstone, 2023). The costs and risks associated with bad supplier practices like forced labor and environmental degradation can be mitigated if a company adopts green purchasing processes and choices. The financial losses associated with green procurement disruptions, such as violations of environmental laws, would also be avoided.

14.5.3 PROFITS

Innovating ecofriendly goods and charging a premium for them, as well as profiting from recycling initiatives, are all ways in which a company can increase its bottom line by adopting green procurement practices.

14.5.4 RESILIENCE

Any supply chain that cannot bounce back swiftly from setbacks can hardly be called resilient or sustainable (Greenstone, 2023).

14.5.5 RESPONSIBILITY

If toughness implies protection against threats to the supply chain, then accountability implies a greater duty to answer for the results of one's actions (Greenstone, 2023). A sustainable business and supply network will have minimal unfavorable effects on their employees, neighbors, and the environment. Integration of sustainability into buying has been shown to be beneficial in the most developed cases (Greenstone, 2023).

14.5.6 POLICIES

An organization's policies can make promises about its future behavior, goals, and success. Suppliers are increasingly viewed as an extension of the organization; therefore, it is the responsibility of the organization to learn about and assess its suppliers to ensure that they, too, adhere to the standards outlined in pertinent policies (Greenstone, 2023).

14.5.7 OPPORTUNITY

If a company's operations are examined from a sustainability perspective, they will gain clarity and, consequently, more opportunities. This can be achieved in a number of ways, including more mutually beneficial long-term partnerships with vendors, innovative approaches to product and service delivery, and greener, more socially responsible business operations (Greenstone, 2023).

14.5.8 MANAGEMENT SUPPORT

Management of the internal atmosphere includes endorsement and encouragement from higher-ups. Companies' internal management is a crucial element in their success in adopting environmentally friendly procedures (Wu and Barnes, 2016). Management is driven to safeguard the environment by employee pressure, positive reinforcement, and environmental advocacy. At the same time, a shift in how people view environmental risks could have a positive impact on their willingness to embrace green practices (Luthra et al., 2016).

14.5.9 CUSTOMER MANAGEMENT

The role of the consumer is crucial and successful in green supply chains (Sar et al., 2017). There is a lot of strain on businesses in developing countries to implement environmentally friendly supply chain practices in order to keep up with consumer demand and remain profitable (Wu and Barnes, 2016). The benefits of green supply chain management become much easier to achieve with customer cooperation.

14.5.10 THE ADMINISTRATION OF SUPPLIERS

The adoption of green supply chain methods requires the involvement of both customers and suppliers (Wu and Barnes, 2016). When companies and their suppliers work together effectively, they can improve incentive systems and speed up the spread of environmentally responsible innovations. Improvements in operational and environmental performance may help businesses reach their economic goals if they adopt technologies, enter into green partnership agreements, and are transparent about implementing new green practices (Sar et al., 2017).

14.5.11 COMPETITIVENESS

Competence and pertinent components may contribute to the implementation of green practices in their supply chain, as shown by a number of studies (Luthra et al., 2016). In recent years, the desire to remain competitive has trumped the desire to safeguard the environment and sustainability among many businesses as the primary motivation for adopting green practices. Firms' adoption of environmentally friendly practices may also be traced to other, noncompetitive, voluntary variables (Sar et al., 2017).

14.5.12 SOCIAL

Several studies have demonstrated the importance of societal variables in achieving the goals of environmentally friendly practices (Luthra et al., 2016). The increasing focus of regulators and consumers on environmental issues requires businesses to share comprehensive data on how their supply chain activities affect local communities and people's daily lives. Pressure from NGOs (nongovernmental organizations), electronic and social media, and other sources is more successful in encouraging businesses to embrace green practices.

14.5.13 REGULATORY

The regulating authorities have tightened environmental laws and policies due to the growing importance of environmental issues (Sar et al., 2017). To combat climate change, global warming, and pollution, governments have enacted stringent environmental laws, and businesses have been obligated to lessen the environmental impact of their supply chains (Sar and Dong, 2017). As a result, it is becoming increasingly crucial for supply chain companies to be in compliance with laws in order to implement environmentally friendly strategies.

14.6 IMPLICATIONS

Hiring a purchasing expert who is familiar with the ins and outs of the advanced technologies, can shape a company's sustainability initiatives, and can help cut operational expenses is a smart investment. To achieve personal and global environmental goals and to develop customer trust, it is necessary to enhance the effect of purchasing as green has become an extremely important priority across all industries. To make the "greenest" choice, procurement staff should weigh the pros and cons of various products and their effects on the environment. To be more specific, when making purchases, they should do the following: adhere to all applicable environmental laws and regulations;instruct vendors and service providers to supply environmentally friendly goods and services at reasonable costs; prompt vendors and service providers to arrange for the return of discarded goods and their subsequent disposal; and instruct service providers to think about how their operations will affect the ecosystem. Leaders in procurement should be agents of transformation. Green initiatives are made possible by better data precision and spending transparency.

14.7 CONCLUSIONS

Short- and medium-term gains, such as increased social effect rather than haphazardly funded causes, are prioritized when companies adopt green procurement practices. Profits and CSR, and thus trust; avoiding ethical, legal, and brand image risks; differentiating themselves to attract and retain customers; and adapting to customers' changing needs. All of the aforementioned goals can be accomplished by businesses with the aid of green buying. Compliance with environmental and social laws is becoming increasingly important for businesses as governments around the globe pass sustainability legislation. Several studies show that cost-cutting, decreased risk, and increased profits are motivating factors for businesses to prioritize sustainability throughout their supply chains. The key to a successful transition to green sourcing is not to try to tackle all of sustainability at once but rather to focus on incorporating just one element at a time while at the same time gradually increasing sustainability-related metrics.

KEYWORDS

- **sustainability**
- **procurement**
- **cost**
- **benefit**
- **green**

REFERENCES

Bohari, A. A. M.; Skitmore, M.; Xia, B.; Teo, M. Green oriented procurement for building projects: preliminary findings from Malaysia. Journal of Cleaner Production, 148, 690–700.

Bohari, A. A. M.; Bo, X. Green Procurement Framework for the Malaysian Construction Industry. In: *The 7th International Conference of SuDBE2015* **2015**, (July), 68–71.

Bidin, Z. A.; Bohari, A. A. M.; Rais, S. L. A.; Saferi, M. M. Green Related Practices for Construction Procurement. *IOP Conf. Ser.: Earth Environ. Sci.* **2018**, *140* (1).

Buniamin, S.; Ahmad, N.; Rauf, F. H. A.; Johari, N. H.; Rashid, A. A. Green Government Procurement Practices (GGP) in Malaysian Public Enterprises. *Procedia Economics and Finance* **2016**, *35* (16), 27–34.

Carroll, A. B. Corporate Social Responsibility: The Centerpiece of Competing and Complementary Frameworks. *Organ. Dyn.* **2015**, *44* (2), 87–96.

Chan, A. P. C.; Darko, A.; Ameyaw, E. E.; Owusu-Manu, D. G. Barriers Affecting the Adoption of Green Building Technologies. *J. Manag. Eng.* **2017**.

De Corbière, F.; Rowe, F.; Habib, J. A Simulation Approach for Analysing the Influence of Information Quality on the Deployment of a Green Supply Chain. In: *Twenty-Fourth European Conference on Information Systems (ECIS)*, 2016; pp 1–16.

De Villiers, G.; Nieman, G.; Niemann, W. *Strategic Logistics Management: A Supply Chain Management Approach*; Van Schaik Publishers: Braamfontein, South Africa, 2017.

European Commission. Green Public Procurement in Europe, 2006. https://ec.europa.eu/environment/gpp/barriers_en.htm

Farrell, J.; Shapiro, C. Upward Pricing Pressure in Horizontal Merger Analysis: Reply to Epstein and Rubinfeld. *BE J. Theoret. Econ.* **2010**, *10* (1), 41.

Fiorini, P. C.; Jabbour, C. J. C. Information Systems and Sustainability Supply Chain Management Towards a More Green Society: Where We Are and Where We Are Going. *Int. J. Inf. Manag.* **2017**, *37* (4), 241–249.

Ford, S.; Despeisse, M. Additive Manufacturing and Sustainability: An Exploratory Study of the Advantages and Challenges. *J. Clean. Prod.* **2016**, *137*, 1573–1587.

Fritz, M. M. C.; Schoggl, J. P.; Baumgartner, R. J. Selected Sustainability Aspects for Supply Chain Data Exchange: Towards a Supply Chain-Wide Sustainability Assessment. *J. Clean. Prod.* **2017**, *141*, 587–607.

Greenstone. Sustainable Procurement, 2023. https://www.greenstoneplus.com/resources/supply-chain-responsible-sourcing/sustainable-procurement

Han, J. H.; Wang, Y.; Naim, M. Reconceptualisation of Information Technology Flexibility for Supply Chain Management: An Empirical Study. *Int. J. Prod. Econ.* **2017**, *187*, 196–215.

Klufallah, M.; Ibrahim, I. S.; Moayedi, F. Sustainable Practices Barriers Towards Green Projects in Malaysia. *IOP Conf. Ser.: Earth Environ. Sci.* **2019**, *220* (1).

Kaur, H.; Singh, S. P. Heuristic Modeling for Green Procurement and Logistics in a supply Chain Using Big Data. *Comput. Operat. Res.* **2017**. http://dx.doi.org/10.1016/j.cor.2017.05.008 accessed 2017/07/23

Li, S.; Lin, B. Accessing Information Sharing and Information Quality in Supply Chain Management. *Decis. Supp. Syst.* **2006**, *42*, 1641–1656.

Luthra, S.; Garg, D.; Haleem, A. The Impacts of Critical Success Factors for Implementing Green Supply Chain Management Towards Sustainability: An Empirical Investigation of Indian Automobile Industry. *J. Clean. Prod.* **2016**, *121*, 142–158.

Mafini, C.; Muposhi, A. The Impact of Green Supply Chain Management in Small to Medium Enterprises: Cross-Sectional Evidence. *J. Transp. Supply Chain Manag.* **2017**, *11* (0), 270–283.

Mosgaard, M. A. Improving the Practices of Green Procurement of Minor Items. *J. Clean. Prod.* **2015**, *90*, 264–274.

Omar, R.; Ramayah, T.; Lo, M. C.; Sang, T. Y.; Siron, R. Information Sharing, Information Quality and Usage of Information Technology (IT) Tools in Malaysian Organisations. *Afr. J. Bus. Manag.* **2010**, *4* (12), 2486–2499.

Pazirandeh, A.; Jafari, H. Making Sense of Green Logistics. *Int. J. Prod. Perform. Manag.* **2013**, *62* (8), 889–904.

Rais, S. L. A.; Bidin, Z. A.; Bohari, A. A. M.; Saferi, M. M. The Possible Challenges of Green Procurement Implementation. *IOP Conf. Ser.: Mater. Sci. Eng.* **2018**, *429* (1).

Rajeev, A.; Pati, R. K.; Padhi, S. S.; Govindan, K. Evolution of Sustainability in Supply Chain Management: A Literature Review. *J. Clean. Prod.* **2017**, *162*, 299–314.

Rostamzadeh, R.; Govindan, K.; Esmaeili, A.; Sabaghi, M. Application of Fuzzy for Evaluation of Green Supply Chain Management Practices. *Ecol. Indic.* **2015**, *49*, 188–203.

Shen, L.; Zhang, Z.; Long, Z. Significant Barriers to Green Procurement in Real Estate Development. *Resour. Conserv. Recycl.* **2017a**, *166*, 160–168.

Shen, L.; Zhang, Z.; Zhang, X. Key Factors Affecting Green Procurement in Real Estate Development: A China Study. *J. Clean. Prod.* **2017b**, *153* (1), 372–383.

Nutburn, M. Five Benefits of a Green Supply Chain, 29 July 2019. https://www.cips.org/supply-management/opinion/2019/july/five-benefits-of-a-green-supply-chain/

Sievo. What Is Green Procurement and Why Is It Important? 27 Feb 2023. https://sievo.com/blog/green-procurement-part1

Slovenska agentura zivotneho prostredia. *Green Public Procurement (GP)*; SAZP: Banska Bystrica, 2014.

Soto, N. S. What Is A Green Procurement Policy? Green Business Bureau Feb 2021. https://greenbusinessbureau.com/blog/what-is-a-green-procurement-policy/

Sar, K.; Dong, Q. Impact of Green Supply Chain Management Practices on Firms' Performance: An Empirical Study from the Perspective of Pakistan. *Environ. Sci. Pollut. Res.* **2017**, *24*, 16829–16844. DOI: 10.1007/s11356–017–9172–5

Sar, K.; Dong, Q.; Wei, S. B.; Khalid, Z.; Yu, Z. Environmental Logistics Performance Indicators Affecting Per Capita Income and Sectoral Growth: Evidence from a Panel of Selected Global Ranked Logistics Countries. *Environ. Sci. Pollut. Res*. **2017,** *24* (2), 1518–1531. DOI: 10.1007/s11356–016–7916–2

Wu, C.; Barnes, D. Partner Selection in Green Supply Chains Using PSO—A Practical Approach. *Prod. Plan. Control* **2016,** *27* (13), 1041–1061. DOI: 10.1080/09537287.2016.1177233

World Bank. Green Procurement An Introduction for Practitioners to Green Procurement in World Bank IPF projects, 2nd edn., 2019. https://thedocs.worldbank.org/en/doc/788731479395390605–0290022019/original/GuidanceonGreenProcurement.pdf

Wu, K. J.; Liao, C. J.; Tseng, M. L.; Lim, M. K.; Hu, J.; Tan, K. Toward Sustainability: Using Big Data to Explore the Decisive Attributes of Supply Chain Risks and Uncertainties. *J. Clean. Prod.* **2017,** *142*, 663–676.

CHAPTER 15

Green Logistics

MOHAMMED MAJEED

Tamale Technical University, Tamale, Ghana

ABSTRACT

"Green logistics" (GL) respond to the societies' decision to go green. This chapter aims to explain (1) the factors affecting the adoption of GL, (2) the benefits of GL, and (3) the strategies of GL. GL can be incorporated into any business strategy to reduce emissions, reduce paper and plastic waste, and increase consumer awareness. It is an excellent starting point, as it will provide short- and long-term benefits to the ecosystem. Integrating these efforts into a larger business plan promotes environmental improvement and appeals to consumers who prefer to support environmentally responsible businesses. The determinants in this review include stakeholders, customers, organizations, and so on. While the strategies include warehouse optimization, inventory optimization, GL partnership, ethical sourcing, eco-conscious strategy, storage facility optimization, innovation, transport optimization, packaging optimization, improved current reverse logistics, and route optimization.

15.1 INTRODUCTION

When a product is required most, it can be delivered quickly and efficiently thanks to logistics. The negative effects of logistics on the natural environment are often disregarded in favor of improving operational efficiency, which is evaluated in terms of streamlined expenses and rapidity of distribution (Murthy and James, 2018). Logistics is the process of getting components, finished products, and individuals where they need to be when they

---

Green Supply Chain Management. Mohammed Majeed, Kirti Agarwal, and Ahmed Tijani (Eds.)
© 2025 Apple Academic Press, Inc. Co-published with CRC Press (Taylor & Francis)

need to be there. Logistics is an expression used to refer to the flow of goods from their initial place of acquisition, through the manufacturing process, and on to the consumer (McKinnon, 2014). Therefore, logistics is an essential part of contemporary transport networks, not just on a national but on a global scale. The spread of globalization fragmentation of manufacturing, and advancements in supply chain ideas all contributed to the growth of logistics (Bekovnik and Jakomin, 2010). In addition to its fiscal viability, "green logistics" (GL) also takes into account its impact on the environment and the community. All efforts to quantify and reduce operations' negative effects on the environment are covered. All processes involved in moving goods, data, and services from their source to their final destination are included here. The objective is to maximize both financial and ecological efficiency to build a business with lasting value. GL has become popular in the supply chain in recent years as a means to reduce negative environmental impacts and to increase brand loyalty among customers who value businesses with a strong dedication to sustainability. When it comes to logistics, "green" means "any" business strategy that lessens the toll on the planet. Sustainable logistics, also known as GL, ensures a healthy profit margin without jeopardizing environmental protection or client service. Smart companies are racing to learn about and implement sustainable transportation management, aided by cutting-edge tools such as artificial intelligence (AI), machine learning (ML), and data analytics (DA). Shippers are under increasing pressure from eco-conscious consumers to reduce carbon dioxide emissions, improve waste disposal and administration, increase the use of recycled materials, and more (Zahava, 2023). Carbon emissions from waste handling and disposal, packaging, recycling, cutting energy use, and other areas are all part of GL. More and more businesses are promising to achieve zero net environmental impact in response to growing customer demand for environmentally conscious products and policies on the part of governments and other international bodies (Zahava, 2023). This chapter, therefore, aims to explain (1) the factors affecting the adoption of GL, (2) the benefits of GL, and (3) the strategies of GL.

Industry around the world must adopt eco-friendly logistics methods because of rapid environmental loss and rising CO_2 emissions. Finally, this research adds new knowledge by exploring the connections between the various causes and effects of GL practices. The search for more environmentally friendly business practices has been prompted by concerns over corporate social responsibility, pollution prevention laws, and the depletion of natural resources (Zhu and He, 2017). Due to this shift, businesses need to make sure their sustainability and competitive advantages are factored into how they assess economic and environmental performance. The progress and development of many developing economies are tied to the availability of their natural resources. Economic development can benefit from green growth if it is implemented in a way that is consistent with the country's current policies on natural resource usage and poverty reduction. The goal of this qualitative single-case research was to investigate the link between green supply chain management (GSCM) strategies and the financial and environmental benefits they provide.

15.2 GREEN LOGISTICS

The term "logistics" is used to describe the chain of events that begins with the procurement, storage, and transfer of the necessary materials. Understanding, managing, and controlling the flow of resources throughout an organization's supply chain is essential for success in any industry, especially in the manufacturing domain. There is a current movement toward transportation practices that minimize their impact on the environment. Achieving a satisfactory degree of environmental responsibility in operations based on both management and technological advances requires inventions along with comprehensive phases of execution (Domagała et al., 2022). GL or eco-logistics is a collection of environmentally friendly guidelines and procedures developed to lessen the negative effects that the logistics industry has on the planet (Zahava, 2023). How products are transported, distributed, and stored are all impacted by this idea in logistics. The term "green logistics" is used to describe the methods and strategies put into place by the logistics and transit sector to improve sustainability, cut down on carbon emissions, and address issues related to the environment (Miashkova, 2022). Experiencing how GL is a crucial part of sustainable supply chain management procedures requires an understanding of how to efficiently circulate information and products while minimizing negative effects on the environment. Sustainable material, product, and data movement from the point of use to the point of reuse or disposal is the purview of GL (Cosimato and Troisi, 2015). Successful company leaders balance the environmental goals of recyclable materials with the financial costs of transportation and reverse logistics (Yang, 2017). Air pollution and the release of greenhouse gases, which are harmful to both ecosystem and human health, are primarily caused by transportation (Asrawi et al., 2017). Goods are delivered to the consumer in smaller quantities and with the help of vehicles that are easier on the atmosphere (Verma et al., 2018). Improving operational and fiscal performance is just one of the many potential outcomes of implementing GL management (Cosimato and Troisi, 2015). The goal of "green" or "sustainable" logistics is to lessen the toll that supply chain activities take on the ecosystem and other nonbeneficial factors. By streamlining processes and eliminating waste, "green supply chains" hope to lessen their negative effect on the ecosystem (World Green Economy Council, 2021). In the setting of humanitarian logistics, "green logistics" calls for everyone involved to think about how their actions will affect the planet. GL aims to meet beneficiary requirements at the "least cost" to the environment by coordinating activities along the supply chain (World Green Economy Council, 2021). It is a vital part of the field of reverse transportation. The word "cost" used to only refer to monetary losses, but now it also encompasses the environmental losses incurred by logistics operations due to things like global warming, air pollution, waste dumping (including packaging waste), soil degradation, noise, vibration, and accidents.

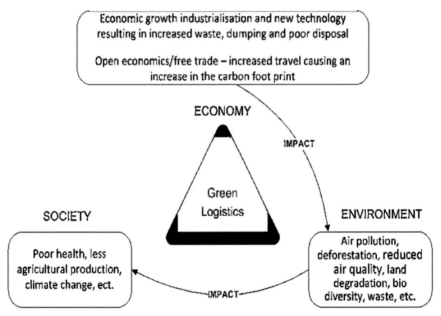

FIGURE 15.1 Effects of GL.

Source: World Green Economy Council (WGEC) (2021). https://wgeco.org/green-logistics/

15.3 FACTORS FOR ADOPTING GL

The efficiency of a GL is affected by factors such as location, clientele, infrastructure, and data. Based on their specific business and financial needs, companies can design and optimize these drivers to strike the best possible balance between speed and efficiency.

15.4 LOCATION/PLACE

If the site driver is looking to be as responsive as possible, they might decide to set up shop in multiple nearby neighborhoods. Fast food franchises, for instance, can increase their responsiveness to customers by strategically placing numerous outlets in densely populated areas. The ability to rapidly respond to customer demand at multiple locations comes at the expense of increased overhead (Kluwer, 2022). Having a small number of hubs from which to run operations is a surefire way to maximize productivity. e-Commerce retailers are a good example of location efficiency because they can service global markets from a small number of strategically placed hubs. This improves the efficiency of individual sites, but it also leaves them vulnerable to disturbances, such as the recent coronavirus epidemic (Kluwer, 2022).

15.5 SUSTAINABILITY OF MATERIALS

The goal of green supply chain projects is to help businesses make the most of the limited resources they have by improving how they currently use those resources (Wang and Gupta, 2011). Some green practices adopted by businesses also promote making full use of all resources (StudyCorgi, 2023). Due to this, refuse recycling has become increasingly common in recent decades. Waste recycling optimizes resource utilization, which in turn boosts a company's bottom line. In addition, it is a practical approach to realizing the goals of business social responsibility. As a result, consumers will have more faith in companies that make an effort to green their supply chain, leading to increased sales and patronage (StudyCorgi, 2023).

15.6 CUSTOMERS

Continuous innovation in goods and how customers are served is driven by a dedication to listening to and meeting the needs of customers. Companies that place a premium on responsiveness are better able to adapt to the unpredictable changes in the marketplace and shifts in consumer preferences (Kluwer, 2022).

15.7 STAKEHOLDERS

Leadership targets and goals are influenced by stakeholders, and these in turn fuel the organizations economic and environmental performance goals. The company can reap the benefits of green supply chain tactics by better utilizing its resources and capabilities (Liu et al., 2017). Positively affecting environmental views through stakeholder pressure (Liston-heyes and Vazquez Brust, 2016). Sustainable restrictions that reflect stakeholders' ecological worries and the financial viability of green investments are intertwined in supply chain environmental decisions. According to Zhu and He (2017), companies should use price rivalry to increase the sustainability of their products and services. Stakeholders who have a say in resource allocation by means of capability distribution, as discussed by Liu et al. (2017) and Liston-heyes and Vazquez Brust (2016), are able to gain a competitive edge. Some of the areas in which business executives have developed their knowledge and abilities are globalization, sustainability, and supply chain integration and innovation.

15.8 INTERNAL INFLUENCES

Make sure factories have spare capacity and employ adaptable production methods to make a broad variety of products with a responsive supply chain (Kluwer, 2022). The ability to rapidly adapt production to changes in consumer demand is made possible by flexibility. Increased buyer demand responsiveness is another benefit of having numerous, smaller production facilities located near distribution centers and customer hubs. On the contrary, having production facilities that are lean and optimized for a narrow variety of products can boost productivity (Kluwer, 2022). Even though some customers' delivery times may increase, centralized production in big central plants improves efficiency due to economies of scale.

15.9 CHANGES IN THE ENVIRONMENT

In the past, companies could operate without worrying about how their activities might affect the ecosystem (Ballou, 2007). Companies were incentivized to disregard environmental conservation efforts due to a dearth of laws requiring them to do so while simultaneously pursuing profit maximization. However, because of the recent climatic changes that have characterized most countries around the world, laws mandating companies' adoption of the concept of social responsibility through conservation are now essential. In response to the detrimental effects of climate change on economies, the majority of nations have enacted laws to protect the ecosystem. Heat waves, rains, snowfall, and hurricanes have all become familiar phenomena in the modern world, and experts in the field of weather research and forecasting have linked these changes to environmental pollution (Zhu et al., 2008). This factor is a major reason why most governments have enacted stringent laws aimed at protecting the ecosystem.

15.10 INVENTORY

When it comes to merchandise, having more of it in more places is usually the best way to maximize responsiveness. Rapid response to changes in demand is made possible by an organized stockpile. The trade-off between the higher storage expenses and increased accessibility should be carefully considered (Kluwer, 2022).

15.11 ORGANIZATIONAL FACTORS

Senior management endorsement and buy-in for GL practice implementation is also crucial, as suggested by Loke et al. (2017) and Murthy et al. (2018). The company's top management makes choices about how those resources will be used, including whether or not to engage in cutting-edge technology. McKinnon et al. (2015) stressed that businesses have a generally positive outlook on GL implementation if doing so benefits the business's social and ecological metrics at the same time as lowering or keeping costs stable. The authors argue that the expenses involved act as both a driver and a barrier. The drivers and challenges in further application of the GL include the desire to be leaders in sustainable development, rising power and fuel prices, greater competitive advantage and differentiation, compliance with existing or prospective legislation, and relatively rising transport costs. Business executives whose organizations have best-in-class environmental management systems can strengthen their supply chain strategies by shaping environmental legislation and policy.

15.12 INFORMATION

As information-gathering and sharing tools improve in accessibility, usability, and cost, so too does information's potential to propel change (Kluwer, 2022). Decisions made with the help of analytics-powered software improve supply chain drivers' efficiency by using both internal and exterior data. For maximum efficiency, the supply chain should gather and share accurate and timely data generated by the aforementioned four drivers (Kluwer, 2022).

15.13 WAREHOUSING

Logistics plays a crucial role in facilitating globalization and the free movement of trade. Since the speed and dependability of deliveries eliminate the need to keep and stockpile, the economies of modern logistics systems are predicated on lowering inventory levels. One of the benefits of transportation is a decreased need for storage space. This, however, implies that some stocks have been moved to the transportation network, particularly the roadways and terminals. Inventories are currently in transport, adding to the already substantial amounts of traffic and pollution. Rather than the logistics companies themselves paying the price, the ecosystem and society do.

15.14 TRANSPORTATION

Air freight, while typically more expensive, allows for quicker delivery periods and more responsiveness (Kluwer, 2022). Both FedEx and UPS use a variety of transit options to ensure that customers receive their orders as quickly as possible, usually within 24–48 hours. Transporting goods in bigger quantities, but less frequently, by bulk carriers like ships or railroads, is a common practice to maximize transportation efficiency. When goods are shipped from one central warehouse rather than many smaller ones, this method of delivery is more effective (Kluwer, 2022).

15.15 BENEFITS OF GL

Everyone in the supply chain, the company's clients, and the general public can benefit from GL. Few examples are listed in the following:

15.15.1 SAVE MONEY

GL is necessary, but it need not come at a high price. Logistics' primary goal is to cut down on spending, particularly in the transportation sector. The former is still the most important logistics expense, but the latter is the cost of keeping goods on hand. Improved service reliability, including adaptability, and labor savings are additional goals. In reality, cutting costs in the supply chain can be achieved without sacrificing environmental concerns. Here are seven strategies for greener and more effective last-mile delivery and logistics (Zahava, 2023). Since environmentally friendly company procedures are centered on increasing productivity and decreasing waste, they frequently go in tandem side with cost savings as businesses go green. Due to the implementation of GL takes on various forms, the cost savings and decreased waste realized by individual companies will also vary. Logistics companies recognize the importance of reducing delivery costs in today's fiercely competitive market. Reduced fuel usage per ton-kilometer is just one of the ecological advantages that can result from transportation cost savings tactics like efficiencies of scale and increased load densities. There are times when logistic companies' attempts to save money directly conflict with externalized concerns about the climate. Therefore, if the advantages of logistics are distributed along the entire supply chain, the users and, ultimately, the consumer, will reap the benefits (Rodrigue et al., 2023). According to studies, businesses that have successfully implemented environmentally conscious supply chains have lower operating expenses (Testa and Iraldo, 2010). Innovations made by such businesses in their pursuit of a pollution-free supply chain are credited with lowering running costs (StudyCorgi, 2023). Efficiency, made possible by the advances, results in substantial financial gain for the businesses. Although there may be no short-term advantages, studies show that long-term benefits are substantial for these companies. The company's bottom line benefits greatly from the purchase and installation of more efficient equipment (StudyCorgi, 2023). Arguments for cost savings are also supported by the decline in penalties levied against businesses for immoral behavior.

15.15.2 COMPETITIVE ADVANTAGE THROUGH PRODUCT DIFFERENTIATION

Logistics can be made more environmentally friendly by adopting measures that lessen their impact on the world at large. Such actions are consistent with the idea of corporate philanthropy, which mandates that businesses ensure the well-being of the areas immediately surrounding the establishment (Sheu and Talley, 2011). Consequently, increasing customer loyalty is a direct result of greening the supply chain and improving the company's public reputation. A company's bottom line benefits when customers are devoted to them (StudyCorgi, 2023).

15.15.3 ADJUSTING TO NEW RULES AND LIMITING DANGER

One of the most pressing ethical concerns confronting modern companies is pollution of the natural environment. As a result, greening the supply chain is one of the initiatives that could aid businesses in avoiding wasteful expenditures in the form of penalties for unethical conduct.

15.15.4 PROFITABILITY GAINS OVER THE LONG RUN

GL reduces costs, emissions, and waste across the entire supply chain, from procurement to final distribution. Although there is an upfront investment needed to reap the benefits of GL, the payoff far exceeds the expense. Recently conducted research showed "evidence that high environmental organizations substantially outperform other companies over a long period, both in the stock market and accounting performance." The bottom line is that an eco-friendly enterprise is a profitable enterprise (SAP, 2023).

15.15.5 RELIABILITY

Logistics relies on the unwavering dependability of its services. The company's success hinges on its punctual delivery of cargo with minimal loss or harm. These goals are typically attained by logistics providers by employing the means that are generally accepted as the most reliable. In terms of punctuality, damage, and security, the least polluting alternatives are typically considered to be the worst options.

15.15.6 RAISE CONSCIOUSNESS AMONG BUYERS

Consumers have proven they care about their environmental impact (Champion, 2022). People care about finding brands that share their values and reducing their overall negative effect on the environment. When companies start using environmentally friendly logistics practices, they should tell their clients about it so they can learn from it and apply the lessons to their operations (Champion, 2022). Be aware of where your goods come from and how they are packaged as a company, and tell your customers how to recycle the packaging at home. It's also a good idea to give customers an annual report detailing the progress made toward environmental goals, such as lowering gas emissions or switching to renewable energy sources (Champion, 2022). Customers are more likely to feel engaged in the green transportation process as a result of these strategies.

15.15.7 DELIGHTED AND LOYAL CUSTOMERS

Both consumers and businesses have come to expect expedited shipping and simple refund policies. They want real-time information about the origin of their goods, the ethics of their sourcing and transportation, and the status of their delivery. Businesses that provide such details attract new clients and retain the loyalty of the ones they already have.

15.15.8 TIME

Time is often of the importance in logistics. Increasing the distribution system's efficiency requires increasing its velocity, which is achieved by decreasing the duration of flows. The most polluting and least energy-efficient forms of transit are primarily responsible for this. Partially due to time limitations imposed by logistical activities, the use of air freight and trucking has increased dramatically. The time constraints are a direct result of the retail industry and the greater adaptability of industrial production systems. The door-to-door (DTD) services provided by logistics providers are frequently combined with just-in-time (JIT) tactics. There is no other method that can adequately meet the needs that arise from such a circumstance. The more DTD and JIT methods are implemented, the more severe the environmental impacts of the resulting traffic. Time management within long-distance supply chains is already difficult, and maritime shipping firms' slow-steaming strategy only makes things worse.

15.15.9 STRENGTHENING THE IMAGE OF RESPONSIBLE BUSINESS PRACTICES

Global warming is seen as a social justice issue, and large corporations are increasingly being forced to account for their role in the problem. Companies can win over the public by touting the benefits of green operations in public. Smart businesses are looking at their impact on the environment on a worldwide and regional scale. Those who refuse to adapt, particularly in the transition away from fossil fuels, place themselves at a competitive disadvantage and risk damaging their reputation (SAP, 2023).

15.15.10 REDUCES WASTE

The reduction of waste is another advantage of sustainable transportation. Instead of maintaining paper files, the majority of businesses are centralizing and digitizing their paperwork, records, and operational data within integrated online systems. As a result, the quantity of paper waste generated during production is drastically reduced, and operations are streamlined by having customer insights, inventory information, and order management in one location (Champion, 2022). The quantity of plastic waste generated during the packaging process is decreased by using GL strategies. Reducing the amount of plastic required for deliveries requires switching to renewable resources and putting recycling best practices into effect. Furthermore, combining purchases into fewer shipments can reduce waste (Khan, 2019). Businesses can give customers the choice of receiving all of their orders in a single package as opposed to being split up among several boxes by optimizing their order flow.

15.15.11 TECHNOLOGIES INFORMATION

New aspects of retailing have been made possible by information technologies. e-Eommerce is one of the most dynamic industries. An integrated supply chain with data exchange between suppliers, assembly lines, and freight forwarders makes this feasible. Online transactions may appear to be completely motionless to the consumer, but they may actually require more energy to distribute than other retail activities. The parcel-shipping businesses that only use air and truck transportation have profited the most from e-commerce's impact on distribution. Applying e-commerce-related information tools to logistics can be beneficial. The circumstance could therefore be seen as paradoxical once more.

15.15.12 LOWERING GAS EMISSIONS

Reduced greenhouse gas emissions are one benefit of green operations. Following environmentally friendly best practices in logistics helps to minimize the delivery chain's carbon footprint (Champion, 2022). This covers everything from cutting energy use to improving the effectiveness of logistics processes.

15.15.13 SIMPLER HIRING

Every corporate advantage counts in the most competitive employment market in decades. Young professionals who want to work for a business that shares their values are more drawn to organizations that focus on GL (SAP, 2023).

15.15.14 BUILDS BRAND REPUTATION

Retailers gain a competitive edge in the market by implementing and sharing concrete steps to improve GL in supply chain management. Customers are already prepared to pay more for goods from companies that use sustainable business practices, according to research (Champion, 2022). Being an eco-aware retailer attracts favorable notice from potential customers and is in line with what modern consumers want.

15.15.15 STRATEGIES FOR FIRMS PRACTICING GL

Logistics companies in any sector can gain from adopting eco-friendly practices. Modifying product sourcing, increasing warehouse efficiency, and decreasing transportation emissions are all examples of typical sustainable logistics activities. These methods are applicable to companies of any size and in any field, whether used singly or in combination.

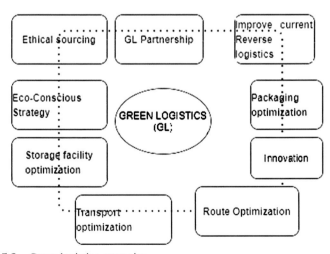

FIGURE 15.2 Green logistics strategies.
Source: Authors.

15.15.16 GL PARTNERSHIP

Partner collaboration is essential for enhancing the supply chain's sustainable performance (Hong and Guo, 2018). Using GL cooperation, top-level executives talk about how to get their teams and departments working together effectively to achieve their goals (Scholten and Schilder, 2015). Green design, environmentally friendly packaging, logistical reversal, and other environmentally friendly procedures increase collaboration between suppliers and consumers in businesses with proactive environmental strategies. Integrating a green supply chain calls for close cooperation between vendors and customers (Wei et al., 2016). Large multinational companies rely heavily on interdepartmental cooperation to achieve their strategy goals, a task that necessitates skills in analysis, interpersonal communication, leadership, adaptability, and project management (Kumar et al., 2017). Due to the greater reach of their marketplaces, multinational corporations place a greater emphasis on brand image (Earnhart, 2017). Supply chain cooperation is proportional to the degree of supply chain alignment and the depth of their collaboration (Sarkis et al., 2016).

15.15.17 ETHICAL SOURCING

Ethical sourcing is a word for the environmentally friendly practice of purchasing goods from businesses that comply with ethical trading standards such as those established by the Ethical Trading Initiative. The Atlantic reports that businesses such as Misfits Market are engaging in ethical sourcing by purchasing "ugly produce" from organic farms that would otherwise go to waste (Kumar et al., 2017).

15.15.18 ECO-CONSCIOUS STRATEGY

In this way, an eco-friendly strategy can help a nation achieve a better balance between its economic and environmental needs (Hong and Guo, 2018). This objective is met, as stated by (Khan, 2019), by incorporating environmental requirements into the formulation of the country's economic and social objectives without hampering business activities and competition. Strategic environmental management is a natural extension of the triple bottom line because it takes all three dimensions into account. According to (Sarkis et al., 2016), a company's environmental plan may be influenced by organizational and managerial factors.

15.15.19 STORAGE FACILITY OPTIMIZATION

Companies can reduce their energy consumption and thus address these issues by employing various GL strategies. Using renewable energy like solar and wind energy to fuel the company's storage facilities is one option. Although changing energy providers may not seem like much, it can have a significant effect by reducing emissions. On-site training for workers is another common strategy for reducing energy consumption. Employees could learn anything from how to properly turn off lights to how to properly recycle while on the job from this instruction (Khan, 2019) In a similar vein, some businesses integrate reduce, reuse, and recycle practices into their workflows, such as using less packaging for goods or printing on both sides of the page to cut down on paper consumption.

15.15.20 INNOVATION

In the realm of information technology, "innovation" refers to any method that results in an improvement. IT-enabled collaboration and information sharing may help businesses outperform their rivals in the long run, as these features are difficult to replicate. Before launching environmentally friendly efforts, businesses can benefit from modeling possible remanufacturing scenarios (Diaz and Marsillac, 2017). Supply chain performance is driven by establishing appropriate metrics, interrelationships, and customer service standards. Developing-world manufacturers and their clients are generally savvy about capitalizing on connections to build creative capacities (Adebanjo et al., 2018). One of the easiest and most dependable ways for businesses to adapt to internal and exterior changes is through innovation. Choosing the most effective methods for decreasing one's carbon impact is facilitated by innovation (Carola et al., 2018). Recognizing how to apply inventiveness to better performance in both the economy and the environment was affirmed by Adebanjo et al. (2018). From the viewpoint of NRBV, an organization's ability to innovate should result in the generation of competitive advantages through the improvement of organizational and ecological improvements without compromising its standing in the market (Adebanjo et al., 2018). Collaboration, capabilities, organizational success, and competitive advantages are all interconnected in a conceptual framework for value-adding innovation.

15.15.21 TRANSPORT OPTIMIZATION

Streamline shipping and delivery processes. Investing in more environmentally friendly vehicles is a straightforward way to green the supply chain, and it is something that some notable delivery companies have started doing. Purchasing electric trucks is a simple move to take, but it also comes with a hefty price tag. It might not be practical for less substantial businesses (Khan, 2019). Even if a company already uses fuel-efficient vehicles, route optimization can still have a significant impact on transit sustainability. Reduced journey distance means less fuel used and less pollution avoided thanks to efficient routing. A transportation management system is frequently used to assist with route optimization. Last-mile delivery optimization is just one aspect of order fulfillment that can benefit from the use of these tools.

15.15.22 PACKAGING OPTIMIZATION

There is a growing demand for recyclable and reusable containers, and two-way freight flows necessitate a rise in packaging streamlining. Less packaging waste and fewer vehicles used due to improved space utilization are two obvious results of packaging optimization that can be expected to have a positive effect on the environment (OptimoRoute, 2022). Minimizing unnecessary packing, increasing the use of biodegradable or returnable packaging, recycling, and reusing are all instances of packaging reductions provided by Khan (2019). As a result, the logistics sector will face greater pressure to cut down on packaging waste in order to make its processes greener.

15.15.23 IMPROVE CURRENT REVERSE LOGISTICS

Improve current methods of backward logistics. Important in the supply chain, reverse logistics involves returning a product to its origin, usually a warehouse or distribution facility, after it has been delivered to a consumer. A company that provides a service similar to a milk delivery service will eventually need to collect the empty glass bottles that contain the milk. In the same way that optimizing a company's delivery methods with a logistics system can increase efficiency and longevity, so can optimizing the company's reverse logistics (OptimoRoute, 2022).

15.15.24 ROUTE OPTIMIZATION

Coordinating a fleet of cars with a limited number of available spots is called route optimization. Finding a route that minimizes the number of trips taken, the total amount of time spent traveling, and the total number of vehicles used is the most effective method to route a fleet. To reduce their environmental impact, logistics firms should reduce the number of shipments they make, the number of times each cargo is handled, the number of times each movement is made, the number of times each route is changed, the number of times each transportation is (Mukupo, 2019). Since the vehicles moving at their optimal speed are less harmful to the environment and they use less fuel, these variables contribute to reduced pollution. Since it makes better use of vehicles and cuts down on miles traveled, optimizing the route helps keep expenses down. The potential for route optimization to significantly reduce carbon emissions makes it a crucial factor to explore in this research. It is a simple thing that can be done to lessen the transportation chain's financial and environmental impact. According to Mukupo (2019), improving routing efficiency and decreasing greenhouse gas emissions requires a strong computer system as well as creative management ideas. We think it's important to look into this because optimizing routes can have major effects on the economy and the ecology.

15.16 DISCUSSION

This chapter aims to explain (1) the factors affecting the adoption of GL, (2) the benefits of GL, and (3) the strategies of GL. Scholarly and managerial interest in how businesses react to today's massive environmental worries has been on the rise (Sarkis et al., 2011). The effects of GSCM techniques on productivity have been the subject of extensive study. According to Chiaw Fen et al. (2020), businesses that implement GL see financial gains. The authors have stressed that a well-planned system of GL application could help reduce waste, transportation costs, and electricity consumption while simultaneously increasing profits through the prudent use of fewer raw materials. Due to these elements, businesses are increasingly adapting to meet the changing needs of their customers.

A GL's flexibility and responsiveness to changing customer requirements are impacted by numerous external factors. Efficiency gains, risk mitigation, and reduced environmental impact are just some of the outcomes of a comprehensive knowledge of how these factors influence corporate environmental strategies and organizational performance. Supply chain partners' adoption of innovation and innovations to cut waste and greenhouse gas emissions is influenced by the length of a product's life cycle. Decisions along the supply chain may be impacted by the pace at which information is shared among participants. By working together, members of the supply chain help their leaders allocate resources where they will have the greatest impact on their stakeholders. When synergies drive strategies that are advantageous to all members of the supply chain, innovation between partners in the supply chain improves. By bolstering integration ties with suppliers and customers, collaboration increases supply chain resilience which allows for greater flexibility and agility in the face of environmental change (Grandiere, 2019). By reducing or eliminating nonvalue-added tasks before their execution, optimization models allow for risk sharing and cut down on waste. Technology advancements facilitate greater information dissemination throughout the supply chain.

15.17 IMPLICATION

This chapter aims to explain (1) the factors affecting the adoption of GL; (2) the benefits of GL and (3) the strategies of GL. Our review of desktop data has significant consequences for managers who are responsible for putting GL practices into action. Firm practitioners can use this study to better understand the most significant challenges to implementing GL strategies. In light of the reality that companies cannot thrive without adopting GL practices, it is imperative that managers investigate the obstacles to doing so. They should devise effective solutions to the issue by weighing the significance of the various groups and obstructions. Without compromising price, quality, dependability, effectiveness, or consumption of energy efficacy, coordinated GL practices lessen the environmental effect (Wei et al., 2016). Authorities in the supply network may boost their company's economic and social standing by implementing GL practices, such as the responsible disposal of goods that have outlived their usefulness and organizational success benefits from GSCM (Shafique et al., 2017). Both Wei et al. (2016) and Shafique et al. (2017) proposed that GL practices aid in saving money and minimizing damage to the ecosystem and society.

When businesses prioritize sustainability and societal responsibility in their decision-making, they gain a leg up on the competition. Environmental projects have compelling profit-maximizing outcomes. Proof that profits can grow in ways besides cutting costs can be found in the capacity to sell more expensive products with greater efficiency. Saving money by using fewer natural materials benefits both businesses and the planet. Insights from this research could be used by corporate decision-makers to advance eco-friendly methods of boosting bottom lines. Leaders in the business world can reduce their negative impact on the climate by adopting strategies and policies that help the economy thrive. It can be difficult for company leaders to know what metrics to use when evaluating performance. The environmental effect or carbon footprint of goods and processes can be evaluated with the aid of the life-cycle assessment (LCA) (Carola et al., 2018). Business executives can learn more about how to implement GSCM strategies by using LCA tool and balanced scorecard.

15.18 CONCLUSION

This chapter aims to explain (1) the factors affecting the adoption of GL, (2) the benefits of GL, and (3) the strategies of GL. GL is used to describe any method implemented by a company to reduce its environmental impact. It is an expansion of conventional logistics that is sometimes referred to as "eco-logistics." The climate is not a priority in conventional logistics, which instead prioritizes efficiency. GL seeks to enhance both the efficiency of business processes and an organization's long-term viability. The goal of GL is to transport and distribute goods at a cost that is affordable while still meeting or exceeding quality standards and causing as little harm to the environment as feasible. It means new ideas were used at every stage of production, from ideation to, in some instances, disposal. GL policies not only help businesses meet environmental laws, but also give them an edge over rivals by repositioning their brands and getting them ready for a future in which they will have to be environmentally friendly. Taking steps to reduce energy consumption is a viable tactic for dealing with increasing supplier costs. The scientific community is making rapid strides in its knowledge of various facets of ecology. Increased environmental and societal regulation is a political priority for many countries. A more all-encompassing strategy for governing the economic, social, and environmental implications of business operations is emerging. As globalization and rivalry increase, businesses are increasingly adopting environmentally friendly logistics practices, which are central to their operations.

Businesses are under continuous scrutiny to create more sustainable practices, and dedication to the preservation of nature is a significant factor in business scenarios. Corporate-level green transportation challenges can come from within or without an organization. Some intriguing results have emerged from the literature review. Managers must first recognize that there are several variables that can shift over time that affect how feasible it is to incorporate environmental concerns into company strategies. Factors that influence whether or not a company implements environmentally friendly transportation procedures include the nature of the business, its location, and the environmental consciousness of its customers. Buyer demands on organizations' ethical conduct is a differentiating factor in the study's findings, which may be related to the various supply chain positions of the companies. Logistics managers should consider technological influences in the future despite the importance of corporate variables in most sectors. Legislative pressure is just one method of encouraging environmentally responsible behavior on the part of businesses; other methods, such as raising managers' environmental consciousness, should also be employed to achieve this long-term goal. GL can be applied to any business strategy to reduce emissions, minimize paper and plastic waste, and raise customer consciousness. It is a good place to begin, as it will benefit the ecosystem in the short and long term. Integrating these efforts into a larger business plan promotes positive environmental change and appeals to customers who prefer to support environmentally responsible companies.

KEYWORDS

- **green**
- **logistics**
- **environment**
- **ecological**
- **eco**
- **efficiency**
- **waste**

REFERENCES

Adebanjo, D.; Teh, P.; Ahmed, P. K. The Impact of Supply Chain Relationships and Integration on Innovative Capabilities and Manufacturing Performance: The Perspective of Rapidly Developing Countries. *Int. J. Prod. Res.* **2018**, *56*, 1708–1721. DOI: 10.1080/00207543.2017.1366083

Agyabeng-Mensah, Y.; Afum, E.; Acquah, I. S. K.; Dacosta, E.; Baah, C.; Ahenkorah, E. The Role of Green Logistics Management Practices, Supply Chain Traceability and Logistics Ecocentricity in Sustainability Performance. *Int. J. Logist. Manag.* **2021**, *32* (2), 538–566. https://doi.org/10.1108/IJLM-05-2020-0187

Ballou, R. *Business Logistics/Supply Chain Management*; Pearson Education: New York, 2007.

Carola, P. T.; Lusa, A.; Coves, A. M. A Proposal for a Green Supply Chain Strategy. *J. Ind. Eng. Manag.* **2018**, *11*, 445–465. doi:10.3926/jiem.2518

Champion, A. 4 Advantages of Green Logistics in Supply Chain Management & How to Apply Them. FlowSpace, 24 Oct 2022. https://flow.space/blog/4-advantages-of-green-logistics-in-supply-chain-management-how-to-apply-them/

Colicchia, C.; Marchet, G.; Melacini, M.; Perotti, S. Building Environmental Sustainability: Empirical Evidence from Logistics Service Providers. *J. Clean. Prod.* **2013**, *59*, 197–209.

Cosimato, S.; Troisi, O. Green Supply Chain Management: Practices and Tools for Logistics Competitiveness and Sustainability. *TQM J.* **2015**, *27* (2), 256–276. doi:10.1108/TQM-01-2015-0007

Domagała, J. Górecka, A.; Roman, M. *Sustainable Logistics: How to Address and Overcome the Major Issues and Challenges*, 1st edn.; Taylor and Francis. https://doi.org/10.4324/9781003304364. https://www.taylorfrancis.com/books/edit/10.4324/9781003304364/sustainable-logistics-joanna-domagała-aleksandra-górecka-monika-roman

Earnhart, D. Corporate Environmental Strategies in Transition Economies: Survey of the Literature. *East. Eur. Econ.* **2017**, *55* (2), 111–145. DOI: 10.1080/00128775.2016.1271279

Grandiere, M. D. D. L. *Optimizing Green Supply Chain Management Strategies*; Walden University, 2019. https://scholarworks.waldenu.edu/dissertations

Hong, Z.; Guo, X. Green Product Supply Chain Contracts Considering Environmental Responsibilities. *Omega* 2018. DOI: 10.1016/j.omega.2018.02.010

Khan, S. A. R. The Effect of Green Logistics on Economic Growth, Social and Environmental Sustainability: An Empirical Study of Developing Countries in Asia. Preprints **2019**, *2019*, 010104.

Kluwer, W. Five Supply Chain Drivers That Make or Break Your Forecasts, 5 Sept 2022. https://www.wolterskluwer.com/en/expert-insights/five-supply-chain-drivers

Kumar, V.; Verma, P.; Sharma, R. R. K.; Khan, F. A. Conquering in Emerging Markets: Critical Success Factors to Enhance Supply Chain Performance. *Benchmark.: Int. J.* **2017**, *24*, 570–593. DOI: 10.1108/BIJ-05-2016-0078

Liston-heyes, C.; Vazquez Brust, D. A. Environmental Protection in Environmentally Reactive Firms: Lessons from Corporate Argentina. *J. Bus. Ethics* **2016**, *135*, 361–379. DOI: 10.1007/s10551-014-2473-4

Liu, Y.; Zhu, Q.; Seuring, S. Linking Capabilities to Green Operations Strategies: The Moderating Role of Corporate Environmental Proactivity. *Int. J. Prod. Econ.* **2017**, *187*, 182–195. doi:10.1016/j.ijpe.2017.03.007

Loke, S.-P.; Khalizani, K.; Rohati, S.; Sayaka, A.; Drivers and Barriers for Going Green: Perceptions from the Business Practitioners in Malaysia. *ASEAN J. Sci. Technol. Dev.* **2017**, *31* (2), 49.

McKinnon, A. C. Options for Reducing Logistics-related Emissions from Global Value Chains, Paper 2014/31, Robert Schuman Centre for Advanced Studies, European University Institute, Florence, 2014.

Miashkova, Y. Green Logistics for Greener Supply Chain Management. Track-Pod, 9 Sept 2022. https://www.track-pod.com/blog/green-logistics-guide/

Mukupo, S. Challenges of Managing Green Logistics in Zambia a Case Study of ZEMA, DHL, Barloworld Logistics and Green Living Movement. Published Thesis. Cavendish University Zambia, 2019. http://155.0.3.194:8080/jspui/bitstream/123456789/157/1/Challenges%20of%20Managing%20Green%20Logistics%20in%20Zambia.pdf

Murthy, D.; James, l. Key Drivers for Adoption of Green Logistics by Organized Retail Sector in Bengaluru. *Int. J. Manag. Stud.* **2018**. http://www.researchersworld.com/ijms/. http://dx.doi.org/10.18843/ijms/v5i2(2)/01

Murthy, P. R. A. D.; Dean, A.; James, L.; Key Drivers for Adoption of Green Logistics by Organized Retail Sector in Bengaluru. *Int. J. Manag. Stud.* **2018**, *2* (April), 1–7.

OptimoRoute. What Is Green Logistics and Why Does It Matter? 3 May 2022. https://optimoroute.com/green-logistics/

Rodrigue, J.; Slack, B.; Comtois, C. B.15—Green Logistics, 2023. https://transportgeography.org/contents/applications/green-logistics/

SAP. Green Logistics: What Is It and Why It Matters, 2023. https://www.sap.com/insights/green-logistics.html#:~:text=Green%20logistics%20includes%20any%20business,well-being%20of%20the%20planet

Sarkis, J.; Bai, C.; Lopes De Sousa Jabbour, A. B.; Jabbour, C. J.; Sobreiro, V. A. Connecting the Pieces of the Puzzle Toward Sustainable Organizations. *Benchmark.: Int. J.* **2016**, *23*, 1605–1623. DOI: 10.1108/bij-04-2015-0033

Scholten, K.; Schilder, S. The Role of Collaboration in Supply Chain Resilience. *Supply Chain Manag.: Int. J. Supply Chain Manag.* **2015**, *20*, 471–484. DOI: 10.1108/scm-11-2014-0386

Sheu, B.; Talley, W. Green Supply Chain Management: Trends, Challenges, and Solutions. *Transp. Res. Part E: Logist. Transportation Rev.* **2011**, *47* (6), 791–792.

StudyCorgi. Advantages and Challenges of Green Supply Chain Management, 23 Feb 2023. Retrieved from https://studycorgi.com/green-supply-chain-advantages-and-challenges/

Testa, F.; Iraldo, F. Shadows and Lights of GSCM (Green Supply Chain Management): Determinants and Effects of These Practices Based on a Multi-National Study. *J. Clean. Prod.* **2010**, *18* (10), 953–962.

Trivellas, P.; Malindretos, G.; Reklitis, P. Implications of Green Logistics Management on Sustainable Business and Supply Chain Performance: Evidence from a Survey in the Greek Agri-Food Sector. *Sustainability* **2020**, *12* (24), 10515.

Verma, D.; Dixit, R. V.; Singh, K. Green Supply Chain Management: A Necessity for Sustainable Development. *IUP J. Supply Chain Manag.* **2018**, *15* (1), 40–58. Retrieved from https://www.iupindia.in/supplychain_management.asp

Wang, F.; Gupta, S. *Green Supply Chain Management: Product Life Cycle Approach*; McGraw Hill Professional: New York, 2011.

Wei, H. L.; Ju, P. H.; Angkasa, Y. A. Implementing Green Supply Chain Management to Achieve Competitive Advantage. In: *2016 5th IIAI International Congress on Advanced Applied Informatics (IIAI-AAI)*, 2016. DOI: 10.1109/iiaiaai.2016.242

World Green Economy Council (WGEC). Green Logistics, 2021. https://wgeco.org/green-logistics/

Yang, C. An Analysis of Institutional Pressures, Green Supply Chain Management, and Green Performance in the Container Shipping Context. *Transp. Res. Part D: Transp. Environ.* **2017,** *61*, 246–260. DOI: 10.1016/j.trd.2017.07.005

Zahava, D. Green Logistics: Strategies for Eco-Friendly Delivery, 2023. https://www.bringg.com/blog/logistics/green-logistics/

Zhu, Q.; Sarkis, J.; Lai, K. Confirmation of a Measurement Model for Green Supply Chain Management Practices Implementation. *Int. J. Prod. Econ.* **2008,** *111* (2), 261–273.

CHAPTER 16

A Study on Green Practices and Strategies in Supply Chain Management

SUJA SUNDRAM[1], CHETAN V HIREMATH[2], MADHU ARORA[3], VARSHA AGARWAL[4], S. SEKAR[5], and SUJA SUNDRAM[1]

[1]Department of Business Administration, Jubail Industrial College, Jubail, Kingdom of Saudi Arabia

[2]Department of Operations and Analytics, Kirloskar Institute of Management, Yantrapur, Harihar, Davangere, Karnataka, India

[3]Uttaranchal Institute of Management, Uttaranchal University, Dehradun, India

[4]ISME, ATLAS Skill Tech University, Mumbai, Maharashtra, India

[5]Department of Commerce (CA), Government Arts College (Autonomous), Salem, Tamil Nadu, India

ABSTRACT

Purpose: Green supply networks, which include environmental sustainability into their operations, are an alternative to traditional supply chains (SCs). The purpose of the study is to understand GSC activities that have been documented in the literature and to utilize that catalog to inform the development of effective green SC strategies.

Research design: The study examined the impact that environmentally friendly SC management practices have on business success. The researcher conducted an extensive literature review of relevant academic literature, databases, and bibliographical lists for this study. The first and most vital step was to conduct a literature review of implemented green supply chain

Green Supply Chain Management. Mohammed Majeed, Kirti Agarwal, and Ahmed Tijani (Eds.)
© 2025 Apple Academic Press, Inc. Co-published with CRC Press (Taylor & Francis)

management (GSCM) methods. The complete focus of our literature search was a number of books, journals, and other publications. The study is empirical. A total of 100 respondents were considered as a sample and data were collected through a questionnaire using Google Forms.

Data analysis and results: SPSS was used for descriptive analysis, which involved computing mean, median, and standard deviation among other descriptive statistics for the variables involved.

Implications: In this part, the findings of a qualitative exploratory study that was conducted to favor of GSCM. The work may be needed to develop a measurable approach to gauging the effect of consumer participation on SC management strategies. Researchers may aid practitioners by providing plausible explanations for why sustainable SC management practices work. By offering a step-by-step framework, this study improved the decision-maker's ability to properly formulate green strategies for GSCM. SC performance in terms of the environment, the economy, and operations is closely related to the strategy chosen for the supply chain (SC).

Originality/value: Researchers may get a comparative understanding of various green SC strategies, and SC decision makers may benefit from a new taxonomic framework that simplifies and enhances green strategy creation.

16.1 INTRODUCTION

SCM involves a variety of stakeholders, including suppliers, manufacturers, distributors, and retailers. Effective SCM is essential for any organization that wants to remain competitive in the modern business landscape. One key strategy in SCM is to establish strong relationships with suppliers. Holt Ghobadian (2009). This can involve negotiating favorable terms for purchasing raw materials or components and collaborating with suppliers to ensure that they meet quality and delivery standards. Another important aspect of supplier management is risk management. This involves balancing the costs of holding inventory against the risks of stock outs or shortages. To achieve this balance, organizations can employ a variety of techniques, including just-in-time (JIT) inventory management and demand forecasting. JIT involves minimizing inventory levels by ordering only what is needed to fulfill customer orders, while demand forecasting involves using data analysis to predict future demand for products or services. Technology can also play a key role in SCM (Zhu and Sarkis, 2007). Companies can use automated systems to track inventory levels, monitor supplier performance,

A Study on Green Practices and Strategies in Supply Chain Management

and identify areas where efficiency can be improved. The use of big data analytics can also help organizations to optimize their SC by identifying patterns and trends in customer demand, supplier performance, and other key metrics. Finally, effective communication is critical to successful SCM (Rath, 2013). Organizations must ensure that all stakeholders in the SC are aware of their roles and responsibilities and that they are able to collaborate effectively to achieve common goals. This requires clear and open communication channels, as well as the use of tools and techniques such as SC mapping and performance scorecards to track progress and identify areas for improvement. By employing strategies such as strong supplier relationships, inventory optimization, technology adoption, and effective communication, organizations can achieve greater efficiency, improve product quality, and ultimately deliver better value to customers.

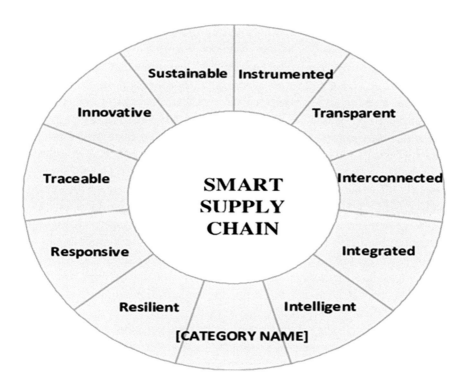

The key green practices and approaches in SCM are listed in the following:

1. Sustainable sourcing: This involves sourcing raw materials and components from suppliers that follow sustainable practices, such

as using renewable energy sources, reducing waste and emissions, and minimizing the use of hazardous substances.
2. Eco-design: This involves designing products and packaging with sustainability in mind, such as using recycled materials, reducing packaging waste, and designing products that can be easily disassembled and recycled.
3. Green logistics: This involves optimizing transportation and distribution networks to reduce emissions and energy consumption, such as using alternative modes of transportation, optimizing routing, and using fuel-efficient vehicles.

16.2 CRITICAL SUCCESS FACTORS IN GSCM: AN OVERVIEW

Critical success factors (CSFs) play an important part in green supply chain management (GSCM) by ensuring that sustainability is considered at each stage of the SC. CSFs are useful because they guarantee that sustainability is prioritized and accounted for at every stage of production. Improving environmental and social performance is a potential outcome of detecting and controlling CSFs in GSCM. By zeroing in on the most important aspects, businesses may pinpoint problem areas and take corrective measures. This has the potential to enhance connections with stakeholders as well as lessen environmental and social consequences (Yan and Xia, 2011). CSF management in GSCM also has the added benefit of assisting businesses with risk management. Organizations may lessen the likelihood of environmental or social incidents in their SC by emphasizing essential success elements such as supplier partnerships and staff training. This might aid in maintaining the company's credibility and standing in the marketplace. CSFs in GSCM must be managed in a methodical and organized fashion for the best results. As part of this process, we will determine the organization's important success criteria, establish goals for each, and track our progress toward those goals. Sustainability is a shared responsibility across the whole SC; therefore, cooperation and open lines of communication are essential at every stage. In conclusion, GSCM projects rely heavily on important success elements (Holt Ghobadian, 2009). They aid in incorporating sustainability into the SC as a whole, which can boost environmental and social performance. Effective management of CSFs requires a structured and systematic approach, as well as collaboration and communication across the SC. By managing CSFs effectively, organizations can promote sustainability and achieve their goals for a more sustainable future. When it comes to managing the internal environment, ethical leadership includes top managements backing and encouragement (Rath, 2013). Organizational management has a crucial role in whether or not a company is successful in going green. Senior management is encouraged and supported in their efforts to conserve the environment in response to pressure from their staff. The public's understanding of the dangers to the environment may also prompt a shift toward more environmentally friendly behaviors.

16.3 GREEN PRACTICES IN SUPPLY CHAIN MANAGEMENT: A BRIEF BACKGROUND

1. Sustainable development approaches, of which green SC activities are prime examples, include the following. This research illustrates a fundamental model of a green SC, and its accompanying text discusses how firms may adopt eco-friendly practices to lessen their negative effects on the environment while boosting their bottom line and productivity. Concepts of SC sustainability and environmental friendliness are advanced by Khan et al. increased productivity and

good environmental effect are realized by businesses that implement many green practices across their operations and SC.

2. Green material sourcing: When components and materials are sourced in a way that minimizes or eliminates their negative effects on the environment, this is called "green sourcing." Rising environmental protection concerns have pushed procurement professionals to reassess their present sourcing. Remanufacturing and recycling play a crucial role in achieving sustainable consumption. Min and Galle highlighted the significance of green sourcing in facilitating waste minimization, recycling, remanufacturing, and other SC activities. They arrived at the following conclusion: The effective implementation of a green buying strategy leads to lower product costs, improved environmental performance, and higher financial and market performance for enterprises (Zailani et al., 2015) found a favorable correlation between environmentally conscious spending and the efficiency and sustainability of businesses. They found that companies' overall performance increased after making green purchases. Waste, air, and water pollution may all be reduced when businesses embrace green buying practices across their SCs and operations. Green material sourcing is an essential aspect of GSCM. Green material sourcing seeks to mitigate these impacts by sourcing materials that are environmentally sustainable and have a reduced environmental footprint. Green materials can include recycled materials, renewable materials, and materials that have been sustainably sourced. By sourcing these materials, organizations can reduce their reliance on nonrenewable resources and reduce the amount of waste generated by their operations. Green material sourcing can also bring economic benefits. For example, recycled materials are often less expensive than new materials and renewable materials can provide a reliable and cost-effective source of energy. To implement green material sourcing, organizations need to take a systematic approach. This includes identifying areas of the SC that can be improved, setting targets for reducing environmental impact, and monitoring progress towards these targets. Collaboration and communication with suppliers, customers, and other stakeholders are also critical for the success of green material sourcing practices. In conclusion, green material sourcing is an essential aspect of GSCM. Adopting environmentally sustainable sourcing practices can reduce costs, improve efficiency, and enhance the reputation of the organization.

To achieve these benefits, organizations must take a systematic approach to implementing green material sourcing practices and collaborate with stakeholders across the SC. By doing so, they can create a more sustainable future for themselves and the planet.

3. Green marketing can include promoting products that are made from environmentally sustainable materials, promoting environmentally sustainable manufacturing processes, and communicating environmental performance data to customers and stakeholders. Green marketing can also bring economic benefits. To implement green marketing practices, organizations need to take a systematic approach. This includes identifying areas of the SC that can be improved, setting targets for reducing environmental impact, and monitoring progress towards these targets. Collaboration and communication with suppliers, customers, and other stakeholders are also critical for the success of green marketing practices (Holt Ghobadian, 2009). However, it is important to note that green marketing can also be subject to criticism if it is perceived as insincere or not backed up by concrete actions. To avoid greenwashing, organizations need to ensure that their green marketing claims are accurate and backed up by concrete actions. In conclusion, green marketing is an essential aspect of GSCM. Adopting environmentally sustainable marketing practices can reduce costs, improve efficiency, and enhance the reputation of the organization. To achieve these benefits, organizations must take a systematic approach to implementing green marketing practices and collaborate with stakeholders across the SC. By doing so, they can create a more sustainable future for themselves and the planet while avoiding greenwashing. It's a collection of things that people like to do, but which also have a low impact on natural beauty. Furthermore, green marketing boosts businesses' competitiveness, financial performance, and environmental impact through improved corporate reputation and image.

4. Green management: When a company adopts green management practices (GMP), it gains access to new data that can be used to further its environmental and financial goals. A company's public perception, productivity, environmental compliance, bottom-line savings, commitment to society, carbon footprint, and other metrics can all benefit from the use of green management methods. Growth that benefits all sectors of society may be achieved via the active participation of stakeholders, particularly customers.

5. Green distribution and warehousing: Waste is reduced, energy consumption is down, and the value of green items stored in warehouses is increased, all of which contribute to an organization's bottom line and public perception. Businesses may benefit from green distribution in several ways, including improved environmental and financial outcomes.
6. Green manufacturing: Green manufacturing is a term used to describe a set of manufacturing practices that are focused on reducing environmental impact, conserving resources, and improving sustainability. In the article, we will explore the concept of green manufacturing in the context of SC management, and discuss some of the strategies that can be used to implement green manufacturing practices. The audit should identify areas where energy, water, and materials can be conserved, and where waste can be reduced or eliminated. One key strategy in green manufacturing is to optimize energy efficiency. Another important aspect of energy efficiency is reducing the amount of energy required to produce goods. This can involve using lean manufacturing techniques to reduce waste or designing products that are more energy-efficient to manufacture. Water conservation is another important aspect of green manufacturing. Companies can reduce water consumption by using water-efficient processes, such as closed-loop water systems, which recycle water for multiple uses, or by implementing rainwater harvesting systems. By reducing water consumption, companies can also reduce the amount of wastewater generated by manufacturing processes, which can help to reduce environmental impact. Reducing waste is also a key strategy in green manufacturing. This can involve implementing recycling programs, or designing products that are more easily recyclable or biodegradable. Companies can also reduce waste by using lean manufacturing techniques, which focus on minimizing waste and improving efficiency. Finally, SC collaboration is critical to the success of green manufacturing initiatives. This requires open communication channels, as well as the use of performance metrics to track progress and identify areas for improvement. In conclusion, green manufacturing is an important concept in SC management, as companies seek to reduce their environmental impact and improve sustainability. As the importance of sustainability continues to grow, green manufacturing will become an increasingly important consideration for companies in all sectors of the economy.

7. Ecological design: Luthra et al. (2016) ecological design in SC management has the potential to mitigate 80% of negative environmental consequences associated with products and production processes. Cleaner technological processes, greener raw materials, and eco-friendly components are only a few of the numerous ideas included in an ecological design. Products with greener designs have less of an impact on the environment over time. Product reuse, recycling, and remanufacturing are all made easier by green design, which benefits the environment and gives businesses a chance to save money.
8. Green transportation: Green transportation refers to the use of environmentally sustainable transportation methods, while reverse logistics involves the management of products and materials that are returned from the customer to the supplier (Ruiz–Benítez et al., 2011). The transportation of goods is responsible for a significant amount of greenhouse gas emissions and pollution. Green transportation methods, such as electric vehicles, bicycles, and public transportation, can help to reduce these emissions and improve air quality. In addition to reducing environmental impact, green transportation can also bring economic benefits. Green transportation methods can also enhance the reputation of the organization and increase customer loyalty. The management of returned materials can be a significant challenge for organizations, as it can result in increased costs and environmental impact. However, by adopting green reverse logistics practices, organizations can reduce these costs and improve their sustainability.
9. Green reverse logistics practices include the recycling and reuse of materials, the reduction of waste generation, and the optimization of transportation routes. By recycling and reusing materials, organizations can reduce the amount of waste that is sent to landfills and conserve natural resources. By optimizing transportation routes, organizations can reduce the number of miles driven and the associated greenhouse gas emissions. Adopting green transportation and reverse logistics practices requires a systematic approach. This includes identifying areas of the SC that can be improved, setting targets for reducing environmental impact, and monitoring progress towards these targets. Collaboration and communication with suppliers, customers, and other stakeholders are also critical for the success of green transportation and reverse logistics practices.

To achieve these benefits, organizations must take a systematic approach to implementing green transportation and reverse logistics practices and collaborate with stakeholders across the SC. By doing so, they can create a more sustainable future for themselves and for the planet.

10. Green production: When making a product, "green production" means doing it in a way that reduces environmental impact and operational expenses. The term "green productivity" refers to a strategy that prioritizes sustainable growth in an industry by increasing productivity and environmental performance. The sector has to leverage the value chain to boost product value. So, it is crucial to lessen environmental effects all along the value chain, from the sourcing of raw materials through the delivery of the finished good. Pollutants released in the process are carried by wind and water throughout the globe. As a result, several nations have worked together under the UNFCCC to reduce carbon emissions, which science has shown to be a major factor in the planetary climate-altering process known as global warming. Manufacturers are now expected to take full accountability for the logistics.

11. Green purchasing: Green SC, sustainability, and green initiatives have all received increased attention as a result of the current uptick in environmental protection awareness. This includes goods and services that are more energy efficient, made from renewable resources, contain no ozone-depleting substances, and run on renewable energy. Green power is energy generated from renewable resources like hydro, solar, and wind that produce negligible amounts of greenhouse gases. Global environmental protection rules inform the selection of eco-friendly providers. From raw material extraction through final product disposal, the laws and regulations cover all the bases of environmental management.

12. Green procurement: Green procurement, also referred as ecologically minded purchasing, is an approach to acquiring goods and services that takes into consideration the possible effects on the environment. Programs for environmentally responsible shopping may be as easy as switching to renewable energy or using recycled paper instead of virgin paper. Supplier and contractor compliance with environmental regulations is an example of a more complicated option. Products and services' environmental impacts must be evaluated across their entire life cycles, and environmental standards must be established

to guide purchasing and contracting decisions. This has led to the establishment of a green purchasing policy, which is assessed on a regular basis and integrated with other efforts. Resource efficiency, manufacturing, markets, pricing, services, and even organizational behavior may all benefit from green procurement policies and initiatives, which aim to reduce costs and waste. The implementation of international accords like the Kyoto Protocol and the Rotterdam Convention can also benefit from these technologies. Many groups, including the International Organization for Standardization, have established guidelines for green purchasing.

16.4 THEORETICAL UNDERPINNING: REVIEW

Green technologies, green products, and sustainable energy are gaining prominence in today's globe. The literature shows the many motivations for customers to purchase green products and engage in more environmentally friendly behaviors. Consumers' propensity to shell out extra money for "green" goods suggests that policymakers should seize the opportunity presented by this market trend (Peattie, 2001). Value, attitude, and conduct were shown to be the three primary factors influencing Chinese consumers' purchasing decisions. After implementing the green IT system, researchers looked to see how much impact mimetic and coercive forces had on managers' actions. Mimetic isomorphism describes an organization's reaction to ambiguity when the best course of action is unclear. This is common when one company benefits from another's adoption of a policy or technology (Kaur, 2021). Because of the pressure from above, as well as from suppliers and customers in the SC, we may conclude that the deployment of the green information system affected the behavior of top executives. Coercive pressure is the norm in the regulated field. Because of this, environmental concerns are considered unfavorable externalities, and senior-level managers are under pressure to improve the company's environmental performance. All companies are subject to the same amount of coercive pressure, which drives them to standardize more effective adaptive processes. Because of the environmental and economic benefits that come from using green IT, managers who are forced to embrace it are likely to change their attitudes and actions in favor of it.

Product creation, manufacture, packaging, and distribution through a network of vendors are all part of supply chain management (SCM), which is crucial to the adoption of sustainability-based practices. It takes the collaboration and coordination of numerous stakeholders to manage the flow of services from suppliers to retailers. Due to the need for healthier options, CSR, and risk assessment and management of unanticipated actions, beverage firms and many retailers are prime candidates for implementing sustainable practices across the supply chain. Hence, environmentally responsible SCM is accomplished through fostering economic growth, social advancement, and stakeholder participation. It's a group endeavor that needs input from everyone involved. Social justice and environmental preservation may coexist if economic considerations are given equal weight. Sustainability is a risk management technique that allows businesses to grow internationally while maintaining their distinct identities at home via iterative improvement, careful stakeholder management, and increased employee and consumer involvement and loyalty. This is done by embracing the social, economic, and environmental components of sustainability for upstream, downstream, or internal channel partners. The study's overarching goal is to learn how sustainable performance is affected by green manufacturing, green purchasing, customer collaboration, and green information systems. The research's overarching objective is to learn more about the company's long-term viability in terms of both its structure and its day-to-day operations. In addition, the moderating idea of institutional pressure has been eliminated from the present investigation. The study is dependent on long-term performance. The study found that businesses' sustainability performance may improve dramatically when they adopt more environmentally friendly production methods (Abdul-Rashid et al., 2017) There are several social issues stemming from both industrial waste and poor manufacturing practices. The author values green manufacturing's contribution to achieving long-term success across the enterprise. In addition, some studies have found that successful sustainability initiatives may have positive effects on an organization's bottom line. Nonetheless, Cankaya and Sezen's (2018) research found that environmentally responsible production holds great potential for future expansion. Green manufacturing methods not only help build future assurance but also help minimize costs and reduce production waste. Previous research has also corroborated this connection (Chin et al., 2015), "green buying has gained great prominence in the past decade with respect to scholarly research," and this has important implications for economic growth.

Moreover, De et al. (2020) said that green buying had a moderating function in the economic growth of any economy since it involves future methods which may be applied by any firm searching for sustainability. Third, the "effect of interaction with consumers on sustainability performance is considerable," as stated in the studies hypotheses. The study's findings indicated that this concept was not of sufficient importance to warrant further investigation. The findings that have demonstrated the worth of the connection support this claim. The research draws on the existing literature to make the case that eco-design is both a means to ensure the safety of the environment and to promote a product's visibility in the marketplace. The researcher tested a working hypothesis on how the green information system affects sustainability (Schoggl et al., 2017) and found that businesses are under increasing pressure from the government to make environmentally friendly purchases such as recycling and composting. The notion of planned behavior provides a useful lens through which future academics might analyze consumers' green purchasing habits. Furthermore, as mentioned in the current research, it may be worthwhile to investigate the possible role of sustainability and digital transition concerns in the green movement

16.5 TAXONOMIC SELECTION OF GSCM STRATEGIES

There are a wide range of strategies that companies can employ to implement GSCM practices, ranging from product design to supplier management to logistics optimization. However, not all GSCM strategies are equally effective or appropriate for all organizations. In this essay, we will discuss the taxonomic selection of GSCM strategies and the factors that organizations should consider when selecting GSCM strategies. Taxonomic selection refers to the process of categorizing different GSCM strategies based on their effectiveness and appropriateness for different organizations. The framework categorizes GSCM strategies into three levels: proactive, reactive, and defensive. Proactive strategies are considered the most effective, as they can result in long-term improvements to environmental performance and can also provide a competitive advantage (Jayaram and Avittathur, 2015). Reactive GSCM strategies involve responding to specific environmental issues or regulatory requirements, such as emissions regulations or waste disposal regulations. Reactive strategies are less effective than proactive strategies, as they are typically implemented in response to specific problems rather than as part of a long-term environmental strategy. However, reactive strategies may be more appropriate for organizations that do not have the resources or expertise to implement proactive strategies. Defensive GSCM strategies involve minimizing the negative environmental impact of supply chain operations, without necessarily improving environmental performance. Defensive strategies are the least effective, as they do not result in any long-term improvements to environmental performance, and may also result in additional costs. However, defensive strategies may be appropriate for organizations that are just beginning to implement GSCM practices, or that are facing significant environmental challenges. When selecting GSCM strategies, organizations should consider a range of factors, including their industry sector, their level of environmental impact, their resources and capabilities, and their long-term strategic goals. Organizations should also consider the potential benefits and costs of each strategy, and should assess the risks associated with each strategy. In conclusion, taxonomic selection is an important consideration in the implementation of GSCM practices. By categorizing different GSCM strategies based on their effectiveness and appropriateness for different organizations.

16.6 STATEMENT OF THE PROBLEM

As global environmental awareness rises, several stakeholders, including the government and customers, put significant pressure on businesses to lessen their harmful effects on the environment. To stay ahead of the competition, businesses in both the service and manufacturing sectors need to consider how they might integrate sustainable business practices into their daily operations (Srivastava, 2007). The implementation of GSCM has the potential to contribute to the long-term viability of an organization (Yan and Xia, 2011). Rising environmental concerns necessitate that GSCM become a continuing community priority in developed nations. As a bonus, it has recently re-energized the green movement in developing countries. Individual green strategies were shown to have a substantial effect on not just material and energy procurement, but also innovative process technologies. Strategies have varying impacts on procurement, production technology, processing capabilities, transport and logistics operations, and performance measurement systems (Simpson and Samson, 2008).

The study aims to

1. investigate the variables that play a role in SCM and
2. quantify how much external influences affect supply-chain management.

16.7 METHODOLOGY

The researcher conducted an extensive literature review of relevant academic literature, databases, and bibliographical lists for this study. The first and most vital step was to conduct a literature review of implemented GSCM methods. The complete focus of our literature search was several books, journals, and other publications (Jayaram and Avittathur, 2015).The study is empirical in nature. A total of 100 respondents were considered sample and data were collected through a questionnaire using Google Forms. While gathering information for a study, the researcher must take into account both the population and the sample. In research, the population refers to the pool of people from which a sample will be drawn (Yan and Xia, 2011). The research used a Google Forms to obtain information from participants using a predetermined set of questions. The questionnaire used was adapted from those of earlier studies and utilized after being reviewed by experts in the area.

16.8 FACTORS THAT INFLUENCE SCM EFFICIENCY

SCM is impacted by several elements, many of which are explained by expert opinion and theory. The duration of the review period, the manner of demand forecasting, lead times, and review periods, as well as the structure of the supply chain itself. The respondents' views on these aspects are sorted using the Friedman method.

TABLE 16.1 Descriptive Statistics.

Factors	Mean	Standard deviation	Mean rank
Energy efficiency	3.18	1.161	4.02
Green certifications	2.94	1.044	4.09
Green procurement	2.72	1.269	3.81
Life cycle analysis	2.96	1.425	3.24
Supply chain collaboration	2.82	1.215	3.56
Sustainable packaging	2.73	1.129	3.87
Sustainable product design	3.25	1.192	4.76

According to the data in the table above, the contribution of sustainable product design (4.76 out of 5) to SCM efficiency is the greatest. Most respondents have also taken into account the importance of green certifications (4.09 out of 5.0) in the supply chain system. Respondents in the sample group also think about energy efficiency (4.02). Sustainable packaging in the supply chain is evaluated in fourth place (3.87). Green procurement (3.81 overall) placed sixth.

TABLE 16.2 Friedman Test.

N	100
χ^2	28.281
df	6
Asymptotic significance	0.001

χ^2 for degree of freedom 6 is determined as 28.281, which is statistically significant at the 1% level, according to the Friedman ranking method. As a result, we know that respondents care most about supply chain structure, variables like product design and certifications, and green credentials.

16.9 FACTORS INFLUENCING SCM STRATEGY

A regression model is used to assess the influence of these elements on SCM. Here, the effectiveness of the SCM serves as the dependent variable, while the aforementioned seven components serve as predictors. The following elucidates the model's findings.

TABLE 16.3 Model Summary.

Model	R	R^2	Adjusted R^2	Standard error of the estimate
1	0.958	0.826	0.871	1.78172

Predictors: (Constant), energy efficiency, green certifications, green procurement, life cycle analysis, supply chain collaboration, sustainable packaging, and sustainable product design.

Dependent variable: SCM

$R = 0.958$ indicates that the model well describes the relationship between the independent and dependent variables. $R^2 = 0.871$, which indicates that the predictors account for 82.6% of the variation in the dependent variables. The external influences have a significant impact. Moreover, analysis of variance (ANOVA) is used to determine if the suggested model is statistically significant.

TABLE 16.4 ANOVA.

Model		Sum of Squares	df	Mean square	F	Significance
1	Regression	2214.657	7	321.094	104.269	0.000
	Residual	291.113	92	3.174		
	Total	2507.790	99			

a. Dependent Variable: SCM

b. Predictors: (Constant), Energy efficiency, Green certifications, Green procurement, Life cycle analysis, Supply chain collaboration, Sustainable packaging and Sustainable product design.

Table 16.4 displays the results of the ANOVA test, which confirm the validity of the model with the F value of 104.269. At the 1% confidence level, significance is seen. So, the coefficient values provide additional context for understanding the predictive power of the model's predictors.

TABLE 16.5 Coefficients.

Model	Unstandardized coefficients B	Unstandardized coefficients Standard error	Standardized coefficients Beta	T	Significance
(Constant)	1.295	0.586		2.164	0.032
Energy efficiency	0.374	0.245	0.082	1.327	0.181
Green certifications	0.241	0.222	0.021	0.983	0.321
Green procurement	1.268	0.323	0.268	3.492	0.002
Life cycle analysis	0.785	0.354	0.201	3.065	0.004
Supply chain collaboration	−0.237	0.289	−0.051	−0.891	0.375
Sustainable packaging	−0.610	0.234	−0.187	−2.555	0.011
Sustainable product design	2.507	0.273	0.591	9.104	0.000

Table 16.5 reveals that energy efficiency, green certifications, green procurement, life cycle analysis, and sustainable product design are significant influence factors on the strategies of SCM. The t-values are determined to be in the range 1.96 to −1.96, and the significance levels are less than 0.05. Hence, it is concluded supply chain collaboration and sustainable packaging are highly influencing the performance of SCM.

16.10 DISCUSSION

GSCM entails implementing environmentally friendly and sustainable methods throughout the product design and sourcing through manufacture and delivery. Some options for implementing green practices in SCM include the following:

- Sustainable product design: Designing products that are environmentally friendly, energy-efficient, and recyclable or biodegradable.
- Green procurement: Selecting suppliers who have demonstrated a commitment to sustainable practices, and who offer environmentally friendly products and materials.
- Energy efficiency: Implementing energy-efficient practices in manufacturing facilities and logistics operations, such as using renewable energy sources, optimizing equipment and machinery, and reducing energy consumption.
- Waste reduction: Implementing waste reduction strategies, such as recycling, composting, and reducing packaging materials.
- Sustainable packaging: Using sustainable packaging materials, such as biodegradable or compostable materials, or reducing the amount of packaging used.
- Water conservation: Implementing water-efficient practices in manufacturing facilities, such as using closed-loop water systems, or harvesting rainwater for nonpotable uses.
- Supply chain collaboration: Collaboration with suppliers and partners to guarantee that everyone in the supply chain is committed to sustainable practices and that everyone is working together to decrease environmental effects.
- Life cycle analysis: Conducting a life cycle analysis of products to identify areas where environmental impact can be reduced throughout the supply chain.
- Green certifications: Obtaining green certifications, such as LEED or ISO 14001, to demonstrate a commitment to sustainable practices and improve brand reputation.

16.11 CONCLUSION

Managing the supply chain is essential in today's corporate environment. The term "green practices in supply chain management" is used to describe eco-friendly procedures at every stage of the supply chain. The SC has a major influence on the environment. Several positive outcomes can result from an organization's adoption of environmentally friendly SCM strategies (Holt Ghobadian, 2009). The lessening of damage to the natural world is a major plus. Greenhouse gas emissions, waste creation, and the depletion of natural resources may all be mitigated if businesses adopt sustainable practices. This has financial and productivity benefits in addition to being good for the planet. GSCM strategies also have the potential to improve an organization's standing in the community (Rath, 2013). Customers are more willing to back businesses that care about the environment now that they are better informed about these concerns. Businesses may boost their image and retain more customers if they adopt sustainable practices. Compliance with environmental rules is another benefit of using GSCM strategies. Businesses in several nations are required to adhere to stringent environmental laws (Jayaram and Avittathur, 2015). Organizations may guarantee they are in compliance with these requirements and avoid fines and penalties by implementing GSCMP. Improving the supply chain entails locating problem areas, establishing goals for lowering environmental effects, and keeping tabs on development. The effectiveness of environmentally friendly SCM strategies also depends on close cooperation and open lines of communication with suppliers, consumers, and other stakeholders (Yan and Xia, 2011). Sustainable techniques implemented throughout the supply chain have been shown to increase efficiency, save costs, and ensure conformity with environmental laws. To reap these advantages, businesses need to adopt green practices methodically and work together with supply chain stakeholders.

KEYWORDS

- **green practices**
- **strategies**
- **supply chain management**
- **green marketing**

REFERENCES

Andic, E.; Yurt, O.; Baltacioglu, T. Green Supply Chains: Efforts and Potential Applications for the Turkish Market. *Resour. Conserv. Recycl.* **2012**, *58*, 50–68.

Carter, C. R.; Rogers, D. S. A Framework of Sustainable Supply Chain Management: Moving Toward New Theory. *Int. J. Phys. Distrib. Logist. Manag.* **2008**, *38* (5), 360–387.

Eltayeb, T. K.; Zailani, S.; Ramayah, T. Green Supply Chain Initiatives Among Certified Companies in Malaysia and Environmental Sustainability: Investigating the Outcomes. *Resour. Conserv. Recycl.* **2011**, *55* (5), 495–506.

Govindan, K.; Khodaverdi, R.; Vafadarnikjoo, A. Intuitionistic Fuzzy Based DEMATEL Method for Developing Green Practices and Performances in a Green Supply Chain. *Expert Syst. App.* **2015**, *42* (20), 7207–7220.

Gunasekaran, A.; Spalanzani, A. Sustainability of Manufacturing and Services: Investigations for Research and Applications. *Int. J. Prod. Econ.* **2012**, *140* (1), 35–47.

Handfield, R.; Walton, S. V.; Sroufe, R.; Melnyk, S. A. Applying Environmental Criteria to Supplier Assessment: A Study in the Application of the Analytical Hierarchy Process. *Eur. J. Operat. Res.* **2002**, *141* (1), 70–87.

Holt, D.; Ghobadian, A. An Empirical Study of Green Supply Chain Management Practices Amongst UK Manufacturers. *J. Manuf. Technol. Manag.* **2009**, *20* (7), 933–956.

Hu, A. H.; Hsu, C. W. Critical Factors for Implementing Green Supply Chain Management Practice: An Empirical Study of Electrical and Electronics Industries in Taiwan. *Manag. Res. Rev.* **2010**, *33* (6), 586–608.

Jayaram, J.; Avittathur, B. Green Supply Chains: A Perspective from an Emerging Economy. *Int. J. Prod. Econ.* **2015**, *164*, 234–244.

Khan, S. A. R.; Dong, Q. L.; Yu, Z. Research on the Measuring Performance of Green Supply Chain Management: In the Perspective of China. *Int. J. Eng. Res. Afr.* **2016**, *27*, 167–178.

Kim, J.; Rhee, J. An Empirical Study on the Impact of Critical Success Factors on the Balanced Scorecard Performance in Korean Green Supply Chain Management Enterprises. *Int. J. Prod. Res.* **2012**, *50* (9), 2465–2483.

Luthra, S.; Garg, D.; Haleem, A. The Impacts of Critical Success Factors for Implementing Green Supply Chain Management Towards Sustainability: An Empirical Investigation of Indian Automobile Industry. *J. Clean. Prod.* **2016**, *121*, 142–158.

Mangla, S. K.; Kumar, P.; Barua, M. K. Flexible Decision Approach for Analyzing Performance of Sustainable Supply Chains Under Risks/Uncertainty. *Glob. J. Flexible Syst. Manag.* **2014**, *15* (2), 113–130.

Mangla, S.; Madaan, J.; Chan, F. T. Analysis of Flexible Decision Strategies for Sustainability-Focused Green Product Recovery System. *Int. J. Prod. Res.* **2013**, *51* (11), 3428–3442.

Min, H.; Galle, W. P. Green Purchasing Practices of US Firms. *Int. J. Operat. Prod. Manag.* **2001**, *21* (9), 1222–1238.

Mousazadeh, M.; Torabi, S. A.; Pishvaee, M. S. Green and Reverse Logistics Management Under Fuzziness. In: *Supply Chain Management Under Fuzziness*; Springer: Heidelberg, Berlin, 2014; pp 607–637.

Peattie, K. Golden Goose or Wild Goose? The Hunt for the Green Consumer. *Bus. Strategy Environ.* **2001**, *10*, 187–199.

Rath, R. C. An Impact of Green Marketing on Practices of Supply Chain Management in Asia: Emerging Economic Opportunities and Challenges. *Int. J. Supply Chain Manag.* **2013**, *2* (1), 78–86.

Rostamzadeh, R.; Govindan, K.; Esmaeili, A.; Sabaghi, M. Application of Fuzzy VIKOR for Evaluation of Green Supply Chain Management Practices. *Ecol. Indic.* **2015**, *49*, 188–203.

Sarkis, J.; Zhu, Q.; Lai, K. An Organizational Theoretic Review of Green Supply Chain Management Literature. *Int. J. Prod. Econ.* **2011**, *130* (1), 1–15.

Schoggl, J.-P.; Baumgartner, R. J.; Hofer, D. Improving Sustainability Performance in Early Phases of Product Design: A Checklist for Sustainable Product Development Tested in the Automotive Industry. *J. Clean. Prod.* **2017**, *140*, 1602–1617.

Shen, L.; Govindan, K.; Shankar, M. Evaluation of Barriers of Corporate Social Responsibility Using an Analytical Hierarchy Process Under a Fuzzy Environment—A Textile Case. *Sustainability* **2015**, *7* (3), 3493–3514.

Srivastava, S. Green Supply-Chain Management: A State-of-the-Art Literature Review. *Int. J. Manag. Rev.* **2007**, *9* (1), 53–80.

Wang, Z.; Sarkis, J. Investigating the Relationship of Sustainable Supply Chain Management with Corporate Financial Performance. *Int. J. Prod. Perform. Manag.* **2013**, *62* (8), 871–888.

Yan, L.; Xia, L.H. A Study on Performance Measurement for Green Supply Chain Management. In: *IEEE International Conference on Cyber Technology in Automation, Control, and Intelligent Systems*, 2011; pp 293–297.

Zailani, S.; Govindan, K.; Iranmanesh, M.; Shaharudin, M. R.; Chong, Y. S. Green Innovation Adoption in Automotive Supply Chain: The Malaysian Case. *J. Clean. Prod.* **2015**, *108*, 1115–1122.

Zhu, Q.; Sarkis, J.; Lai, K. H. Green Supply Chain Management Innovation Diffusion and Its Relationship to Organizational Improvement: An Ecological Modernization Perspective. *J. Eng. Technol. Manage.* **2012**, *29* (1), 168–185.

Index

A

Accountability
 issues, 179
Accounting for customers, 247
Accuracy of stock, 142–143
Additive manufacturing, 28
Adopting, 22
Alliance formation, 246
Artificial intelligence (AI), 30
Awareness, 244

B

Boost efficiency, 146–147
Brand reputation, 250
Budget cuts, 155

C

Chain agility, 192
Clean transportation, 27–28
Closed-loop supply chains, 175–176
Closed-loop supply cycle (CLSC), 241
Cloud computing, 204–205
Committed leadership, 24
Coordinated efforts, 244
Corporate social responsibility (CSR), 188
Customer management, 253

D

Data extraction, 179
Decision making, 205–207
Decreased fuel use, 96
 clean up air, 96
 reduces traffic, 96–97
 shorter travel times, 97

E

Eco-alliance, 107–108
Eco-design, 107
Ecofriendly procurement, 222–223
Ecologic buying practices, 174

Electric motorcycles, 94
 biofuel, 95
 sustainable transportation, 95
Electric-powered stackers, 137
Emergency rooms, 142
Employee safety, 141
Energy management system, 137
E-procurement, 241–242

F

Factors/Determinants of green supply chain
 management (GSCM), 19
 additive manufacturing, 28
 clean transportation, 27–28
 constraints, 29
 cost, 25–26
 infrastructure, 27
 innovative, 27
 knowledge, 26
 literature, 21–22
  adopting, 22
  committed leadership, 24
  environmental aspects, 23–24
  external, 23
  internal factors, 22–23
  stakeholder insistence, 23
  technologies, 24–25
  unique brand culture, 25
 logistics networks, 28–29
 putting money, 28
 reducing, 27
 scientific study, 30–31
 stockpiling carbon emissions, 29
 technology, 29
  artificial intelligence (AI), 30
  internet of things (IOT), 30
  robotics, 30
 trends, 26–27
Fashion firms
 costs, 177–178
 government, 177
 large clothing firms, 177

market, 176
top management support, 176–177

G

Green distribution, 77
  literature, 79–80
    areas, 80
    benefits, 84–85
    marketing, 82
    packaging, 82–84
    procurement, 80
    storage, 80–81
    warehousing, 81–82
Green innovation (GI), 111
Green logistics (GL)
  benefits, 266
    builds brand reputation, 271
    competitive advantage, 267–268
    conscienceless, 268–269
    delighted and loyal customers, 269
    eco conscious strategy, 272
    ethical sourcing, 272
    GL partnership, 272
    implication, 276–277
    innovation, 273
    lowering gas emissions, 270
    packaging optimization, 274
    profitability gains, 268
    reliability, 268
    responsible business practices, 269–270
    reverse logistics, 274
    route optimization, 275
    rules and limiting danger, 268
    save money, 267
    simpler hiring, 271
    storage facility optimization, 273
    strategies for, 271
    technologies information, 270
    time, 269
    transport optimization, 274
    waste, reduction, 270
  customers, 263–264
  defined, 261
  effects of, 262
  environment changes, 264–265
  factors FOT adopting, 263
  internal influences, 264
  inventory, 265

location/place, 263
organizational factors, 265
stakeholders, 264
sustainability of materials, 263
transportation, 266
warehousing, 266
Green manufacturing (GM), 153
  barriers, 161
  electricity conservation, 160
  exemptions from taxes, 160
  financial, 162–163
  generate interest, 162
  implication, 164–165
  insufficient internal knowledge, 162
  insufficient monitoring, 161
  lack of innovation, 163
    competition, 164
    customers, 164
    drivers, 163
    society, 164
    suppliers, 164
  lack of supplier, 161
  lessening of contamination, 160
  literature, 154–155
    benefit, 155
    budget cuts, 155
    creating a recognizable image, 156
    customer needs, 158
    employment available, 157
    government partnerships, 156
    improvements, 158
    lessen discarded material, 158
    raise employee spirits, 157
    raise revenues, 157
    safe components, 158–159
    savings on expenses, 159
    secure office, 158
    social standing, 159
    spend less, 156
    sustainable energy practices, 156
  reduce firm's, 160
  regulations, 162
  resulting minimal carbon impact, 159
Green marketing, 103
  benefits, 116
  competitive, 118
    aggressive, 123
    challenges, 121

Index

consumers, 123
consumption-based skepticism, 122
customer gains, 118
discussion, 124–126
economy, 120
environmental benefits, 119
green washing, 124
high prices, 121, 124
implication, 126–127
insufficient uniformity, 123
long suffering, 122
lowering supporting expenses, 121
novel idea, 123
positive effects, 119
product, 119
sales, 120–121
stopping "green myopia," 122–123
strategy, 120
sustainable materials, 120
truthful claims, 124
unanticipated, 122
literature, 105–106
  CSR, 107
  eco-alliance, 107–108
  eco-design, 107
  packaging, 108
  practices, 106
money, 116–117
positioning, 108–109
  advertising, 109–110
  disposal, 110
  eco-labels, 109
  green innovation (GI), 111
  mix, 111
  organizational greening, 110–111
  place, 114–115
  price, 113–114
  product, 112–113
  promotion, 115–116
societal problems, 117
  emotional connection, 118
  enhances credibility, 117
  new market entry, 117–118
Green myopia, 122–123
Green procurement (GP), 237
barriers of
  accounting for customers, 247
  alliance formation, 246
  attractiveness, 248
  awareness, 244
  brand reputation, 250
  coordinated efforts, 244
  ecological goods, 242–243
  ecologically sound industry, 251
  employee health, 250–251
  environmental issues, 245, 246
  environmental laws, 243
  extensive and time-consuming, 243
  health and social advantages, 248–249
  high-quality materials, 248
  inadequate instruction, 243
  innovation, 249
  materials and labor, 250
  monetary constraints, 244
  outcomes, 243
  Procurement Directives, 244
  profit-boosting outcomes, 251
  reputation enhancement, 246
  resources, 247
  reverse supply network, 248
  risk, 247
  safety improved, 250–251
  short supply, 244–245
  social, 245
  total cost of ownership, 249–250
  workers, 249
benefits, 245
drivers for
  administration of suppliers, 253–254
  competence and pertinent, 254
  cost reduction, 251
  customer management, 253
  management support, 253
  opportunity, 253
  policies, 252–253
  profits, 252
  regulating authorities, 254–255
  resilience, 252
  responsibility, 252
  risks, 252
  societal variables, 254
implications, 255
literature review
  buying, 239–240
  green procurement, 239–240
  procurement, 238–239

purchasing, 239–240
methods
　closed-loop supply cycle (CLSC), 241
　e-procurement, 241–242
　ethical procurement, 242
　lean supply, 240–241
　reverse supply chain (RSC), 242
　triple-bottom line (TBL), 241
triple bottom line (TBL), 238
Green structural capital
　competitive advantage, 188–189
　corporate social responsibility (CSR), 188
　hypothesis development
　　chain agility, 192
　　environmental sustainability, 191
　intangible asset, 189
　intellectual capital, 190
　reduced costs, 188
　regulatory compliance, 189
　research methodology
　　Green Supply Chain Agility (GSCA), 192, 193
　supply chain agility, 188
Green supply chain management (GSCM), 1, 170, 219
　benefits
　　company reputation, 180
　　financial gains, 179–180
　　market leadership, 180
　　strong industry dominance, 180
　challenges
　　accountability, issues, 179
　　data extraction, 179
　　difficulty, 179
　　fast change, 178–179
　　stakeholder pressure, 178
　contribution, 3–4
　critical success factors (CSFs), 286
　　organizational management, 287
　factors influencing
　　efficiency, 298–299
　　strategy, 299–300
　fashion firms
　　costs, 177–178
　　government, 177
　　large clothing firms, 177
　　market, 176
　　top management support, 176–177

global environmental awareness, 297
hotels
　benefits of, 227–228
　ecofriendly procurement, 222–223
　green design, 224
　green inventory, 223
　green waste management, 222
　information technology, 225–226
　logistics, 224–225
　marketing, 226–227
　practices in, 222
　reverse logistics, 225
implications, 14, 181
just-in-time (JIT) inventory management, 284
literature, 219, 220
　benefits, 7–11
　challenges, 12–14
　concept, 5–6
　fashion industry, 171–172
　green supply, 4–5
　ISO14001 quality systems licensing, 172
　organizational capabilities, 172
　SCM, 4
methodology, 298
practices
　closed-loop supply chains, 175–176
　ecologic buying practices, 174
　green design, 174–175
　logistics, 173
　production focuses, 175
　reverse logistics, 175–176
SCM, 284, 285, 286
　green practices, 287–293
strategies
　taxonomic selection, 296
　theoretical underpinning, 293–295
Green transportation, 89
　bicycle and pedal powered, 93–94
　consumer devotion, 98
　costs less, 97–98
　decreased fuel use, 96
　　clean up air, 96
　　reduces traffic, 96–97
　　shorter travel times, 97
　electric car, 92
　electric motorcycles, 94
　　biofuel, 95
　　sustainable transportation, 95

Index

employment opportunities, 98
enhances road safety, 98–99
fosters physical, 95
honesty goal, 99
literature, 91
maintains open space, 97
mode
   hybridized vehicles, 92
   public and mass, 91–92
monorail, 94
reduces pollution output, 95–96
reduces wasted time, 98
saves energy, 99
solar, 94
train, 92–93
   pedestrians and walking, 93
   vehicles with several occupants, 93
Green warehousing practices, 133
benefits
   boost efficiency, 146–147
   customer satisfaction, 145–146
   functionality, 147
   improved procedures, 146
   less waste, 148–149
   manufacturing, 147–148
   new technology, 146
   reputation of companies, 147
   running expenses, 148
   safer practices, 145
   space occupied, 145
implications, 149–150
literature, 134–135
   accuracy of stock, 142–143
   biodiversity, 143
   building materials, 138
   climate change, 138
   controlling shift schedules, 142
   eco-friendly, 144–145
   electric-powered stackers, 137
   emergency rooms, 142
   employee safety, 141
   energy management system, 137
   harvesting rainwater, 135
   inbound processes, 140
   inventory control, 140
   landscaping, 144
   location proximity, 135–136
   man-made lights, 143–144
   outbound, 141
   paperless system, 138–139
   reliable stock-keeping, 139
   renewable energy sources, 137–138, 144
   retrieval, 144
   reusable plastic, 143
   roofing, 139
   sensors, 136
   space-saving data storage, 139
   storage, 139–140
   superior efficiency lighting, 136
   training of employees, 141
Green waste management, 222
Green washing, 124

H

Harvesting rainwater, 135
High-quality materials, 248
Hypothesis development
   chain agility, 192
   environmental sustainability, 191

I

Industry 4.0 tools, 198
   customers, 201
   literature review, 202
      cloud computing, 204–205
      decision making, 205–207
      distribution function, 207–208
      robotics, 203–204
   smart factories, 200
   unmanned aerial delivery, 200
Insufficient internal knowledge, 162
Insufficient uniformity, 123
Internal influences, 264
Internet of Things (IOT), 30
ISO14001 quality systems licensing, 172

J

Just-in-time (JIT) inventory management, 284

K

Key drivers, 57
literature, 59–60
   cognitive drivers, 60–61
   external, 61–67
   internal, 67–72

Key practices, 35
   discussion, 49–50
   distribution, 48
   eco-friendly procurement, 40–41
   environment-friendly, 39–40
   green design, 38–39
   green manufacturing, 44–45
   GSCM, 37
   implications, 50–51
   internal, 43–44
   life cycle management, 47–48
   packaging, 46
   reverse logistics (RL), 41–43
   sustainable logistics, 48–49
   transportation, 47
   warehousing, 46–47

L

Lack of innovation, 163
   competition, 164
   customers, 164
   drivers, 163
   society, 164
   suppliers, 164
Lack of supplier, 161
Large clothing firms, 177
Lean supply, 240–241
Lessen discarded material, 158
Lessening of contamination, 160
Logistics networks, 28–29
Lowering gas emissions, 270

M

Management support, 253
Man-made lights, 143–144
Monetary constraints, 244
Monorail, 94

P

Positioning
   in green market, 108–109
      advertising, 109–110
      disposal, 110
      eco-labels, 109
      mix, 111
      organizational greening, 110–111
      place, 114–115
      price, 113–114
      product, 112–113
      promotion, 115–116
Procurement Directives, 244
Profit-boosting outcomes, 251

R

Reliable stock-keeping, 139
Responsible business practices, 269–270
Reverse logistics, 225, 274
Reverse supply chain (RSC), 242
Reverse supply network, 248
Robotics, 203–204
Route optimization, 275

S

Simpler hiring, 271
Societal issues, 117
   emotional connection, 118
   enhances credibility, 117
   new market entry, 117–118
Space-saving data storage, 139
Stakeholder insistence, 23
Storage facility optimization, 273
Superior efficiency lighting, 136
Sustainable energy practices, 156

T

Top management support, 176–177
Total cost of ownership, 249–250
Transport optimization, 274
Triple bottom line (TBL), 238, 241

U

Unique brand culture, 25
United Nations (UN) development goals, 170
Unmanned aerial delivery, 200

V

Vehicles with several occupants, 93

W

Warehousing, 81–82, 266